AFRICAN AMERICAN MEN IN COLLEGE

Michael J. Cuyjet and Associates

JOSSEY-BASS
A Wiley Imprint
www.josseybass.com

Published by Jossey-Bass
A Wiley Imprint
989 Market Street, San Francisco, CA 94103-1741   www.josseybass.com

Jossey-Bass books and products are available through most bookstores. To contact Jossey-Bass directly
call our Customer Care Department within the U.S. at 800-956-7739, outside the U.S. at 317-572-3986,
or fax 317-572-4002.

Jossey-Bass also publishes its books in a variety of electronic formats. Some content that appears in
print may not be available in electronic books.

Library of Congress Cataloging-in-Publication Data

African American men in college / [edited by] Michael J. Cuyjet.— 1st ed.
    p. cm.
  Includes bibliographical references and index.
  ISBN-13: 978-0-7879-6460-3 (cloth)
  ISBN-10: 0-7879-6460-3 (cloth)
  1. African American men—Education (Higher) 2. African American male college students—Services
for—Case studies. I. Cuyjet, Michael J.
  LC2781.A39 2006
  378.1'982996073
                             2005036414

Printed in the United States of America
FIRST EDITION
HB Printing   10 9 8 7 6 5 4 3 2 1

TABLE OF CONTENTS

In producing this book, I salute every African American man who has persevered to obtain a college degree. For some, who had fortunate opportunities and the assistance of family and friends, it was relatively easy, but a significant accomplishment nonetheless. For others it was a mighty struggle, many obstacles to overcome, and a major battle to be won.

This book is dedicated to each of you, but in particular it is dedicated to the fond memory of one very special African American male college graduate who has been the primary mentor of my life—John Felix Cuyjet (1916–2000), bachelor of science in mechanic arts, cum laude, West Virginia State College, June 2, 1941.

Thanks, Dad.

PREFACE

The recruitment, retention, and graduation of African American men in U.S. colleges and universities are ongoing concerns of many administrators and faculty. One of the unfortunate—and often overlooked—effects of the efforts to increase college attendance and graduation by African Americans is that these efforts seem to have benefited women in significantly greater numbers than men. The fact that, among higher education attendees, African Americans continue to have the lowest male-to-female ratio of all ethnic demographic groups (white, African American, Asian American, Latino/Latina, American Indian) belies these efforts in recent years. Many books and journal articles address concerns about recruiting, retaining, and graduating increasing numbers of underrepresented ethnic minority undergraduate and graduate students, particularly African American students. However, few of these works separate men and women and focus on the differences in their issues, their different needs, and the growing difference in their demographic representation among the U.S. college and university population. In Roach's (2001) article "Where Are the Black Men on Campus?" he offers an anecdotal example of this phenomenon in describing the attendance at Dillard University. Roach cites Dillard's president, Dr. Michael Lomax, who explains that while his institution enjoyed a 26 percent rise in enrollment in just three years, these figures included a 30 percent increase for females and only a 14 percent increase for males. In fact, the number of Black men on campus increased by only 55 while the number of women increased by 349 over the same time span.

PURPOSE AND FOCUS

The primary purpose of this book is twofold. First, it is intended to contribute information on the status of African American men in institutions of higher education, particularly at predominantly white colleges and universities. Second, it presents both (1) specific examples of programs and activities that have been attempted at colleges across the country with some relative success and (2) a suggestion of the circumstances under which those programs or activities might succeed on other campuses. One particularly noteworthy contribution of this book is the attention it calls to the difficulties encountered by African American men in undergraduate matriculation that are not experienced by African American women or members of other ethnic minority groups of either gender.

This book arose out of a perceived need for specific discussion of issues pertaining to the undergraduate college matriculation of African American men. (Certainly there are other issues faced by African American males in the United States, starting with their first encounters with the public education system in preschool programs. However, we leave the discussion of those topics and the development of remedies to others.) The popularity of a number of recent books that do focus on the plight of African American men in postsecondary education evidences the concern of members of the higher education community about this topic of African American men's successful matriculation. Most of these works, however, address topics peripheral to the issues that impact undergraduate African American male matriculation. *Brothers of the Academy: Up and Coming Black Scholars Earning Our Way in Higher Education* (Jones, 2000) focuses on faculty, not students. *Success Factors of Young African American Males at Historically Black Colleges* (Ross, 1998) is limited to historically Black institutions. Several other books, such as *African American Males in School and Society: Practices and Policies for Effective Education* (Polite & Davis, 1999) and *The War Against Boys: How Misguided Feminism Is Harming Our Young Men* (Sommers, 2000), look at African American males in the educational system, but tend to focus more on elementary and secondary education. As such, those books do not include the detail on the postsecondary educational environment that is presented here.

These postsecondary topics were addressed in *Helping African American Men Succeed in College* (Cuyjet, 1997). Although that volume addressed a number of salient issues related to the retention and graduation of African American men, it did not offer more than a few representative examples of viable programs that have been successfully tried on college campuses and found to be helpful in providing support for the matriculation of African American men. Our book is intended to be a sequel to that book. We add some new information to some of the general topics addressed in the earlier volume and offer a limited, but revealing, reiteration of the important issues and theoretical constructs it raised. However, this book makes a particularly valuable contribution to the body of knowledge on this topic by offering examples of viable programs and activities in use on various campuses to enhance the college environment for African American men. We present these in a format that explains their function, structure, and outcomes—offering what we hope is sufficient information for those readers who may wish to replicate any of these programs on their own campuses to do so successfully.

The primary audiences for this book are student affairs and higher education professionals at colleges and universities across the country. Although the most obvious consumers of this book are those who have direct responsibility for making various aspects of the campus environment more comfortable and nurturing for students, because of the perceived breadth of the concern over this issue of low matriculation rates by African American men, higher education officials in all areas of the university administrative structure are potential consumers of this book. Also, the inclusion of material relative to some special college environments (such as community colleges, and HBCUs) expands the book's potential audience beyond just those professionals whose work focuses on undergraduate students at predominantly white institutions.

A secondary audience for this book includes faculty and graduate students in student affairs or higher education preparation programs. Many preparation program curricula include course work on the American student or on multicultural diversity among the general college student population. This book can be used in conjunction with other text materials to provide data on African American male students within either or both of these contexts. An additional segment of this secondary audience may be faculty in other academic programs who teach courses that focus on issues related to African American college students and their matriculation, who might use it to provide data on this particular segment of the African American population. A possible tertiary audience includes individuals at federal or state government agencies or private agencies outside the campus who are interested in the circumstances of African American college students, particularly males.

Whoever the readers may be, it is the intention of the authors included in this book to share our ideas and suggestions for ways to better understand the issues that present particular challenges to African American college men. Moreover, we hope these ideas help readers develop ways to surmount and reduce these challenges such that the journey for these young men is made easier and the numbers of those succeeding increases significantly.

SYNOPSIS OF THE BOOK CHAPTERS

In Chapter One, Michael Cuyjet shares some of the demographic data about African American men in the United States and in U.S. colleges in particular. He then offers an overview of some of the more significant issues facing African American male undergraduates and the people who are attempting to assist them in their matriculation. Particular attention is paid to the skewed numbers of African American women and men in college and the impact that imbalance has on colleges and on society as a whole.

In Chapter Two, Fred Bonner and Kevin Bailey identify and examine a number of factors that have been found to promote a climate of academic success among African American men, such as peer group influences, relationships with faculty members, the importance of support from family, the enhancement of self-perception, and the impact of the overall institutional environment.

In Chapter Three, Charles Brown discusses how involvement in extracurricular activities can create a more positive social climate for African American men on the campus. In addition to making some general observations on the activities in which African American college men tend to engage, he explains the results of a study that identified several specific activities found to support retention and graduation.

In Chapter Four, Shaun Harper considers the positive outcomes associated with African American male participation in leadership roles in out-of-class organizations and activities. He discusses the developmental advantages these can give participants, including

enhanced communication skills, basic leadership skills such as organizing meetings and delegating, positive relationships with administrators and community leaders, and greater political astuteness.

In Chapter Five, Michael Sutton looks at mentoring from both
an instructional and a developmental perspective and describes
how the developmental mentoring experience, in particular, positively impacts African American college men. He uses one exemplary program to demonstrate how college and university
administrators can use developmental mentoring to improve the
lives of their African American male students.

In Chapter Six, Lemuel Watson explores the nature of spirituality and religion among African Americans, particularly among
African American men. He then explains the impact of spirituality and religious activity on educational outcomes of African American men. He also presents the results of a study that reports what
African American college men say about their own spirituality and
how it affects their self-concept.

The book's next three chapters examine three particular subpopulations among African American male college students: fraternity members, athletes, and gay and bisexual men. In Chapter
Seven, Shaun Harper and Frank Harris discuss the positive and
negative influences of membership in social fraternities on African
American men in college. They cite various studies indicating that
fraternity membership provides significant social support and
enhances various aspects of development including identity, leadership skills, and cognitive ability. They also explore some of the
negative aspects of fraternity participation, including declining
public perception, poor academic performance, and the persistent
and very serious issue of hazing.

In Chapter Eight, Kenya LeNoir Messer describes some of the
particular conditions that define the environment for African
American men involved in intercollegiate athletics and how that
particular circumstance presents both advantages and disadvan-
tages to these young men. She also explores a number of strategies
to enhance the graduation rates of African American male college
athletes.

In Chapter Nine, Jamie Washington and Vernon Wall examine
the challenges for gay African American men in the college environment. They discuss the process of identity development for

African American gay men, particularly as these individuals explore the multiple aspects of being Black, male, and gay. Washington and Wall also look at the impacts of religion, role models, and the significance of what gay men name themselves.

The two chapters that follow focus on the issues salient to two particular academic settings by exploring the circumstances of African American men at historically Black college and universities (HBCUs) and at community colleges. A look at the particular climate that may exist at HBCUs is merited, as the majority of African American college graduates prior to the last quarter of the twentieth century were educated at HBCUs and these institutions still produce a high percentage of all African American college graduates compared with predominantly White institutions (PWIs). And because the majority of all African American students today are matriculating on community college campuses, it is particularly useful to see the issues that arise in those environments.

In Chapter Ten, Walter Kimbrough and Shaun Harper reveal the findings from a qualitative study using focus groups at HBCUs to examine how African American men fare on those campuses. They also discuss which of the HBCU-attending African American men's environmental, academic, and social issues are similar to those of their peers at PWIs and which impact them differently. Of particular note in this discussion is the matter of relationships between men and women on HBCU campuses.

In Chapter Eleven, Myron Pope acknowledges that the climate at most community colleges is quite different from the environment at typical four-year PWIs. As such, the impact of those community college environments has some interestingly different effects on African American men. In particular, this chapter will explore the diminishing emphasis on preparing students to transfer to four-year institutions and how that phenomenon has affected the educational experiences of African American men.

Chapter Twelve contains a summary by Michael Cuyjet of the major topics and salient ideas from the material presented in the book's first part. Particular emphasis is placed on suggestions of particular activities, programs, and interventions that campus administrators, staff, and faculty might employ to provide support to their African American male students.

The book's second part profiles a number of programs that either are currently in operation on college campuses or have recently ceased operation. All are examples of efforts that our colleagues across the country have developed to support African American men on their campuses. We have tried to identify a range of types of programs, from large, complex, comprehensive programs that provide a wide range of support systems and materials to their participants to small, informal, periodic gatherings of students to share stories and ideas and support each other. The examples included also represent a diversity of institutions.

References

Cuyjet, M. J. (Ed.). (1997). *Helping African American men succeed in college*. New Directions for Student Services, no. 80. San Francisco: Jossey-Bass.

Jones, L. (Ed.). (2000). *Brothers of the academy: Up and coming black scholars earning our way in higher education*. Sterling, VA: Stylus.

Polite, V. C., & Davis, J. E. (Eds.). (1999). *African American males in school and society: Practices and policies for effective education*. New York: Teachers College Press.

Roach, R. (2001). Where are the Black men on campus? *Black Issues in Higher Education, 18*(6), 18–24.

Ross, M. J. (1998). *Success factors of young African American males at historically Black colleges*. Westport, CT: Bergin & Garvey.

Sommers, C. H. (2000). *The war against boys: How misguided feminism is harming our young men*. New York: Simon & Schuster.

ACKNOWLEDGMENTS

My greatest fear, in trying to name everyone who has assisted me somehow in the development of this book project, is that I will omit the name of someone who provided assistance. So, despite my deepest appreciation to everyone who helped in some small way, I am not going to try to name all of you. To the colleagues and students who contributed ideas and information and to the coworkers who tolerated my distraction while working on this project, I express my gratitude and appreciation. Along with my heartfelt thanks, please accept my earnest apology for not generating a list of your names here—you know who you are.

There are, nonetheless, several people whom I must thank individually for their assistance in this effort. First, I wish to acknowledge the tremendous effort of each of the authors who contributed his or her work to this project. Your names are listed in the table of contents, so I will not repeat them here; but I cannot begin to express how much I respect your creative efforts and your willingness to share your knowledge with others through this medium.

Second, I need to thank the people at Jossey-Bass Publishers, particularly David Brightman, whose unflappable support and infinite patience with my missed deadlines has sustained me through this entire undertaking. Also, thanks to Sona Avakian and Cathy Mallon, who guided me through the final process of book production when time was short and tasks were many.

I would also like to acknowledge the significant contributions of the three "anonymous" reviewers—Mary, Stan, and Michael—whose careful analysis of the manuscript and valuable comments and suggestions have made this work so much better because of their efforts.

Finally, I wish to acknowledge the support and contributions of the individual who served as my personal copy editor, my severest critic, and most enduring fan—my wife, Carol.

THE AUTHORS

Kevin W. Bailey is the assistant vice president for student affairs at Tulane University. He held administrative positions at Millersville University, Bowling Green State University, and the University of North Carolina at Charlotte before assuming his current role. He received his undergraduate degree in management information systems and master's degree in student affairs in higher education from Indiana University of Pennsylvania. His doctorate in higher education administration is from Bowling Green State University. Bailey has been active on the regional or national levels of the National Association of Student Personnel Administrators (NASPA) and the American College Personnel Association (ACPA), where he has served as a facilitator for the African American Male Summit pre-conference at both associations' national conventions. He is the current director of the membership services core council of ACPA. In addition to this work on African American males, Dr. Bailey's other interests include leadership development and organization development. He is a member of Kappa Alpha Psi Fraternity, Inc.

Earnestine Baker has served at the University of Maryland, Baltimore County (UMBC), since 1983. She is executive director of the Meyerhoff Scholarship Program, a nationally recognized program for talented students interested in pursuing terminal degrees in the sciences, mathematics, and engineering and computer science. She received a bachelor's degree in home economics and general science from Hampton Institute and a master's degree in secondary education from Prairie View A&M University. Previously, Baker served as coordinator of minority recruitment in the Office of Admissions and associate director for scholarships at UMBC. She has been a high school teacher in the Lancaster, Pennsylvania, city schools; a chemistry teacher in the Alief Independent School District, Houston, Texas; and an adjunct instructor in the Upward Bound Program at Millersville State University in Pennsylvania. She serves on several advisory boards, including Hampton

University/University of Pittsburgh Cancer Institute; the Science and Everyday Experiences (SEE) Initiative, funded by the National Science Foundation; and the Federation of American Society for Experimental Biology, funded by the National Institutes of Health. She is a member of Delta Sigma Theta Sorority, Inc.

Tyrone Bledsoe is the special assistant to the president at the University of Toledo and executive director of the Student African American Brotherhood (SAAB), whose national headquarters are in Toledo, Ohio. He is the founder of SAAB, which was established in 1990 to enhance the experiences of African American males in grades K–12 and at the college and university level. He received a bachelor's degree and a master's degree from Mississippi State University. He graduated from the University of Georgia with a doctorate in counseling and student affairs administration and in 1993 was chosen as the Outstanding Doctoral Student in the state of Georgia; in 2002 he was recognized as the Outstanding Doctoral Alumnus by the University of Georgia. He has served more than twenty years in the profession of student affairs and as an appointed faculty member at several institutions. He serves as a regular faculty member and facilitator for the African American Male Summit pre-conferences at both NASPA and ACPA and on the board for Ohio's Commission on African American Males (CAAM). He served as a guest lecturer at the Oxford University Roundtable Institute to discuss his research and practical experience with African American men.

Fred A. Bonner II is an associate professor of higher education in the Department of Educational Administration and Human Resource Development (EAHR) at Texas A&M University. He received a bachelor's degree in chemistry from the University of North Texas in 1991, a master's degree in curriculum and instruction from Baylor University in 1994, and a doctorate in higher education administration and college teaching from the University of Arkansas-Fayetteville in 1997. Bonner has been an ACE Fellow and the recipient of both the American Association for Higher Education Black Caucus Dissertation Award and the Educational Leadership, Counseling, and Foundation's Dissertation of the Year Award from the University of Arkansas College of Education. Bonner has served as an assistant editor of the *National Association of Student Affairs Professionals Journal*. He is completing a research fellowship with the Yale University Psychology Department (PACE Center), focusing on issues that impact academically gifted African American male college students. Bonner is also completing a book that highlights the experiences of postsecondary gifted African American male undergraduates in predominantly White and historically Black college contexts.

Charles Brown is the vice chancellor for student affairs at the University of South Florida, St. Petersburg. He received his bachelor's degree in sociology and education from Blackburn College and his master's degree in educational administration and his doctorate in higher education from Illinois State University. He has held several leadership positions in student affairs. Brown served as the vice president for student development and campus life and as an associate professor at Wayne State University and as an assistant, associate, and senior associate vice president for student affairs at the University of Alabama. In addition to his administrative positions at Alabama, he was also an associate professor in the College of Education. His publications have focused on campus life issues such as alcohol consumption, leadership development, diversity, and multiculturalism. He is an active member of NASPA and other local and national student affairs professional organizations.

Tobias Q. Brown is a junior at Central State University (CSU) in Ohio, where he currently serves on the university's board of trustees. Among numerous campus involvements, Mr. Brown also serves as president of the CSU chapter of the Student African American Brotherhood and as co-captain of the men's tennis team; he is also a student teacher for Junior Achievement, an active member of the National Association of African American Programs, and a member of the Marketing Club. He has been on the dean's list for seven consecutive quarters and received numerous awards, such as the 2003–2004 ROTC Leadership and Excellence Award, the 2003–2004 and 2004–2005 Rigor and Excellence Awards from the Honors Program, the Southwestern Ohio Council for Higher Education Student Scholar Award 2003–2004, the 2004–2005 Academic Athlete of the Year Award, the 2004–2005 Central State University President's Award, and the 2005 Arthur Ashe Student Scholar Award. Brown is currently publishing his first book, *It's Easier Than You Think: A Guide to Constant College Success and Balance for Any Student.* After graduating from Central State University in May 2006 he plans to enter a doctoral program.

Christopher C. Catching is an assistant director in the Rutgers College Department of Student Development and College Affairs at

Rutgers University in New Brunswick, New Jersey. He has served as a student affairs administrator and instructor at several institutions including Seton Hall University, Fairleigh Dickinson University, and Bloomfield College in New Jersey. Catching received a bachelor's degree in history from Montclair State University and a master's degree in student personnel administration in higher education from New York University. He is currently a doctoral student in the Social and Philosophical Foundations of Education program at Rutgers University. Catching has served in several student affairs professional associations including the Association for Fraternity Advisors (AFA) and the American College Personnel Association (ACPA), where he is currently the chairperson of the Pan-African Network. He has also been the recipient of several awards in the profession, including the 2004 Val DuMontier New Professionals Award for LGBT advocacy (ACPA). In addition to his research interests on African American males, Catching's other interests include the experiences of African American women, the P–16 educational pipeline, and the social, political, and economic forces affecting educational institutions. He is a member of Iota Phi Theta Fraternity, Inc.

Michael J. Cuyjet is an associate dean of the Graduate School and an associate professor in the College of Education and Human Development at the University of Louisville in Louisville, Kentucky. For the 2005-06 academic year, he is serving as acting associate provost for student life and development at the University of Louisville. He received a bachelor's degree in speech communications from Bradley University and a master's degree in counseling and a doctorate in counselor education from Northern Illinois University. He served more than twenty years as a student affairs practitioner before becoming a member of the faculty and coordinator of the college student personnel master's and doctoral programs at Louisville in 1993. His numerous published articles, chapters, and books include the mongraph *Helping African American Men Succeed in College,* published by Jossey-Bass. Dr. Cuyjet has held numerous offices in a number of professional organizations, including the National Association for Campus Activities (NACA), ACPA, and NASPA; he has served on the board of directors of each of those organizations at some time in his career. In 1995, he was awarded the Bob E. Leach Award for Outstanding Service to Students by NASPA's Region III. He has received the ACPA Annuit

Coeptis award twice—as an outstanding new professional in 1981 and as an outstanding senior professional in 1998.

Amanda A. Farabee is a graduate student in the Educational and Counseling Psychology College Student Personnel program at the University of Louisville in Louisville, Kentucky. She earned her bachelor of arts degree in government and Spanish from Centre College (Kentucky) in 2002, and she is pursuing her master of education degree in Louisville's College of Education and Human Development. Her student affairs experience lies within career services, Greek life, and orientation. Amanda has worked at Jefferson Community College for over two years and will be serving as the graduate assistant of Recognized Student Organizations and Greek Life at the University of Louisville during the 2005–2006 academic year.

Shaun R. Harper is an assistant professor and research associate in the Center for the Study of Higher Education at Pennsylvania State University. He earned his bachelor's degree in education from Albany State, a historically Black university in Georgia, and his doctorate in higher education administration from Indiana University. He has served as a faculty member and executive director of the doctor of education program at the University of Southern California (USC). He has authored several articles and book chapters and has presented over sixty sessions at national higher education conferences since 2000. The Andrew W. Mellon Foundation recently awarded him a grant to study the effects of mentoring on increasing African American male representation in highly selective graduate and professional schools. Harper was awarded the 2004 USC Rossier School of Education's Socrates Professor of the Year Award for Outstanding Teaching and the 2005 Faculty Excellence in Mentoring Award from the USC Center for Excellence in Teaching. He also received NASPA's 2004 Melvene D. Hardee Dissertation of the Year Award for his study of high-achieving African American undergraduate men. In addition, he is recipient of the 2005 Emerging Scholar Award, presented by ACPA.

Frank Harris III is associate director of the Center for Urban Education and a doctoral candidate in higher education administration at the University of Southern California, Rossier School of Education. He holds bachelor's and master's degrees in communication studies from California State University Northridge and Loyola Marymount University, respectively. He has served as an advisor and special projects coordinator in the office of the vice president for student affairs. He has also worked extensively with African American male undergraduates at USC, having served in the capacities of assistant director of the Center for Black Cultural and Student Affairs and advisor to several student organizations, including 100 Black Men of USC, the National Pan-Hellenic Council, and Alpha Phi Alpha Fraternity, Inc. In addition to his experience as a student affairs professional, Harris has also served as a faculty member at Los Angeles Trade Tech College and Loyola Marymount University. He actively participates in NASPA and the Association for the Study of Higher Education (ASHE), and he has published a theoretical model on college men in the *NASPA Journal*. Harris's dissertation research examines the meanings college men make of masculinity and corresponding effects on behaviors, outcomes, and gendered environmental norms.

Pamela Safisha Nzingha Hill is the director of education for Scholars Academy, an African-centered school that is a component of *The Act of Change, Inc., Institute of Cultural Arts* in Dallas, Texas. Hill is also an adjunct professor in the Higher Education program at a local metropolitan university. She writes a weekly column titled "Speak, Sistah, Speak" for the Houston-based Black newspaper *African American News & Issues*. Dr. Hill holds degrees from Langston University, Northeastern State University, and the University of Missouri-Columbia. She holds membership in Delta Sigma Theta Sorority, Inc. and the National Coalition of Blacks for Reparations in America. Hill has lectured at a number of student leadership and professional conferences and at various campuses across the country. She is the author of *An Afrocentric Perspective Towards Black Student Development: From Theory to Practice*. Forthcoming books include *Peace, Power and Blessings: For Sistas on the Journey to Blackwomanhood* and *Speak, Sistah, Speak: Notes from a Serious Sistah*. Additionally, she is writing a series of curriculum books geared towards African-centered schools.

Lasana O. Hotep is the program coordinator for the African American Men of Arizona State University (AAMASU) Program at Arizona State University, Tempe campus. He received his bachelor's degree from Texas State University–San Marcos in 1997 with a double major in speech communications and history. As the founder and lead consultant of Lasana O. Hotep Consultants, Hotep is committed to developing programs and strategies that positively impact the world African community. His areas of expertise include hip-hop history, Pan-Africanism, and African American male retention.

Hotep has served as a primary school instructor at the New World Learning Center in San Antonio, Texas, a Council of Independent Black Institutions (CIBI) school.

Carl Humphrey is the chapter liaison manager of the 100 Black Men of America, where he serves the 103 chapters of the organization and provides support nationwide from the World Headquarters in Atlanta, Georgia. In this role, he endeavors to create consistency of operations and programs throughout each of the national chapters. Humphrey is an Atlanta native and a graduate of North Carolina A & T State University. He recently graduated from the Dekalb County Micro-Business Institute (Georgia). He received top honors for his business presentations, business plans, and was voted top operator by his classmates. Humphrey has been a young successful entrepreneur and has traveled to China to expand his knowledge in distribution opportunities. Humphrey is a member of Big Bethel A.M.E. Church and The Brotherhood. In his spare time, he coaches basketball at Landmark High School. His hobbies include traveling, basketball, computer programs, real-estate, and automotive refurbishment.

Alonzo Jones is the director of multicultural student services at Arizona State University (ASU), Tempe campus. He received a bachelor's degree in justice studies from ASU and a master's degree in developmental education from Southwest Texas State University. He has served since 1981 as a student affairs practitioner and administrator, managing and developing programs within higher education to combat the problematic enrollment, retention, and graduation rates of Black, Latino, and Native American youth. In addition to his work within higher education, Jones is founder of Apoch Programs, an educational and African American cultural training program for high school and college-centered organizations.

Walter M. Kimbrough serves as the twelfth president of Philander Smith College in Little Rock, Arkansas. Prior to Philander Smith, he served at Albany State University in Georgia, Old Domin-ion University in Virginia, and Georgia State University and Emory University, both in Atlanta. He earned a bachelor of science degree in biology from the University of Georgia, a master's degree in college student personnel services from Miami University in Oxford, Ohio, and a doctorate in higher education from Georgia State University. Kimbrough has established a national reputation as an expert on historically Black fraternities and sororities. He has served as consultant to national

publications including the Associated Press, the *Washington Post,* and the *Chronicle of Higher Education.* He has also been a guest on the National Public Radio show *Talk of the Nation.* Kimbrough is the author of the book *Black Greek 101: The Culture, Customs and Challenges of Black Fraternities and Sororities.* After five months the book was an *Essence* magazine top ten best seller; it is currently in its sixth printing.

Edward L. Laster (also known as Mr. Ed) is the director of the Multicultural Academic Enrichment Programs Office at the University of Louisville. He received his bachelor's degree in guidance and counseling and a master's degree in college student personnel from the University of Louisville. Laster has worked in student services programs for more than twenty years, and he has experienced the university from numerous perspectives—not only as a student, but also as a member of the U of L's Board of Trustees. He recently served two terms as chair of the President's Advisory Commission on Diversity and Racial Equality.

Christian A. Mattingly is a graduate student in the College Student Personnel program of the Department of Educational and Counseling Psychology at the University of Louisville in Louisville, Kentucky. She will be graduating in May 2006. She earned her bachelor's degree in communication from the University of Louisville in 2003. Her student affairs experience includes work in the areas of Greek life, orientation, and disability services. Mattingly has previously worked as the associate director of finance at Sigma Kappa Sorority National Headquarters and currently serves as the disability resource center graduate assistant at the University of Louisville. She is a member of NASPA and ACPA.

Kenya LeNoir Messer is vice president for student development and enrollment management and dean of admissions at Wilberforce University in Wilberforce, Ohio. She received a bachelor's degree in psychology from Union College, New York, a master's degree in counseling and student personnel administration from Teachers College, Columbia University, and was selected as one of eight scholars representing the university as part of the US/UK Exchange Program at the University of London. She is currently completing a doctorate in higher education administration at Teachers College, Columbia University. Her dissertation focuses on retention and persistence of students of color in American higher education with a specific concentration on African American male student athletes. She has served as a preconference facilitator at NASPA and ACPA on

the subject of African American male student athletes; has presented at the National Conference on Black Student Retention and at the University of Nebraska's conference on Different Perspectives on Majority Rules; and coauthored a chapter in the 1997 Jossey-Bass monograph *Helping African American Men Succeed in College.* In addition to her work on African American male student athletes, her research interests include issues of access and levels of participation by African American students in international education.

Myron L. Pope is assistant vice president of student services at the University of Central Oklahoma. He received a bachelor's degree in history and English and his master's and doctoral degrees in higher education administration from the University of Alabama. During his career he has worked in the community college system of Alabama as a talent search counselor, at the University of Alabama as the director of recruitment for the College of Education, and at the University of Oklahoma as a faculty member in the Adult and Higher Education Program. Pope has conducted a variety of research on higher education–related issues, including community college student and administrative issues, minority student concerns, faculty governance issues, and institutional trust. He has published in scholarly journals and books and also presented regionally, nationally, and internationally on these topics. He has been active at the regional and national levels of ACPA, ASHE, CSCC, and NASPA. He is a member of Phi Beta Sigma Fraternity, Inc.

Kevin D. Rome, Sr. is the vice president for student services at Morehouse College. He received a bachelor's degree in English from Morehouse College, a master's in education in college student personnel from the University of Georgia, and a doctorate in higher education administration from the University of Texas at Austin. He has worked in higher education administration for the past sixteen years in California, Texas, Indiana, and Georgia. He has been active in NASPA, ACPA, SAAB, Brothers of the Academy, Phi Beta Sigma Fraternity, Inc., and several other professional organizations. In 2001 he participated in the Oxford International Roundtable in Oxford, England. Rome received the National Orientation Directors Association's Norman K. Russell Scholarship Award and the Margaret C. Berry Award for outstanding contributions to student life at the University of Texas at Austin. His areas of interest include African American male development, leadership training, diversity education, and change management.

E. Michael Sutton serves as assistant provost for undergraduate programs at Winston-Salem State University in North Carolina. He received a bachelor's degree in history from Winston-Salem State University, a master's degree in higher education from Southern Illinois University at Carbondale, and a doctorate in higher education administration from Iowa State University. Prior to his current appointment, Dr. Sutton held faculty appointments at Appalachian State University in Boone, North Carolina, and at the University of South Carolina. He has also served in various administrative positions in the student affairs profession, ranging from residence hall director to dean of students. He has presented, as well as published, several articles relating to issues surrounding minority students and Black Greek-letter organizations. He has served in numerous leadership positions within NASPA, as associate editor for the *College Student Affairs Journal,* and as executive committee member at large for the Southern Association of College Student Affairs (SACSA). Sutton's current research interests include utilizing the portfolio method as an alternative pedagogic tool for minority students and issues impacting minority administrators at the community college.

Vernon A. Wall is an independent consultant and a senior consultant for the Washington Consulting Group, an agency specializing in multicultural organizational change. He has over twenty years of professional student affairs experience at Iowa State University, the University of Georgia, and the University of North Carolina at Charlotte and at Chapel Hill. Wall received his bachelor's degree in political science from North Carolina State University and his master's degree in college student personnel administration from Indiana University. He has received several awards for his contributions to the quality of student life, is a nationally known speaker in the areas of diversity/oppression and leadership styles, and is one of the founders and facilitators of the Social Justice Training Institute. Vernon has also served as a trainer for the Martin Luther King Center for Non-Violent Social Change in Atlanta, Georgia. He has served on the Executive Council of the American College Personnel Association and was the 2000 Diamond Honoree recipient and the 2005 Esther Lloyd Jones Professional Service award recipient for outstanding contributions to the field of student affairs. He is co-editor of *Beyond Tolerance: Gays, Lesbians and Bisexuals on Campus* (1991) and *Toward Acceptance: Sexual Orientation Issues on Campus* (2000).

Jamie Washington is the president and founder of the Washington Consulting Group, a multicultural organizational development firm in Baltimore, Maryland. He earned his bachelor's degree in therapeutic recreation and music from Slippery Rock State College; a double master's degree in higher education administration and counseling from Indiana University–Bloomington; a doctorate in college student development from the University of Maryland College Park; and completed the Master of Divinity program at Howard University School of Divinity in May 2004. Washington is a founding faculty member of the Social Justice Training Institute, a trainer development program focusing on diversity awareness, and is a lead faculty member with the LeaderShape Institute and the National Certified Student Leader Program. Some of Dr. Washington's honors include a Mayoral Citation as one of Baltimore's Men of the Year, the 2001 American College Personnel Association Diamond Honoree award for significant contribution to higher education and student affairs work, and a 2002 Voices of Inclusion Award for his work in the area of social justice education. He was ordained in October of 2005 and serves on the ministerial staff of Unity Fellowship Church of Baltimore.

Lemuel W. Watson is professor of higher education and chair of the Department of Counseling, Adult, and Higher Education at Northern Illinois University in DeKalb, Illinois. He holds a bachelor's degree in business from the University of South Carolina, a master's degree from Ball State University, and a doctorate of education from Indiana University. Watson's research interests include educational outcomes, faculty development issues, and social and political issues that affect schools, community, and families with regard to economic development and advancement. He was a Fulbright Scholar at Belarusian State University at the National Institute of Higher Education. Watson is editor for the *Illinois Committee on Black Concerns in Higher Education Journal* and associate editor for both the *National Association of Student Affairs Professionals Journal* and the *College Student Affairs Journal,* and he continues to serve on the board for two other journals in higher education. He is currently writing a book, *Work Is Love Made Visible—A History of National Association of Student Affairs Professionals: A National Leadership Model* and is serving as editor of the book *21st Century Leadership: A Practical Guide for Survival in Dynamic Environments.*

PART ONE

ISSUES AND IDEAS

CHAPTER ONE

AFRICAN AMERICAN COLLEGE MEN

Twenty-First-Century Issues and Concerns

Michael J. Cuyjet, University of Louisville

Several years ago, I had what I describe as "epiphany" experiences while attending two events at the end of another academic school year: the junior year awards ceremony at my daughter's high school and the commencement ceremony at the university at which I work. Although somewhat different in focus and scope, these two events had a few similarities. One very apparent aspect they shared was the almost complete absence of African American men among the honorees.

The first half hour of the high school program consisted of about two dozen special awards for academic achievement. Only one African American male was among those honored. During the latter portion of the program, when each student was called to be recognized, very few of the African American males were cited for any "academic" honors or achievements. At my university's commencement event, the first students recognized were the doctoral degree recipients, who were individually hooded by their mentors. No African American men were among the fifty or so new doctorates conferred that day.

Although this is a wholly anecdotal and very unscientific assessment method, these two events nonetheless provided me with an epiphany by giving witness to an important issue in higher education today: the relative absence of African American men matriculating in college as well as the relatively small pool of academically well-prepared high school students preparing to enter our colleges and universities. The image of these high school and college populations, almost devoid of Black men, with which I was left on each of these days is one borne out by more reliable statistical and demographic measurements, some of which will be reported in this and other chapters in this book. What is less apparent is the impact that the lower percentage of college education among African American men, compared to other groups in our American population, has on a significant number of elements in our society and our communities across the nation.

The issues related to the condition of African American men in American society are far-reaching and complex. Many individuals have addressed various aspects of this broad topic, from the general social conditions that affect African American males to specific instances that have special impact. Particular concerns related to African American men in elementary education, high school education, employment, the criminal justice system, interracial social interactions, and intraracial social interactions have all been examined in both academic literature and the mainstream press. Yet the condition of African American men in higher education seems to have received less attention than some of these other topics, possibly because of the proportionally lower number that are, in fact, part of the condition itself. Among those works that have addressed the concerns of African American men in the college environments, much attention seems to be directed toward faculty and staff rather than undergraduate students. This book focuses attention on a number of issues that affect African American male undergraduate students' matriculation. In doing so, it also identifies some of the efforts being made on campuses across the country to impact these men's lives positively and explores how those programs achieve their success.

This chapter attempts to accomplish several things. First, after a brief examination of some of the statistical information that helps present a picture of the current status of African Americans in American society—particularly at U.S. colleges and universities—it takes a closer look at the dramatic disproportion of African American men and women in college and describes some of the consequences of that imbalance. It also introduces some material about Black men (sometimes referred to as "manhood" issues) that gives evidence of the differences between Black men and Black women, such that the reader can appreciate the need to see these two populations in light of the differences that exist between them and (more important) can understand that the interventions used to assist them may need to be applied differently. Finally, this chapter introduces a number of the various topics to be explored in more detail in the ensuing chapters of the book.

IDENTIFYING THE POPULATION

In a data-driven society like ours, there are endless ways to count and measure things and endless ways to compare the results. In these next few pages we look at some of the numbers that inform us about different groups of people in the United States in ways that help us understand the relationships among those groups.

The 2000 census revealed that, at the time of that enumeration, there were 281,421,906 people in the United States (U.S. Census Bureau, n.d.). Of that population, 143,368,343 were women and 138,053,563 were men, so in the general population women represented a 50.9 percent majority. Breaking that total number down into segments, using the official U.S. racial and ethnic designations, proved somewhat more complicated in 2000 than in previous U.S. census enumerations, because in 2000, for the first time, when individuals were asked to identify their race they were permitted to indicate more than one choice. However, because 97.57 percent of the populations chose to use only one racial identifier, examining just the numbers for that segment of the population to generate a picture of racial mix of the country is fairly accurate. Using the six racial categories employed in the census, we see that 211,460,626 (75.14 percent) identified themselves as White, 34,658,190 (12.32 percent) identified as Black or African American, 2,475,956 (0.88 percent) identified as American Indian and Alaska Native, 10,242,998 (3.64 percent) identified as Asian, 398,835 (0.14 percent) identified as Native Hawaiian and Other Pacific Islander, and 15,359,073 (5.46 percent) identified as Some Other Race. The census separately asked individuals if they identified as Hispanic or Latino since that category is designated an ethnic group rather than a racial group. In the 2000 Census, 35,305,818 (12.55 percent) claimed to be members of this classification.

These numbers present a rough benchmark against which comparisons can be made later in this chapter and throughout other portions of this book to see whether the presence of African American men and women in colleges and in other aspects of life in the United States (such as in prisons) are similar to their representation in the general population.

Interestingly, of the 6,826,228 people who identified themselves with two races or more, 6,368,075 named only two races. Thus the single race group and those that used two races account for 99.84 percent of the total population. Of those identifying with two races, 39.69 percent chose White and one other choice, 11.94 percent chose Black or African American and one other choice, 11.14 percent chose American Indian and Alaska Native and one other choice, 11.11 percent chose Asian and one other choice, 2.54 percent chose Hawaiian and Other Pacific Islander and one other choice, and 23.57 percent chose Some Other Race and one other choice. When added to the much larger number of persons who identified themselves with only one race, these numbers change the general proportions only slightly. Thus, for discussion, we will use the single-identity numbers and percentages. However, it is curious that Whites, who represent more than three quarters of the total population, comprise only two-fifths of those who identify using two races. One wonders if this group is more certain of its heritage than other groups, ignorant about possible multiracial heritage, or in denial about possible non-White ancestors.

The census numbers of greater significance to the topic of this chapter are not so much the ratios of the various racial or ethnic groups to each other, but the proportions of males and females in each group. Of the 34,658,190 citizens who identified as Black or African American, 47.5 percent were male (16,465,185) and 52.5 percent were female (18,193,005). This presents a male-to-female ratio of 90.5. In comparison, the male-to-female ratio for the U.S. population as a whole was 96.3 (49.01 male/50.99 female); the ratio for Whites, 96.4 (49.1 male/50.9 female); for American Indians or Alaska Natives, 99.4 (49.8 male/50.2 female); for Asians, 93.5 (48.3 male/51.7 female); for Native Hawaiians and Other Pacific Islanders, 103.3 (50.8 male/49.2 female); and for Hispanics or Latinos, 105.9 (51.4 male/48.6 female). These figures, showing African Americans with the lowest male-to-female ratio among the groups measured, present one telling indicator of social difference for African American men in relation to the general U.S. society.

Given these numbers, one might assume that, if opportunities were relatively equitable, the ratio of African American college men to African American college women might be similar to the ratio in the general population. An examination of data on collegiate enrollment in the United States in 2000 reveals that women do indeed continue to attend college in greater numbers than men, but their proportion is somewhat greater than their percentage in the general population, as indicated by the 2000 census data. According to the information compiled in 2005 by the *Chronicle of Higher Education Almanac* (2005), of the 16,611,700 college students enrolled in 2002, 43.4 percent were men and 56.6 percent were women. The *Chronicle* breaks these data into six racial or ethnic categories, with the male/female percentages as follows: American Indian, 39.6 percent men/60.4 percent women; Asian, 46.9 percent men/53.1 percent women; Black, 35.8 percent men/64.2 percent women; Hispanic, 42.1 percent men/57.9 percent women; White, 44.0 percent men/56.0 percent women; and Foreign, 55.3 percent men/44.7 percent women. (The *Chronicle* data do not allow for the multiple identifications offered in the 2000 federal census; the numbers associated with these percentages total 16,611,700.) It is quite evident in these enrollment figures that African American men in 2002 not only attended college in a proportion lower than their percentage in the U.S. African American population, but they also still represented the most skewed male/female ratio of any racial/ethnic group—they were outnumbered in colleges by African American women by almost two to one. There is no indication that this trend has changed since these data were published.

As another point of comparison for the relatively low numbers of African American male college students, the question of whether or not there are more African American men in college or in prison has been debated for years. As an example of the figures available to document these claims, Clarence Page, a columnist for the *Chicago Tribune*, wrote in 2002:

> There are now more black men behind bars in America than in its colleges and universities. So says the Justice Policy Institute, a

Washington-based research center, which found a black inmate population explosion over the past two decades, an era of booming prison construction and get-tough-anti-crime legislation. In 1980 there were three times more black men enrolled in colleges and universities (463,700) than in prisons (143,000), the study said. By 2000, black male numbers grew to 791,600 in prison, but only to 603,032 on campus. Although the two groups are not directly comparable, since the college figures count a narrower student-age population, the numbers do dramatize a disturbing trend.

THE DISPROPORTION OF AFRICAN AMERICAN MEN AND WOMEN

Although the number of African American college men in the *Chronicle* data previously cited is slightly higher than the number cited by Page in his 2002 article, the *Chronicle* number is still well below the number of African American men in prison. Which category—prisons or colleges—has the larger population at any particular time is less important than the fact that such a comparison gives stark evidence that the number of African American men in postsecondary educational institutions is so much lower than it should be if their representation were anywhere near what it ought to be if that number were proportional to the percentage of African American men in the U.S. population as a whole. Examples span our culture—from the dramatic disproportion of African American males in "behavior disorder" classrooms in almost every urban public school district to the extremely low percentage of African American men in corporate boardrooms. We can see it every day—that is, if we overcome our tendency to ignore it. For example, walking into the faculty club on the campus, I can choose simply to read the menu and pay no attention to the servers' ethnicity, or I can observe the very apparent fact that the clientele is predominantly white and the wait staff is predominantly African American, then decide how best to voice concern why more of these Black men are not in my classes instead of bringing me iced tea.

This is an extremely important concern for American society for several reasons. First, the disproportion of any one segment of our population in any particular demographic component has far-reaching effects on U.S. society as a whole. Consider for a moment how the disproportion of African American and Latino families concentrated in the lowest economic quadrant of American society casts racial and ethnic overtones onto almost all economic, political, and social policies of federal, state, and municipal government. (This phenomenon was starkly evident among the most severely affected victims of Hurricane Katrina's devastation of New Orleans in 2005.) Logic dictates that if opportunities and resources were available equally and freely to all U.S. residents, the proportional distribution of representatives of various ethnic cultures would be spread across economic levels, throughout occupations, across educational levels, in corporate power structures, and in local, state, and national political arenas. To the contrary, as an example of the existing disproportion, U.S. census data reveal that in 1999, 39.7 percent of African American households and 38.6 percent of Latino households had incomes below $25,000, compared to only 17.8 percent of white households at that level (Wilson, 2000b). Whether or not this issue of the demographic representation of African American men and the places they occupy—or do not occupy—in various components of U.S. society is evidence of institutional racism is a larger and more complex topic than this volume will address. However, the impact of race and economics is one significant reason why some higher education researchers argue for paying close attention to the status of African American men in our colleges and universities—and why they are striving to improve their numbers of attendance and successful matriculation (Arnold, 2001; Brownstein, 2000; Wilson, 2000a).

IMPACTS OF THE MALE-FEMALE IMBALANCE

First, a disclaimer of sorts—although I feel strongly that the significantly low proportion of males among the African American college population has some serious effect on the lives of most African Americans—and perhaps on all Americans in numerous social and cultural arenas—there is currently not much empirical research to prove or disprove this opinion. Thus, a number of the factors examined in this section are not yet supported in the literature and warrant additional research.

RELATIONS BETWEEN MEN AND WOMEN

One result of the low proportion of African American men on the typical four-year college or university campus (this imbalance occurs at HBCUs as well as at PWIs) is the impact on the social climate of the institution, which has several aspects. First, the most apparent result of the proportionally low numbers of African American men on campus is the rather dramatic imbalance of the relative populations of African American men and African American women on the typical campus. As indicated earlier in this chapter, the proportion of men to women among African American undergraduates is more skewed than among any of the other governmental ethnic categories (*Chronicle of Higher Education,* 2005). Dillard University, for example, reported in 2004 a female-to-male gender ratio of 74 percent to 26 percent (Foston, 2004). Despite an increase in interracial dating over the past few years (Hughes, 2003), the fact remains that many African American women seek African American men as potential partners (Porter & Bronzaft, 1995). The relatively low number of these men on the typical campus makes the social dating process on many campuses out of balance. In some cases African American women refuse to date non-African American men and either simply do not date or, if they are fortunate enough to be on a campus in reasonable proximity to a local black community, they seek potential partners off campus. This alternative often proves unsatisfactory as well, since the proportion of men to women in many non-college African American communities is already skewed toward a higher number of women than men, causing competition with the other women in the community. Also, in many cases the available men have less education and a lower socioeconomic status than the college-going females. This may not be a concern of all the women, but it is an issue for many of them (King, 1999).

Although there is little supporting empirical evidence, it seems reasonable to assume that the increasing incidence of interracial dating among African American women at PWIs is exacerbated by the relatively low numbers of African American men among the student body. Some African American college women may indeed select their dating partners with little or no consideration for the person's race (if that is truly possible to do in the U.S.), but others would doubtless admit that they would prefer dating African American men, and that they date others only because of the limited availability of African American men in their environments (Hughes, 2003). Depending on the reactions from their peers on campus, their families, or the surrounding community, these women may perceive interracial dating as preferable to not dating at all, but a stressor nonetheless.

Another issue that adds to the complexity of college dating relationships as they are affected by the low proportion of African American men arises when African American men try to take advantage of their "scarcity" and fail to treat their dating partners with respect. If there is truth to the anecdotal stories of African American women enduring physical or psychological mistreatment, intimidation to engage in sex, and their partners' open dating of others, then these episodes represent another negative consequence of the numerical imbalance of African American men and women on our campuses.

Relations Between Blacks and Whites

The low numbers of African American men on campus at PWIs has another impact on the environment that affects others beyond the African American community. Many schools profess to a desire for a diverse student body, with the expectation that members of the campus community—student, faculty, and administrators included—would thus have opportunities to interact and learn from each other culturally as well as intellectually. Although there is some debate about whether or not students from different cultures actually interact on PWI campuses—even where there are sufficient numbers of students from different ethnic cultures for this to occur—the fact remains that, in order for any such interactions to transpire, there must be sufficient numbers of students representing the various cultural groups. If we do not recognize that there are cultural differences between African American men and African American women, particularly as to how they interact with whites, we may tend to overlook the detrimental effect the low numbers of African American men on PWI campuses can have on this desired cultural interaction.

Of particular concern is the need to counter the often negative stereotypes that the dominant culture—and the African American culture, too—perpetrate about African American men, which can only truly be dispelled by experiencing the positive traits of African American men through face-to-face interactions. In the absence of this experience, we form our perceptions and opinions about members of other social groups from the limited information we obtain from other sources (Sigelman & Tuch, 1997). If these sources—the news media, fictionalized entertainment in books or television or films, or stereotypical images passed from person to person—contain false information, then that is what we accept until provided contradictory, corrective data.

The relative absence of African American men on college campuses lessens the opportunities for non-African Americans to engage in face-to-face interactions that provide experiential learning about the true nature of other people. Obviously, if there are no African American students on a particular campus, the other students will not have a chance to learn firsthand about African Americans. However, even on a campus with a respectable number of African Americans, if that population is overwhelmingly female, the negative stereotype of African American men being culturally dominated by African American women can unwittingly be reinforced. An example of this might be the PWI at which many visible, traditional leadership positions—president of the black student union, representatives to student government, committee chairs in the programming board—are filled by African American women, with at best an occasional token African American man in one of these roles, mainly because of the low numbers of these men in the campus population. Both male invisibility *and* female dominance can easily be inferred from such situations if one is not careful to examine the intervening circumstances affecting the African American men on the campus.

One additional reason for wanting to increase the number of African American men on campus and, therefore, the number of encounters they will inevitably have with members of other ethnic/racial cultures is what I refer to as the "anti-invisible man" factor. As Ralph Ellison tried to explain in his 1952 novel *The Invisible Man,* White people who exist in a world with few if any Black people tend to make Black folks invisible on those few occasions when they do encounter them. Thus, the more opportunities one has for interracial encounters, the less likely one is to retain the ability to render other people "invisible." One result of a skewed imbalance among men and women in the campus African American population is that White people may perceive African American women as "visible" while still failing to see African American men.

Student peers are not the only ones who need the opportunity for positive interactions with African American college men. Faculty, staff, and administrators can harbor stereotypes of African American men from the general media and from the images they see on campus. However, every one-on-one interaction with an African American male, particularly if the resulting impression is a positive one, helps to break down the negative stereotypes and open individuals' eyes to the falsehood of such negative stereotypical images. Obviously, the more African American men on the campus, the more these interpersonal contacts will occur and the quicker students, faculty, staff, and administrators from various cultural backgrounds will learn about each other.

MEN AND WOMEN ARE DIFFERENT

There is an important need for non-Blacks to have these intercultural interactions with both African American women and African American men precisely because they *are* different from each other. In a previous work (Cuyjet, 1997), this author described some of the apparent differences in perceptions and behaviors of African American men and African American women on college campuses. By examining responses to the College Student Experiences Questionnaire (CSEQ) from more that 6,700 African American men and women in the database maintained by the Center for Postsecondary Research and Planning at Indiana University, it was concluded that men and women had substantially different percentages of responses to questions in a range of topical areas (Kuh, Vesper, Connolly, & Pace, 1997). Among the wide variety of topics included were course learning (academics), use of recreational facilities, and grades. For example, almost two-thirds of the African American women in the sample indicated they often or very often took detailed notes in class, whereas fewer than 45 percent of the men did, and twice the percentage of men as women indicated they never took detailed notes in class. More than one third of African American men often or very often played games in the student union or center; less than one in five women did so. In the CSEQ category on the use of athletic and recreational activities, African American men indicated much greater participation than did African American women in each of the ten items; for most items, the percentages of men's "often" or "very often" responses were two or three times that of the women. When asked to indicate their grades in the institution, nearly a quarter of African American women indicated that they were receiving A, A–, or B+, whereas fewer than one in six African American men made that assertion. On the other hand, almost one in five African American men admitted receiving C, C–, or lower, whereas only 12 percent of women made that admission (Cuyjet, 1997).

In one other phenomenon that seems to be particular to African American men, on some campuses at which there are small but stable numbers of African American men, often a large majority of these individuals are intercollegiate athletes; in many cases they are members of the football or basketball team. Person and LeNoir (1997) reported that "about one out of every nine African American male students at predominantly white four-year institutions is an athlete" (p. 79). Although any means that helps to bring African American men to the college campus should be commended, on those campuses where the majority of the African American male students are athletes, several variables can interfere with the kinds of involvement within the broad campus environment that researchers such as Astin (1993) have shown to have positive effects on the general student body. First (as Kenya Messer will explore in Chapter Eight), African American male athletes already must contend with a number of their own particular issues—one of which is a certain amount of isolation from the general campus environment in order to devote hefty amounts of time to practices, travel, and competition for their sport, not to mention sufficient time to keep up with their studies. A second issue is the reinforcement of persistent stereotypes, such as "Black male equals athlete" or "Black male equals dumb jock" or other racially derogatory images (Hall, 2001). On campuses where the majority of African American male undergraduates *are* athletes, or on campuses where athletes are the most visible of the African American male students, it is difficult to promote the perception of African American males as scholars, as intellectuals, or as campus leaders in nonsports activities. For these reasons, any institution facing the situation in which its African American male athletes actually are, or even appear to be, the majority of the Black men on campus must redouble its effort to recruit and retain nonathlete African American men, particularly those who can demonstrate strong academic scholarship.

POSSIBLE INTERVENTIONS

Although chapters two through eleven in this book—each exploring a different aspect of college life for African American men— offer some suggestions for efforts that institutions can take to enhance the enrollment and successful matriculation of African American men, nonetheless a few observations about both direct and indirect intervention by the institution and its officers are warranted in this chapter. One general undertaking by campus leaders should be to develop a clear understanding of the numbers and general characteristics of African American men present on the campus. As has been suggested several times already in this chapter, at most institutions the ratio of men and women is more skewed among African Americans than in other demographic populations. If administrators are not accustomed to breaking down their students' ethnic identifications into gender subunits, the number of African American females can leave them unaware of the size of the African American male population and, possibly, of how fragile that number really is.

IDENTIFYING SPECIFIC CULTURAL CHARACTERISTICS

A major part of this effort to recognize fully the African American men on campus must be an attempt to learn about the particular sociocultural characteristics of this student population itself. To be effective in assisting African American men's matriculation, one must have a reasonable understanding of that population. Three aspects of this knowledge should be addressed briefly here. First, although certain general characteristics can be attributed to African American college men, any population of African American men is not a monolithic body with little or no within-group diversity. In a previous work, this author stated that "the characteristics of each of these men consists of three equally important factors: his common human traits shared with all men and women, his Black male cultural attributes, and his unique individuality" (Cuyjet, 1997, p. 3). It is possible that some of the African American males coming to our institutions now are as likely to be from predominantly white suburban schools as from inner city ones, as likely to be of middle-class backgrounds as of lower socioeconomic means, and as likely to be academically talented as to be academically underprepared. So although we cannot ignore the generalizations that can alert us to some of the problems African American male students may face in adapting to the culture and environment of our campuses and that can prepare us to address those needs, we must not make the mistake of applying these characteristics (and our proposed solutions) universally to each African American man who enrolls. Interventions must include opportunities inclusive of high-achieving African American men as well (Fries-Britt, 1997; Harper, 2003).

Second, to the extent that we can accurately identify African American male culture as "different" from other identifiable groups, an effort to understand those cultural values and behaviors is beneficial. We do often recognize that an understanding of those "Black male cultural attributes" that are different from comparable characteristics of other identifiable groups (White males, for instance) is important to our ability to assist African American men through their matriculation and can be helpful in not labeling these different behaviors and values as deficient or deviant. Lee and Bailey (1999) tell us that because African American men are frequently denied the means of achieving the dominant American culture's manifestations of manhood (such as economic success, head-of-household status, traditional civic involvement), they adopt alternate behaviors to demonstrate manhood attainment—behaviors that are often at odds with those of the dominant culture. Among various authors who have described some of these behaviors, one of the better characterizations of young black manhood is the description of "cool pose" by Majors and Billson (1992). As they explain it,

> Cool pose is a distinctive coping mechanism that serves to counter, at least in part, the dangers that black males encounter on a daily basis. As a performance, cool pose is designed to render the black male visible and to empower him. . . . Cool pose is constructed

from attitudes and actions that become firmly entrenched in the black male's psyche as he adopts a façade to ward off the anxiety of second-class status. . . . By acting calm, emotionless, fearless, aloof, and tough, the African American male strives to offset an externally imposed "zero" image. Being cool shows both the dominant culture and the black male himself that he is strong and powerful. (p. 5)

In addition to this description of cool pose, Majors and Billson offer explanations of other phenomena in the search for expressions of manhood among many African American adolescents through masculinity rituals that are occasionally destructive. These rituals include "black masking" (also referred to as "impression management")—a suppression of natural feelings and assumption of a mask of affable compliance with the role Whites expect Blacks to play; "shucking"—a manner of talking and physical movements designed to construct a façade to accommodate White expectations; "playing the dozens"—a highly stylized verbal repartee of mock insults and bragging; and what Majors and Billson call the "cool cat life style"—adopting particular clothing, automobiles, and other possessions, and speech patterns, physical behaviors, and other activities that are culturally prescribed as highly acceptable by other "cool" young African American men. Familiarity with these behaviors can provide useful insight into the beliefs and values of some of the young African American men entering our institutions.

The third aspect of understanding the different cultural characteristics of African American men is to recognize the self-esteem issues that become evident as one encounters these students and their daily circumstances. The numerical frailty of the African American male student population has already been mentioned; however, this issue speaks to the psychological frailty of many members of this group. Generally speaking, the image of the African American man as a threatening figure has been so institutionalized in American culture that most African American men perceive themselves as being part of a permanently marginalized population (Schlossberg, 1989), and to some extent they have deeply internalized that perception (Freire, 1993). So they come to the campus community at a psychological disadvantage in that they often perceive themselves as "less than" the others they meet. Thus, some of the energy necessary to succeed academically is often directed at other pursuits, such as achieving "manhood" status among other

African American men on the campus and achieving status with African American females. One example of this status-seeking behavior is the amount of time that African American males typically devote to intramural sports competition on campus. This is a culturally acceptable way to demonstrate prowess, ability, and status both in the African American community and, ironically, to non-African Americans as well. Unfortunately, when the time devoted to sports interferes with academic achievement, the ultimate impact on matriculation can be ruinous. For those African American men who come from a high school background in which academic success was devalued, the problem of devoting adequate time to studies is exacerbated. Ways to promote African American male students' academic success are examined in Chapter Two. Other chapters in this book also address ways to increase their involvement in a variety of extracurricular activities and to enhance the opportunities for leadership roles and the positive traits that develop from such endeavors. I encourage you to explore those topics in their respective chapters.

EXPLORING SPIRITUALITY

One additional characteristic of African American men that has not yet been mentioned here is also explored in greater detail later in this book—the topic of spirituality (see Chapter Six). Although it is a relatively new area of interest among student affairs professionals on campuses that are not religiously affiliated, we are beginning to recognize that to understand more fully the maturation of all college students (including African American men), we must acknowledge the impact of spiritual development on them. In attempting to understand the cultural complexity of African American college men, it is helpful to take note of their spiritual inclinations, their faith development, and their involvement in religious activities and organizations—although these three are definitely not synonymous. A number of researchers have begun exploring the spiritual nature of college students in general (Bryant, Choi, & Yasuno, 2003; Love, 2002; Watt, 2003), and several others have examined spirituality as it pertains to various aspects of African American students' lives, such as identity development (Stewart,

2002) and coping skills (Constantine, Wilton, Gainor, & Lewis, 2002). In an article describing the psychosocial development of African American college students, McEwen, Roper, Bryant, & Langa (1990) identified spirituality as one of nine important factors related to developmental tasks of African American college students that "either have not been addressed adequately in the psychological theories or need to be considered in more complex ways" (p. 430). Adding to these facts about increasing spirituality in the lives of African American college students, the influence of the church in the African American community provides more than enough incentive for us to explore how today's college administrators can use knowledge about African American men's spirituality and faith development to enhance the quality of their matriculation experience.

AFFECTING GRADUATION

To conclude this discussion of direct or indirect interventions by the institution and its administrators, the third approach is to establish mechanisms that actually can effectively enhance the successful matriculation and graduation of African American men. These efforts will differ greatly from institution to institution, depending on a number of variables, including the nature of the African American male population and its relation to other student populations, particularly African American females. One key element of this effort is to launch an overt examination of what factors contribute to degree completion for African American men on any particular campus. Studies like the one conducted by Hamilton (2005) at several schools in southern California demonstrate how such assessments can be fruitful. The character of such efforts will also depend on the resources available—on the campus and in the surrounding community—and on the desired outcomes for helping African American men: impacting the social climate, enhancing the academic environment, increasing leadership opportunities, reducing incidences of racism and prejudice, or all of these. It is hoped that the material presented elsewhere in this book, particularly the examples of viable programs in Part Two, will be helpful in achieving this desired outcome.

CONCLUSION

This chapter has begun the discussion of African American men in college by examining some of the demographic data of that group. First, we looked at the numbers and percentages of African American men in the U.S. population and made some comparisons with the male segment of other racial/ethnic groups. We have seen that, not surprisingly, African American men often demonstrate less favorable social conditions when compared to White males. To cite just a few more examples, according to Bureau of Justice statistics in 2001, 16.6 percent of all U.S. adult Black males had been incarcerated at least once, compared to 4.9 percent of White men (Wilson, 2003). The U.S. Department of Health and Human Services (HSS) reports that in 1998, the age-adjusted rate of death from prostate cancer for African American men was 48.7 per 100,000, compared with a rate of 19.6 per 100,000 for White males (U.S. Department of Health and Human Services, 2002). HSS also has reported that in 1997–98, the death rate by homicide for young African American men (age 19 years or younger) was 23.8 per 100,000, compared to a rate of 3.8 per 100,000 for the comparable White group (U.S. Department of Health and Human Services, 2003).

This chapter has also drawn attention to the disproportion of African American men and women in most colleges. Women represent about 51 percent of the total U.S. population, and although the general ratio of men to women in college is 43.9 percent to 56.1 percent, African Americans have the most skewed ratio of all the racial/ethnic groups—36.7 percent men to 63.3 percent women (*Chronicle of Higher Education*, 2005). This imbalance has a number of identifiable impacts. Perhaps the most apparent is the effect on the socialization of African American men and women on the campus. Dating patterns between African American men and women and between African Americans and partners from other racial/ethnic groups are significantly affected by the ratio of men to women in the campus community (Foston, 2004). Moreover, the social experiences on the campus can impact the attitudes that these students, particularly the women, take with them as they leave the campus and develop social relationships in their post-college lives—attitudes that may have been permanently altered in response to the reduced availability of potential African American partners (Porter & Bronzaft, 1995).

This chapter has also introduced what may be considered a central premise for the discussion in the subsequent chapters of this book that address the needs of African American college men—the fact that African American men and women are very different in some ways, with discernible differences in perceptions and behaviors (Cuyjet, 1997). Admittedly, some of the characteristics of African American male students are shared with other students—commonalities for the Black community shared with African American women, for example, or typical male behaviors shared with White men—and readers will no doubt observe this as they proceed to explore the material presented by these authors. Yet readers are also encouraged to recognize that African American men and women are different in a number of ways. Although a particular effort to assist all African American students (perhaps even all underrepresented minority students) may have a positive effect across the entire population, student affairs professionals need to be open to the possibility that the same intervention may have a dramatically different impact on each gender group and that, in some cases, entirely different actions are needed.

A number of specific interventions have been proposed here. The first action is to endeavor to learn the cultural characteristics of African American men. Paradoxically, the first lesson in this effort is to recognize that although there are indeed some characteristics that most African American men may share, there are others that are affected by external sociological and psychological factors, such that each man we encounter is ultimately, uniquely individual. Probably the best advice offered in this chapter is to make the conscious effort to examine the African American male students on a particular campus or set of similar campuses to discover which specific factors contribute to degree completion and which detract from it. Ideally, the material presented in this book will provide provocative ideas on how to conduct such an assessment and how to use the results to make a positive impact on this particularly important population of African American men.

References

Arnold, M. V. (2001). Making a way out of no way: Defining success in a young African American man. *Dissertation Abstracts International, 61*(11-A), 4294.

Astin, A. W. (1993). *What matters in college: Four critical years revisited.* San Francisco: Jossey-Bass.

Brownstein, A. (2000, November 3). Are male students in short supply, or is this "crisis" exaggerated? *Chronicle of Higher Education, 47*(10), A47–A48.

Bryant, A. N., Choi, J. Y., & Yasuno, M. (2003). Understanding the religious and spiritual dimensions of students' lives in the first year of college. *Journal of College Student Development, 44*(6), 723–745.

Chronicle of Higher Education Almanac (2005–6). College enrollment by racial and ethnic group, selected years. Retrieved November 14, 2005, from http://chronicle.com/weekly/almanac/2005/nation/0101503.htm.

Constantine, M. G., Wilton, L., Gainor, K. A., & Lewis, E. L. (2002). Religious participation, spirituality, and coping among African American college students. *Journal of College Student Development, 43*(5), 605–613.

Cuyjet, M. J. (1997). African American men on college campuses: Their needs and their perceptions. In M. J. Cuyjet (Ed.), *Helping African American men succeed in college* (pp. 5–16). New Directions for Student Services, no. 80. San Francisco: Jossey-Bass.

Fries-Britt, S. (1997). Identifying and supporting gifted African American men. In M. J. Cuyjet (Ed.), *Helping African American men succeed in college* (pp. 65–78). New Directions for Student Services, no. 80. San Francisco: Jossey-Bass.

Foston, N. A. (2004, September). Campus dilemma: Coping with the acute male shortage. *Ebony, 59*(11), 128–131.

Freire, P. (1993). *Pedagogy of the oppressed.* New York: Continuum Publishing Company.

Hall, R. E. (2001). The ball curve: Calculated racism and the stereotype of African American men. *Journal of Black Studies, 32*(1), 104–119.

Hamilton, J. P. (2005). Reasons why African-American men persist to degree completion in institutions of higher education. *Dissertation Abstracts International,* A65 (10), 3717.

Harper, V. R. (2003). Most likely to succeed: The self-perceived impact of involvement on the experiences of high-achieving African American undergraduate men at predominantly White universities. *Dissertation Abstracts International,* A64 (6), 1995.

Hughes, Z. (2003). The flip side: Why some sisters only date whites & "others." *Ebony, 58*(7), 55–56, 58.

King, A.E.O. (1999). African American females' attitudes toward marriage: An exploratory study. *Journal of Black Studies, 29*(3), 416–437.

Kuh, G. D., Vesper, N., Connolly, M. R., & Pace, C. R. (1997). *College student experiences questionnaire: Revised norms for the third edition.* Bloomington,

IN: Center for Postsecondary Research and Planning at Indiana University.

Lee, C. C., & Bailey, D. F. (1999). Counseling African American male youth and men. In C. C. Lee (Ed.), *Multicultural issues in counseling: New approaches to diversity* (2nd ed.) (pp. 123–154). Alexandria, VA: American Counseling Association.

Love, P. G. (2002). Comparing spiritual development and cognitive development. *Journal of College Student Development, 43*(3), 357–373.

Majors, R., & Billson, J. M. (1992). *Cool pose: The dilemmas of Black manhood in America.* San Francisco: New Lexington Press.

McEwen, M. K., Roper, L. D., Bryant, D. R., & Langa, M. J. (1990). Incorporating the development of African American students into psychosocial theories of student development. *Journal of College Student Development, 31*(5), 429–436.

Page, C. (2002, September 1). When prisons lure more than colleges. *Chicago Tribune,* http://chicagotribune.com/archives.

Person, D. R., & LeNoir, K. M. (1997). Retention issues and models for African American male athletes. In M. J. Cuyjet (Ed.), *Helping African American men succeed in college* (pp. 79–91). New Directions for Student Services, no. 80. San Francisco: Jossey-Bass.

Porter, M. M., & Bronzaft, A. L. (1995). Do the future plans of educated Black women include Black men? *The Journal of Negro Education, 64*(2), 162–170.

Schlossberg, N. K. (1989). Marginality and mattering: Key issues in building community. In D. C. Roberts (Ed.), *Designing campus activities to foster a sense of community* (pp. 5–15). New Directions for Student Services, no. 48. San Francisco: Jossey-Bass.

Sigelman, L., & Tuch, S. A. (1997). Metastereotypes: Black perceptions of Whites' stereotypes of Blacks. *Public Opinion Quarterly, 61,* 87–101.

Stewart, D. L. (2002). The role of faith in the development of an integrated identity: A qualitative study of black students at a white college. *Journal of College Student Development, 43*(4), 579–596.

U.S. Census Bureau. (n.d.). http://factfinder.census.gov/servlet/.

Watt, S. K. (2003). *Come to the river: Using spirituality to cope, resist, and develop identity.* New Directions for Student Services, no. 104. San Francisco: Jossey-Bass.

Wilson, M. (2000a, October 26). Reversing the plight of African American male college students. *Black Issues in Higher Education, 17*(18), 175.

Wilson, M. (2000b, November). Black and Hispanic median income levels reach all-time high. *Marketing to the Emerging Majorities,* no. 11. New York: EPM Communications.

Wilson, M. (2003, September 5). One in every 37 Americans has served time. *Research Alert,* no. 21. New York: EPM Communications.

CHAPTER TWO

ENHANCING THE ACADEMIC CLIMATE FOR AFRICAN AMERICAN COLLEGE MEN

Fred A. Bonner II, Texas A&M University
Kevin W. Bailey, Tulane University

Gunnar Myrdal (1944), in his attempts to conceptualize the minority experience in the United States, coined the term *an American dilemma.* What Myrdal viewed as the nation's espoused approach of promoting equality for all while truly embracing this concept for only a select few, parallels the current experiences of many African American students in education. For the African American student in general and the African American male student in particular, experiences in the K–12 and higher education contexts have been at best chilly and at worst hostile. According to Hrabowski, Maton, and Greif (1998), "Almost everything we read and hear about young Black males focuses on the problems of crime, violence, drugs, teenage pregnancy, and poor academic achievement" (p. 3). Hence, the operating framework used by schools to interface with African American males is often constructed based on lists of perceived problems, using an approach that identifies pathologies instead of promoting promise.

Fostering academic achievement and promise among African American males in public schools continues to be a formidable task. Hopkins (1997) found that at K–12 institutions, Black male student populations experienced political, cultural, and economic inequalities almost daily. The outcomes of these disparities continue to result in significant numbers of these students failing, stopping out, dropping out, or generally losing interest in scholastic endeavors (Gibbs, 1988; Hale-Benson, 1986; Hrabowski, Maton, & Greif, 1998; Irvine, 1990).

Past experiences of African American males in public schools mirror much of what exists for this population today. White and Cones (1999) found that "From the middle of elementary school and continuing into high school, Black males lead all other groups of students in suspensions, expulsions, behavioral problems, and referrals to special classes for slow learners. In most inner-city high schools, the dropout rate for Black males is over 50%, and those who remain in school are four to five grades behind in reading and math" (p. 259).

Like its K–12 educational predecessor, higher education too has presented a major stumbling block for many African American males. Allen (1992) asserted that among African American and White collegians, significant differences were found in areas of persistence rates, academic achievement levels, enrollment in advanced degree programs, and overall psychosocial development. These differences translate into what Cuyjet (1997) has referred to among African American males as "'underpreparedness' for the academic challenges of postsecondary education" (p. 6). Further evidence supporting this claim is the ever-widening chasm between African American females and African American males within the academy, the former representing a 24 percent higher enrollment rate than the latter (Nettles & Perna, 1997).

Although the myriad issues African American males face span the educational continuum, context notwithstanding, the confluence of a number of very specific factors has been found to promote a climate of success for these men. This chapter illuminates each of these critical factors: peer group influence, family influence and support, faculty relationships, identity development and self-perception, and institutional environment. Each factor is discussed in turn to provide the reader with information regarding its relative impact on the institutional climate experienced by the African American male college student. In addition, policy and programmatic recommendations are described that should encourage the development of initiatives leading to positive academic outcomes, particularly as they relate to the creation of higher-quality education climates engendering African American college student success (Watson et al., 2002).

Peer Group Influence

Peer groups constitute an important source of support for students attempting to negotiate the rigors of the undergraduate experience. According to Astin (1993), "The single most powerful source of influence on the undergraduate student's academic and personal development is the peer group . . . the amount of interaction among peers has far-reaching effects on nearly all areas of student learning and development" (p. 8). Pascarella and Terenzini (1991) also suggest that peer groups influence college student attitudes, occupational choices, and persistence decisions. These groups are important in that they often expose students to viable social circles of similar achievement-oriented peers, thereby reifying these students' aspirations and goals (Bonner, 2001).

The peer group essentially serves as an audience, a virtual training ground to test out assumptions and ideas, strategies and plans within an encouraging and safe environment. The peer group for the African American student in college takes on an even greater level of significance in their matriculation experience. Unlike the postsecondary experiences shared among their nonminority peers, for most African American students there is the added burden of establishing a sense of agency within a milieu that differs quite markedly from their ethnic, cultural, and socioeconomic background. In particular, what ostensibly is accepted behavior (such as assertiveness, aggressiveness, candor) among White male collegiate populations is often viewed as unacceptable behavior among African American male collegiate populations (Wilson-Sadberry, Royster, & Winfield, 1991). Therefore, it is the peer group that serves to "meet the need for belonging, feedback, and new learning experiences" (White & Cones, 1999, p. 214).

The need for belonging is often addressed within the African American peer enclave through the establishment of key social clusters—fraternities, athletic groups, student associations, and academic study groups. Both the frequency and quality of student interactions in these clusters are found to be positively associated with persistence (Astin, 1993). Also, a key consideration for these students is being connected to peers who will provide them with critical feedback related not only to their academic progress, but also to their nonacademic progress. These sociocultural influences are often cited as being more critical to the success of African

American students in educational settings than the more intellectual pursuits traditionally highlighted (Tracey & Sedlacek, 1985). Finally, peer group influences on new learning experiences for African American males become manifest through increased levels of academic development, problem-solving skills, critical thinking skills, and cultural awareness found in these student-to-student exchanges (Astin, 1993). Educators must also continue to play a role by emphasizing high academic achievement and encouraging peer support and peer reinforcement for academic success.

By attempting to understand the composition, structure, and mission of peer group subcultures, institutions of higher education will be better equipped to meet the needs of all student communities. In speaking to the topic of "what works" in campus diversity efforts, it was Smith (1997) who posited, "Opportunities for interaction between and among student groups are desired by virtually all students and produce clear increases in understanding and decreases in prejudicial attitudes. Such opportunities also positively affect academic success. The conditions under which interactions among individuals are likely to be beneficial include institutional support, equal status, and common goals" (p. vi).

Hence, ensuring that positive interactions occur within and between peer groups on college campuses is an important part of the matriculation process. Although this is a necessary goal to implement for institutions across various cultural groups, it is particularly important for those student populations that, much like the African American male, are attempting to integrate both academically and socially into an environment that for all intents and purposes does not coincide with their constructed worldviews.

One way to ensure that men are spending more of their time pursuing academic growth and less time learning interpersonal coping strategies is to form a Black male support group that functions much like a freshman seminar, with the purpose of enlightening and exposing all Black men to the tribulations of a predominantly White campus. If men are informed about what to expect and are able to use each other to share experiences and provide support, fewer will voluntary leave school (D'Augelli & Hershberger, 1993; Hood, 1992), and more can focus their attention on intellectual pursuits without a cloud of deception. In addition, the support group allows its members to take pride in academic achievement and intellectual competence without the added burden or stigma of feeling as if they are "acting White" (Fordham & Ogbu, 1986).

FAMILY INFLUENCE AND SUPPORT

White and Cones (1999) reported that, from a psychological perspective, the family meets needs for safety, emotional security, affection, and guidance—the family is the very first unit to which humans are exposed. These familial units serve as key sources of support for African American male college students. Numerous studies (Allen, 1992; Fleming, 1984; Hughes, 1987; Pascarella & Terenzini, 1986; Wilson & Constantine, 1999) have documented the relative impact of the connection among African American collegians and their families on issues such as psychosocial development, racial identity, academic success, resilience, and self-esteem. According to Wilson and Constantine, familial relationships for many African American students have a particular impact on the development of a positive Black racial identity. The establishment of a positive identity for the African American male student is significant in that it serves as the foundation upon which the student can develop some sense of agency and in turn determine where he "fits" within the academy.

Ostensibly, this notion of fit and of belonging is often experienced quite differently for African American male collegians than for White males and for all females, primarily due to the reasons previously articulated—alienation and isolation, absence of peer connections, and a lack of support. According to Harris and Nettles (1996), "Minority students' efforts to cope with feelings of alienation and isolation take various forms. Many students withdraw psychologically from the university but continue to complete basic tasks in a perfunctory manner" (p. 337). It can be a challenge to find the necessary agents within the institution who are capable of connecting with these students on a very personal level to circumvent these feelings. Tracey and Sedlacek (1985) posited that for many African American students, finding a viable support structure and a sense of belonging typically occurred away from the campus (that is, with family). Therefore, the familial network is used as a frontline defense unit to assist the student in strategically moving through the postsecondary minefield. It is this unit, this cultural and community framework (Fries-Britt, 1998), that provides these students with some sense of familiarity and support, ultimately promoting their development.

Research has also documented the influence of family on not only the psychosocial and social development, but also the academic development of African American male college students. Several studies (Cuyjet, 1997; Fleming, 1984; Wilson-Sadberry, Royster, & Winfield, 1991) attempt to dichotomize the matriarchal and patriarchal influence; however, the unifying theme across all studies in this area is that familial influence from one or both parents is a significant factor in these students' matriculation success. Encouragement and support from the family unit, through accolades and admonishment, is translated into student academic commitment and persistence.

Familial support structures for African American male college students develop during their precollegiate matriculation (Hrabowski, Maton, & Greif, 1998), and these structures are carried forth into their postsecondary experiences. The familiar refrains "hang in there" and "you can do it" often provide the extra push to spur these students on to academic success. It is the complex combination of these nonacademic and noncognitive variables (Tracey & Sedlacek, 1985) that also provides these students with the wherewithal to tackle deep-seated issues such as campus-based racism and prejudice (Wilson & Constantine, 1999), while simultaneously achieving academic success.

In order to make the family a viable component in the collegiate matriculation experience of the African American student, institutions must be proactive in their approach. As one set of plausible strategies to address this issue, Bonner (2001) asserts,

> Orientation officials at the university-wide and departmental level should promote initiatives that include family members and parents in the admissions and retention process. Bridging the knowledge and expertise of the student affairs professional in the area of campus-based orientation programming with the acumen and intuition of the academic affairs professional in the area of department/domain specific orientation programming could serve to meet the varied developmental needs of all students. Bridging should be enacted with the family serving as the supportive scaffolding, primarily through their participation in programming initiatives. (p. 15)

FACULTY RELATIONSHIPS

African American students who attend predominantly White institutions (PWIs) often describe the classroom and institutional environments as inhospitable (Smith, 1997). According to Sedlacek (1999), this inhospitality often stems from the inability to get straightforward information from faculty concerning their academic progress. Berry (1983) reported that Black students in college classrooms are often excluded from informal conversations among their White classmates and complain of being ignored in class discussions. Gossett, Cuyjet, and Cockriel (1996) indicated that Black students experienced feelings of being marginalized in the classroom due to perceived pressures of having to serve as the spokesperson for their race. Additionally, Sedlacek (as cited by Gregory, 2000) found that faculty was less likely to provide praise to African American students commensurate with the degree and quality of praise provided to their nonminority peers.

Davis (1999) acknowledged the isolation that Black men often feel due to their unwillingness to interact with faculty or classmates outside of the classroom. These feelings are usually based on negative in-class relationships. In a recent qualitative study of Black students attending a PWI, Fries-Britt and Turner (2001) reported that 100 percent of the participants in the study perceived that there was a "proving process" required in the classroom setting, essentially to validate their intellectual competence. In particular, many Black men inherited the burden of having to rebuff stereotypes regarding their status as athletes in addition to having to prove their intellectual competence.

To circumvent many of the problems African American males are experiencing in college, purposive initiatives aimed at pairing these students with viable faculty mentors are essential. According to Pascarella and Terenzini (1979), the frequency of student-faculty informal contact accounted for increases in freshman year persistence. Astin (1993) further added that, second only to the peer group, faculty-student interaction represents the most significant aspect of a student's undergraduate development and institutional commitment. By inference, Black men should benefit from these interactions as all other students do, despite the special efforts that may be required to ensure that it happens.

Unfortunately, Black men (1) are perceived by society to have poor academic socialization and low expectations for their academic achievement (Gordon, 1994), (2) are less likely to seek out faculty for assistance (Hood, 1992), and (3) assume they will be subjected to some form of mistreatment by faculty (D'Augelli & Hershberger, 1993)—thus, a purposeful attempt at bringing these two groups together must be the guiding modus operandi.

Although not always possible, the optimal arrangement would be to connect African American male students with African American male faculty. It is imperative that the Black male faculty selected to participate in these programs serve in a dual capacity, as both academic escort and social nurturer. Unfortunately, Black male retention is also a problem in the faculty ranks, so a critical mass of mentors may be lacking in the PWI. Black students have been calling for the increase of Black faculty and staff at PWIs for many years, yet the call sometimes falls on deaf ears.

In the absence of viable African American faculty to serve as mentors and advisors to African American students, it is imperative for institutions to develop cadres of non-African American faculty to serve in these roles. Although many students lament the lack of availability of faculty who share common gender, cultural, ethnic, and racial background experiences, the bottom line is that some sense of connection with a faculty person, regardless of background experiences, is better than none. In a research investigation by Lee (1999), she discovered that for African American students, "having an African American faculty mentor was less important than having a mentor in their career field. Students reasoned that they could get the cultural connection they needed outside of the university, when necessary, by simply going home" (p. 33).

To overcome the frequently negative impact of the issues facing African American males in the K–12 system, researchers cite a multicultural curriculum as one viable means of ensuring their success in college. An added benefit of having African American faculty—or faculty who are at least apprised of the background experiences these students bring to the academic setting—is their willingness to integrate the worldviews of these student cohorts into existing classroom curriculum (Bowser & Perkins, 1991; Goddard, 1990; Ogbu, 1981; Osborne, 1999; Smedley, Myers, & Harrell, 1993; Taylor, 1994). Specifically, the lived experiences of African

American males are integrated into the classroom environment to facilitate learning. In addition, teachers must infuse their presentation of the curriculum with cultural perspectives. Identifying the accomplishments of African Americans in the sciences, history, politics, and mathematics aids students in realizing the endless possibilities of their educational pursuits, and it can fend off the onset of academic disengagement.

Foster and Peele (1999) supported the integration of Black males' personal experiences within the classroom environment. They added that those who successfully teach Black males must be caring and persistent, and they must develop productive relationships focusing on the efforts students have expended rather than solely on their actual abilities or academic achievements. In a qualitative investigation of Black and Hispanic high school students (sophomores, juniors, and seniors), Bowser and Perkins (1991) reported that mentors who took a personal interest in these students and in some cases treated them as members of their families enriched their high school experiences. These findings parallel the experiences of these same student cohorts in higher education, and it becomes readily apparent that it is the combination of culturally relevant curricula and student-centered teachers who genuinely care about their students that will potentially assist in countering the academic problems facing African American males in the elementary and secondary educational systems.

Fostering positive classroom environments is yet another important means of ensuring the successful matriculation of African American male college students. Dawson-Threat (1997), in her research highlighting strategies to enhance the in-class academic experiences for African American men, suggests that faculty must concern themselves with three major issues: including a safe space for expression of personal experience, facilitating and promoting the understanding of difference, and providing the opportunity to explore Black manhood issues. Although faculty may feel some sense of uneasiness in tackling these issues, they must be addressed to ensure that these students identify viable pathways leading to success (1997). Through a concerted effort to understand the needs of this student cohort, faculty members can create student-faculty liaisons that establish a basis for a shared sense of understanding and trust (Adams, 1992).

IDENTITY DEVELOPMENT AND SELF-ESTEEM

Researchers have identified several environmental conditions that can explain why African American males perform poorly in elementary and secondary schools: academic disidentification, lack of academic resilience, stereotype threat, and cool pose. Steele (1992) advanced the concept of disidentification, which he defined as the absence of a relationship between self-esteem and academic performance. Students found to exhibit low levels of academic performance were also found to exhibit low levels of motivation to succeed. Essentially, it was noted that their self-esteem was directly linked to academic performance. These students are neither rewarded for good academic performance nor punished for poor academic performance and are at a higher risk for falling through the cracks and dropping out of school.

Although all students, regardless of race, are susceptible to academic disidentification, students of color have the additional anxiety of combating negative stereotypes about their academic ability. Osborne (1997) used the concept of academic disidentification in a study comparing African American, Hispanic, and Caucasian high school students. His results clearly support the notion of race as a factor in the academic disidentification of African American males. Although all students except Hispanic females demonstrated some level of disidentification between tenth and twelfth grades, Black males demonstrated a statistically significant and dramatic increase in disidentification, which began at the eighth grade and escalated as they progressed toward their senior year. Osborne (1999) reported that this dramatic disidentification gap among African American male populations has not always existed. Osborne first observed this widening disidentification gap in a similar study of high school seniors between the years 1972 and 1992. These results parallel findings cited by other researchers (Demo & Parker, 1986; Lay & Wakstein, 1985), who also found a correlation between low academic performance and low self-esteem among ever-increasing numbers of African American students.

Self-esteem is also linked to the concept of academic resilience. Resilient students develop positive behaviors that improve their chances of being successful in school despite their membership in an at-risk group (Finn & Rock, 1997). Resilient students are found to engage in behaviors that correlate with higher levels of self-esteem than those students who do not exhibit engaging behaviors—"coming to class and school on time, being prepared for and participating in class work, expending the effort needed to complete assignments in school and as homework, and avoiding being disruptive in class" (p. 231).

Still another concept posed by Steele (1997) has also been reported to have an impact on how African American males perceive their institutional environments. This concept, *stereotype threat*, "is a situational threat—a threat in the air—that, in general form, can affect the members of any group about whom a negative stereotype exists . . . members of these groups can fear being reduced to that stereotype and for those who identify with the domain to which the stereotype is relevant, this predicament can be self-threatening" (p. 614).

If the threat becomes pervasive, it can trigger academic disidentification. Students who have high self-esteem and are performing well academically are more susceptible to stereotype threat. According to Osborne (1999), "for these individuals, a wrong answer is not only personally damaging but also confirms the negative group stereotype" (p. 557).

Finally, Majors and Billson (1992) suggested that when African American males are faced with situations that question or jeopardize their manhood, affirm racial stereotypes, or damage their sense of identity or worth, they adopt cool behaviors as coping mechanisms. Cool pose empowers Black males and gives them control. It is an attitude that conveys strength, visibility, and security despite obstacles and situations that would lead to the contrary. Cool pose is defined as "a ritualized form of masculinity that entails behaviors, scripts, physical posturing, impression management, and carefully crafted performances that deliver a single, critical message: pride, strength, and control" (p. 4). Cool behaviors were adopted during slavery to help Blacks to survive and subsequently have influenced popular culture through music, clothing, sports, and the media. Given the previously articulated educational difficulties facing African American males, it is likely that cool behavior is used by males to empower them in the classroom, an environment in which they are perceived by most to be powerless.

INSTITUTIONAL ENVIRONMENT

Once African American males enter college, their interaction with the educational system does not get easier. Some of the issues, such as self-esteem (Constantine, Robinson, Wilton, & Caldwell, 2002; Demo & Parker, 1986; Lay & Wakstein, 1985), stereotype threat (Steele, 2000), teacher neglect (Berry, 1983; Sedlacek, 1999), and a homogenous curriculum (Bourassa, 1991; Dawson-Threat, 1997; Love, 1993; Sedlacek, 1999) are recapitulated throughout their matriculation experiences. However, students have an additional burden of coping and adjusting to an environment that may be less hospitable to their presence, particularly if they attend PWIs as opposed to HBCUs (Allen, 1992; Bonner & Murry, 1998; Cheatham, Slaney, & Coleman, 1990; Cokley, 2001; Davis, 1994; DeSousa & Kuh, 1996; D'Augelli & Hershberger, 1993; Fleming, 1981, 1984; Flowers, 2003; Fries-Britt & Turner, 2001; Harper, Carini, Bridges, & Hayek, 2004; Hughes, 1987; MacKay & Kuh, 1994; Pascarella & Terenzini, 1991; Person & Christensen, 1996; Smith, 1997).

Although the literature is replete with information about the experiences of African American college students, it is bereft of specific attention to the issues impacting African American males (Cokley, 2001; Davis, 1999) or the differences these students experience on HBCU campuses compared with PWI settings (Jackson & Swan, 1991). This is quite a surprising commentary, given the societal, economic, and political pressures facing African American males that have been described in the literature and in the media over the last several years.

At HBCUs African American students, in general, report higher levels of academic achievement than do their counterparts attending PWIs (Allen, 1992; Fleming, 1984; Flowers, 2002; Nettles, 1988; Pascarella & Terenzini, 1991). In particular, African American men are cited as being able to focus more on their academic pursuits without the distractions facing their peers who attend PWIs (Fleming, 1984, DeSousa & Kuh, 1996; Pascarella & Terenzini, 1991). Berger and Milem (2000) found that African American men who attend HBCUs are at an advantage in developing self-concept—as defined by psychosocial wellness, academic ability, and achievement orientation—compared with their African American female counterparts. Allen (1992) reported that African American men have higher occupational aspirations than African American females. The implication is that men aspire to more high-status, high-paying occupations than women. Additionally, Fleming (1984) added that Black men at HBCUs improve their competitive abilities and exhibit power and an intellectual presence in the classroom. In sum, HBCUs have demonstrated their ability to provide a quality academic experience for African American students (Bohr, Pascarella, Nora, & Terenzini, 1995; Harper, Carini, Bridges, & Hayek, 2004), despite having fewer financial resources and faculty.

On the other hand, at PWIs African American students face an array of environmental issues that impinge upon their academic success. The literature is saturated with accounts of Black students who perceive the environment at PWIs as hostile (Allen, 1988, 1992; Allen & Haniff, 1991; Bennett & Okinaka, 1990; Davis, 1999; Fleming, 1984; Fries-Britt & Turner, 2001; Love, 1993; Nettles, 1988, 1991; Pascarella & Terenzini, 1991). Fleming (1981) wrote, "for Blacks college will be the greatest exposure to an integrated social environment" (p. 282). Yet what many African American students find in this integrated social environment is a strange and foreign atmosphere of cutthroat competition. According to Hughes (1987), "Such orientations are least likely to produce the best environment for Black students, for whom socially oriented climates are crucial for learning and growth" (p. 535). Thompson and Fretz (1991) added that competitive classrooms limit opportunities for Black students to share opinions and inspire others to learn about culturally diverse perspectives on a particular subject. In fact, "cooperative classroom settings may prove particularly valuable for Black students in White schools because traditional measures for evaluating performance . . . may limit their stylistic impact on the class and on the teacher" (p. 440).

Another major negative in the academic experiences of African American students is the stigma often associated with special academic support services tailored to meet their individual and collective needs. Providing academic assistance to help with the overall scholastic integration process is often a necessary component in promoting a successful transition for these students. Unfortunately, many campus constituents view these provisions as indicators of African American students' lack of ability. Others view these provisions as manifestations of affirmative action mandates gone wrong. In speaking to this issue as it pertains to the experiences of African American men, Dawson-Threat (1997) asserts, "African American male college students are concerned about the negative stereotyping that overshadows their genuine identity as intelligent, young Black men on the rise" (p. 38).

Thus, it is imperative for programming and policy initiatives aimed at meeting the academic needs of African American students to not be cast in a negative light among campus-based constituencies. Differences cannot be touted as deficiencies; academic integration, not only for minority student groups but also for nonminority student cohorts, must be viewed as a viable part of the student learning, growth, and development processes. According to Moses (1994), there are a number of misconceptions reifying the notion that diverse student populations have an adverse impact on institutional quality—including the pervasive belief that "admissions policies are discriminatory in favor of diverse students, because there are 'set asides' or special admissions status for them" (p. 12).

At the core of the environmental issues that impinge upon student academic success is the concept of "student-institution fit" (Tinto, 1975). According to Tinto's model, the more a student assimilates into the college's social and academic systems, the more committed the student will be to the college. The initial strength of a student's commitment to an individual campus is linked to the successful matching of that student's background and the college campus (Paulsen, 1990). For example, Flowers (2004) discovered that not all student experiences of involvement positively influence the educational outcomes of African American students, and the involvement of these students is typically lower than that of their White counterparts. Although Flowers does not specify differences between men and women, anecdotal evidence indicates limited male involvement in extracurricular activities other than intramural sports or time engaged in informal games of basketball with peers in the campus recreation center.

African American students often struggle to develop coping strategies to fit in and succeed in PWIs, due to the lack of successful matching between their background experiences and the collegiate context. Consequently, many African American men become resistant to adopting strategies that would lead to their successful matriculation (Hughes, 1987). According to Hughes, this pervasive mode of resistance is often due to the African American male's alignment with "masculine 'macho' principles" that they felt were necessary to defend instances of real and perceived racism" (p. 541).

Hughes' findings are analogous to the cool pose construct employed by African American adolescents, described by Majors and Billson (1992). In both instances, the end result is regaining a sense of control and power in an environment in which their inability to cope may lead to withdrawal, retreat, or dropping out. Also, the same stereotype threat that Steele (1997) applied to Black high school students can be attributed to college students, resulting in a further sense of isolation and alienation from the institutional context. Further, Steele (2000) reported that stereotype threat among college students could lead to the same academic disidentification articulated for high school students, yet for the collegian the stakes are often higher and the consequences more dire: namely, the loss of both personal and professional aspirations.

CONCLUSION

To create academic climates that foster the success of African American men, higher education institutions must focus on a number of issues that defy solutions of a singular nature. This chapter has attempted to shed light on the most salient factors impacting the success of these collegians. Although the role of the peer group has been investigated for college populations on a more generalized scale, particular attention must be dedicated to the special function these cohorts serve in the lives of the African American male college student. Negotiating membership within cultural and ethnic microcultures must be examined in terms of their overlap and influence dictated by broader university macrocultures. Are the peer groups these students belong to becoming integrated into the fabric of the institution, or are they relegated to academe's periphery?

An implication for academic as well as student affairs officials is the need to identify, in collaboration with these men of color, initiatives of interest. Perhaps capitalizing on many of the social (recreational sports, video games, card tournaments) as well as academic (study sessions, group library meetings) venues in which these students naturally engage could create more participation and involvement. Additionally, it is critical not to overlook the old-fashioned approach (which is often marginalized in our fast-paced, technologically advanced society)—that is, making direct contact and a personal request for student involvement.

The institution must encourage a concentrated effort to focus not only on student-student interactions but also on student-faculty interactions. As the scholarly literature reports, it is the relationship that students develop with faculty that so often serves as the primary factor in their retention and success. For the African American male, identifying and connecting with faculty provides him with a knowledgeable liaison capable of assisting him with matters of academic importance. Depending on the nature of the relationship, this connection may even extend to matters beyond academics—issues involving psychosocial and social development could also be considered.

Again, both academic affairs and student affairs personnel can play a pivotal role in fostering these relationships among students and faculty. One means of accomplishing this task is to create residential student learning communities. A symbiotic relationship among faculty and student affairs is created in their efforts to meet these students' needs. An underlying message to the student is that the institution does not believe in the artificial boundaries that are often temporally as well as structurally created between these areas, but rather recognizes that the student is not at certain times academic and at other times social, but always some combination of both. Through these residential learning communities, the African American male student is provided with the opportunity to interface with the faculty member on a much smaller scale and in a more authentic setting. Note that these communities are not meant to circumvent the faculty members' need to connect with students in more traditional settings: classrooms, recitation sessions, and office hours.

The chapter also speaks to the importance of the family in the success of African American male college students. By continuing to cast a blind eye on the contributions of the family, higher education will keep missing the mark with this group of matriculants. As we have attempted to show in this chapter, the role of the family must fit squarely into any equation designed to generate a successful outcome. Finding a way to integrate the family into various aspects of the student's postsecondary experience will only add to his chances of academic success and in turn promote goodwill between the family unit and the institution. It's very important to promote "family days" that expose the student and his family to the institution as a whole. Academic sessions aimed at providing insight on how to negotiate the programmatic, departmental, and collegiate-level terrain could be combined with student affairs assemblies that highlight the various student development opportunities on campus.

Finally, the last two factors, identity development and institutional environment, are in many ways connected. According to Lewin (1951), it is the interaction of individual and environmental variables that produces requisite behaviors. Thus the establishment of a positive identity for African American male collegians rests on their ability to establish some sense of agency within these milieus—one that not only recognizes the importance of the identity development process but also supports this process through altruistic dialogue. Both academic and student affairs personnel can initiate this process by "equipping themselves with the skill base to interact, teach, serve, and counsel students from a global and contextual perspective that takes into account their culture" (p. 110). A logical starting point might be constructing town-hall meetings or departmental forums that would allow students from these diverse backgrounds to essentially "speak their temporal realities into existence" for the uninformed masses. At a minimum, this opportunity would create an institutional climate in which these students feel that their voices and worldviews are not particularistic but part of the normal structure of the academy.

References

Allen, W. R. (1988). The education of Black students on White college campuses: What quality the experience? In M. T. Nettles (Ed.), *Toward Black undergraduate student equality in American higher education* (pp. 57–86). New York: Greenwood Press.

Allen, W. R. (1992). The color of success: African-American college student outcomes at predominantly White and historically Black public colleges and universities. *Harvard Educational Review, 62*(1), 26–44.

Allen, W. R., & Haniff, N. Z. (1991). Race, gender, and academic performance in U.S. higher education. In W. R. Allen, E. G. Epps, & N. Z. Haniff (Eds.), *College in Black and White: African American students in predominantly White and in historically Black public universities* (pp. 95–110). Albany, NY: State University of New York Press.

Astin, A. W. (1993). What matters in college. *Liberal Education, 79*(4), 4–15.

Bennett, C., & Okinaka, A. M. (1990). Factors related to persistence among Asian, Black, Hispanic, and White undergraduates at a predominantly White university: Comparison between first and fourth year cohorts. *The Urban Review, 22*(1), 33–60.

Berger, J. B., & Milem, J. F. (2000). Exploring the impact of historically Black colleges in promoting the development of undergraduates' self-concept. *Journal of College Student Development, 41*(4), 381–394.

Berry, M. F. (1983). Blacks in predominantly White institutions of higher education. In J. D. William (Ed.), *The state of Black America* (pp. 295–318). New York: National Urban League.

Bohr, L., Pascarella, E. T., Nora, A., & Terenzini, P. T. (1995). Do Black students learn more at historically Black or predominantly White colleges? *Journal of College Student Development, 36*(1), 75–85.

Bonner, F. A. (2001). *Gifted African American male college students: A phenomenological study.* Storrs, CT: National Research Center on the Gifted and Talented.

Bonner, F. A., & Murry, J. W. (1998). Historically Black colleges and universities: A unique mission. *National Association of Student Affairs Professionals, 1*(1), 37–49.

Bourassa, D. M. (1991). How White students and students of color organize and interact on campus. In J. C. Dalton (Ed.), *Racism on campus: confronting racial bias through peer interventions* (pp. 13–24). New Directions for Student Services. San Francisco: Jossey-Bass.

Bowser, B. P., & Perkins, H. (1991). Success against the odds: Young Black men tell what it takes. In B. P. Bowser (Ed.), *Black male adolescents: Parenting and education in community context* (pp. 183–200). New York: University Press of America.

Cheatham, H. E., Slaney, R. B., & Coleman, N. C. (1990). Institutional effects on psychosocial development of African-American college students. *Journal of Counseling Psychology, 37*(4), 453–458.

Cokley, K. O. (2001). Gender differences among African American students in the impact of racial identity on academic psychosocial development. *Journal of College Student Development, 42*(5), 480–487.

Constantine, M. G., Robinson, J. S., Wilton, L., & Caldwell, L. D. (2002). Collective self-esteem and perceived social support as predictors of cultural congruity among Black and Latino students. *Journal of College Student Development, 43*(3), 307–316.

Cuyjet, M. J. (Ed.). (1997). *Helping African American men succeed in college.* New Directions for Student Services, no. 80. San Francisco: Jossey-Bass.

D'Augelli, A. R., & Hershberger, S. L. (1993). African American under-graduates on a predominantly White campus: Academic factors, social networks, and campus climate. *Journal of Negro Education, 62*(1), 67–81.

Davis, J. E. (1994). College in black and white: Campus environment and academic achievement of African American males. *Journal of Negro Education, 63*(4), 620–633.

Davis, J. E. (1999). What does gender have to do with the experiences of African American college men? In V. C. Polite & J. E. Davis (Eds.), *African American males in schools and society: Practices and policies for effective education* (pp. 134–148). New York: Teachers College Press.

Dawson-Threat, J. (1997). Enhancing in-class academic experiences for African-American men. In M. J. Cuyjet (Ed.), *Helping African American men succeed in college* (pp. 31–42). New Directions for Student Services, no. 80. San Francisco: Jossey-Bass.

Demo, D. H., & Parker, K. D. (1986). Academic achievement and self-esteem among Black and White college students. *Journal of Social Psychology, 127*(4), 345–355.

DeSousa, D. J., & Kuh, G. D. (1996). Does institutional racial composi-tion make a difference in what Black students gain from college? *Journal of College Student Development, 37*(3), 257–267.

Finn, J. D., & Rock, D. A. (1997). Academic success among students at risk for school failure. *Journal of Applied Psychology, 82*(2), 221–234.

Fleming, J. (1981). Special needs of Blacks and other minorities. In A. W. Chickering & Associates (Eds.), *The modern American college: Respond-ing to the new realities of diverse students and a changing society* (pp. 279–295). San Francisco: Jossey-Bass.

Fleming, J. (1984). *Blacks in college: A comparison study of students' success in Black and White institutions.* San Francisco: Jossey-Bass.

Flowers, L. A. (2002). The impact of college racial composition on African American students' academic and social gains: additional evidence. *Journal of College Student Development, 43*(3), 403–410.

Flowers, L. A. (2003). Effects of college racial composition on African American students' interaction with faculty. *The College Student Affairs Journal, 23*(1), 54–63.

Flowers, L. A. (2004). Examining the effects of student involvement on African American college student development. *Journal of College Student Development, 45*(6), 633–654.

Fordham, S., & Ogbu, J. (1986). Black students' school success: Coping with the burden of "acting White." *Urban Review, 18,* 176–206.

Foster, M., & Peele, T. B. (1999). Teaching Black males: Lessons from the experts. In V. C. Polite & J. E. Davis (Eds.), *African American males in schools and society: Practices and policies for effective education* (pp. 8–19). New York: Teachers College Press.

Fries-Britt, S. L. (1998). Moving beyond Black achiever isolation: Experiences of gifted Black collegians. *Journal of Higher Education, 69*(5), 556–576.

Fries-Britt, S. L., & Turner, B. (2001). Facing stereotypes: A case study of Black students on a White campus. *Journal of College Student Development, 42*(5), 420–429.

Gibbs, J. T. (1988). *Young, Black, and male in America: An endangered species.* Auburn, NY: Auburn House.

Goddard, L. L. (1990). You can teach wisdom: Ways to motivate Black male adolescents. In B. P. Bowser (Ed.), *Black male adolescents: Parenting and education in community context* (pp. 201–213). New York: University Press of America.

Gordon, E. T. (1994). Social science literature concerning African American men. *Journal of Negro Education, 63*(4), 508–531.

Gossett, B. J., Cuyjet, M. J., & Cockriel, I. (1996). African Americans' and non-African Americans' sense of mattering and marginality at public, predominantly White institutions. *Equity & Excellence in Education, 29*(3), 37–42.

Gregory, S. T. (2000). Strategies for improving the racial climate for students of color in predominantly White institutions. *Equity & Excellence in Education, 33*(3), 39–47.

Hale-Benson, J. E. (1986). *Black children: Their roots, culture, and learning styles.* MD: The Johns Hopkins University Press.

Harper, S. R., Carini, R. M., Bridges, B. K., & Hayek, J. C. (2004). Gender differences in student engagement among African American undergraduates at historically black colleges and universities. *Journal of College Student Development, 45*(3), 271–284.

Hood, D. W. (1992). Academic and noncognitive factors affecting the retention of Black men at a predominantly White university. *Journal of Negro Education, 61*(1), 12–23.

Hopkins, R. (1997). *Educating Black males: Critical lesson in schooling, community, and power.* New York: State University of New York Press.

Hrabowksi, F. A., Maton, K. I., & Greif, G. L. (1998). *Beating the odds: Raising academically successful African American males.* Oxford: Oxford University Press.

Hughes, M. S. (1987). Black students' participation in higher education. *Journal of College Student Personnel, 28,* 532–545.

Irvine, J. J. (1990). *Black students and school failure: Policies, practices, and prescriptions.* Westport, CT: Greenwood Press.

Jackson, K. W., & Swan, L. A. (1991). Institutional and individual factors affecting Black undergraduate student performance: Campus race and student gender. In W. R. Allen, E. G. Epps, & N. Z. Haniff (Eds.), *College in Black and White: African American students in predominantly White and in historically Black public universities* (pp. 127–141). Albany, NY: State University of New York Press.

Lay, R., & Wakstein, J. (1985). Race, academic achievement, and self-concept of ability. *Research in Higher Education, 22*(1), 43–65.

Lewin, K. (1951). *Field theory in the social sciences.* New York: Harper & Row.

Love, B. J. (1993). Issues and problems in the retention of Black students in predominantly White institutions of higher education. *Equity & Excellence in Education, 26*(1), 27–36.

MacKay, K. A., & Kuh, G. D. (1994). A comparison of student effort and educational gains of Caucasian and African-American students at predominantly White colleges and universities. *Journal of College Student Development, 35*(3), 217–223.

Majors, R., & Billson, J. M. (1992). *Cool pose: The dilemmas of Black manhood in America.* New York: Lexington.

Myrdal, G. (1944). *An American dilemma: The Negro problem and modern democracy.* New York: Harper.

Nettles, M. T. (1988). Factors related to Black and White students' college performance. In M. T. Nettles (Ed.), *Toward Black undergraduate student equality in American higher education* (pp. 17–34). New York: Greenwood Press.

Nettles, M. T. (1991). Racial similarities and differences in the predictors of college student achievement. In W. R. Allen, E. G. Epps, & N. Z. Haniff (Eds.), *College in Black and White: African American students in predominantly White and in historically Black public universities* (pp. 75–94). Albany, NY: State University of New York Press.

Nettles, M.T., & Perna, L. W. (1997). *The African American Education Data Book (Vol I).* Frederick D. Patterson Research Institute.

Ogbu, J. U. (1981). Black education: A cultural-ecological perspective. In H. P. McAdoo (Ed.), *Black families* (pp. 139–154). Thousand Oaks, CA: Sage.

Osborne, J. W. (1997). Race and academic disidentification. *Journal of Educational Psychology, 89*(4), 728–735.

Osborne, J. W. (1999). Unraveling underachievement among African American males from an identification with academics perspective. *Journal of Negro Education, 68*(4), 555–565.

Pascarella, E. T., & Terenzini, P. T. (1979). Student-faculty informal contact and college persistence: A further investigation. *Journal of Educational Research, 72,* 214–218.

Pascarella, E. T., & Terenzini, P. T. (1991). *How college affects students.* San Francisco: Jossey-Bass.

Paulsen, M. B. (1990). *College choice: Understanding student enrollment behavior.* ASHE-ERIC Higher Education Report no. 6. Washington, DC: George Washington University School of Education and Human Development.

Person, D. R., & Christensen, M. C. (1996). Understanding Black student culture and Black student retention. *NASPA Journal, 34*(1), 47–56.

Sedlacek, W. E. (1999). Black students on White campuses: 20 years of research. *Journal of College Student Development, 40*(5), 538–550.

Smedley, B. D., Myers, H. F., & Harrell, S. P. (1993). Minority-status stresses and the college adjustment of ethnic minority freshmen. *Journal of Higher Education, 64*(4), 434–452.

Smith, D. G. (1997). Diversity works: The emerging picture of how students benefit. Washington, DC: Association of American Colleges and Universities.

Steele, C. M. (1992). Race and the schooling of Black Americans. *The Atlantic Monthly, 269*(4), 68–78.

Steele, C. M. (1997). A threat in the air: How stereotypes shape intellectual identity and performance. *American Psychologist, 52*(6), 613–629.

Steele, C. M. (2000). Stereotype threat and Black college students. *AAHE Bulletin, 52*(6), 3–6.

Taylor, R. L. (1994). Black males and social policy: Breaking the cycle of disadvantage. In R. G. Majors & J. U. Gordon (Eds.), *The American Black male: His present status and his future* (pp. 147–166). Chicago: Nelson-Hall.

Thompson, C. E., & Fretz, B. R. (1991). Predicting the adjustment of Black students at predominantly White institutions. *Journal of Higher Education, 62*(4), 437–450.

Tinto, V. (1975). Dropout from higher education: A theoretical synthesis of recent research. *Review of Educational Research, 45,* 89–125.

Tracey, T., & Sedlacek, W. E. (1985). *A comparison of White and Black student academic success using noncognitive variables: A LISREL analysis* (research report). College Park, MD: University of Maryland, Counseling Center.

Watson, L. W., Terrell, M. C., Wright, D. J., Bonner, F. A., Cuyjet, M. J., Gold, J. A., Rudy, D., & Person, D. R. (2002). *How minority students experience college: Implications for planning and policy.* Sterling, VA: Stylus Publishing.

White, J. L., & Cones, J. H. (1999). *Black man emerging: Facing the past and seizing a future in America.* New York: Freeman.

Wilson, J. W., & Constantine, M. G. (1999). Racial identity attitudes, self-concept, and perceived family cohesion in Black college students. *Journal of Black Studies, 29*(3), 354–367.

Wilson-Sadberry, K. R., Royster, D., & Winfield, L. F. (1991). Resilience and persistence of African American males in postsecondary enrollment. *Education and Urban Society, 24*(1), 87–103.

CHAPTER THREE

THE IMPACT OF CAMPUS ACTIVITIES ON AFRICAN AMERICAN COLLEGE MEN

Charles Brown, University of South Florida St. Petersburg

Few issues involving students in higher education are as serious and complicated as the lack of improvement in African American male enrollment on college campuses. The trend has been relatively unchanged over the past fifteen years. It is imperative for higher education to address this crisis, as resolving it is essential to the social, political, and economic stability of the African American and larger community.

Even those few institutions experiencing success in enrolling higher numbers of African American male students are also wrestling with retaining African American males through to graduation. The campus climate, particularly outside of the classroom, is often referenced as one of the major reasons that these institutions have struggled to keep these students. Addressing the overall campus environment is the only way to impact retention positively and effectively. Many student affairs professionals who advise, counsel, and work with students, especially in cocurricular campus activities and programs, report that the current cohort of African American male students continues the ongoing trend of

minimal involvement of African American men in campus organizations and at institution-sponsored activities and events and a
lack of African American males in campus leadership roles.

This chapter examines campus activities and programs identified by a group of African American male college students that
encouraged them to become involved in campus life. The discussions and findings were gathered through focus group sessions and
discussions with African American male college students attending
a southern university.

ASSESSING THE CURRENT CONDITION

A continuous assessment of campus environments by higher education institutions as they relate to the recruitment, retention, and
graduation of African American males should be integrated into
enrollment and retention strategic plans. The campus leaders—
usually student affairs educators—who are responsible for assessing campus climate must pay more attention to the social climate
outside of the classroom to ensure that the quality of campus life
has a positive impact on the successful recruitment, retention, and
graduation of African American males. They must identify and
address those barriers in the campus environment that impede
these students' ability to have a positive college experience. A campus social climate that encourages involvement and participation
by African American male students is paramount to the academic
success of these students. To make this goal a reality, faculty, staff,
and administrators must understand and enhance diversity in the
cocurriculum as it relates to all students, especially African American males. Becoming familiar with the developmental needs of
African American males is also important in promoting the involvement of African American men in the campus community, and it
is important for student affairs educators to take the lead in providing an overall understanding of these students' needs as well as
viable opportunities for them to satisfy those needs through
involvement on the campus.

Student affairs educators are usually the most active and visible individuals in the academy when it comes to teaching and practicing the need to appreciate, understand, and embrace diversity.
Their role places them on the front line in addressing this particular issue. On most campuses, they are responsible for retention

programs, advising student organizations, and other out-of-class activities that teach and encourage civility, develop leadership skills, and give students the opportunity to meet faculty, staff, administrators, and other campus leaders. In these roles, they can be the principals in creating a campus climate that is nurturing and receptive to all students, especially African American males. They are critical to and play a prominent role as members of the campus climate assessment team because of their training in student development theory. Nevertheless, some scholars believe that today's student affairs educators, although trained in student development theory, still lack the necessary skills and expertise to effectively address the needs of all segments of their student population. (Johnson, 2003; McEwen et al., 1996; Howard-Hamilton, 1997) They take this position because student development theory evolved from traditional European psychology and the findings are drawn from studies with mostly white males. However, over the past ten years numerous national and campus-based institutes and workshops have been offered to better prepare and assist student affairs educators in their efforts to address the needs of African American male students. Participants in these institutes and workshops, who are responsible for working with these students, can better understand and respond to the needs, concerns, and issues Black men bring to campus. A common theme emerging from these institutes is that societal problems faced by African American males in the general U.S. population are just as prevalent among many of those who enter higher education. Participating in these forums enables student affairs educators to develop the necessary skills to be effective and successful in getting these students acclimated and involved in campus life. Because we know that campus involvement and participation by students creates an attachment and sense of belonging, it is critical that student affairs educators are dedicated to building a campus environment that is perceived as nonthreatening and receptive to the presence of African American male students (Allen, 1992; Davis, 1994).

LACK OF INVOLVEMENT

Current literature indicates that African American students at predominantly White institutions (PWIs) experience a high degree of isolation, alienation, and hostility (Love, 1993; Allen, 1992). The

efforts made by these students to feel accepted are sometimes compounded by the stresses they encounter based on their own doubts
about their abilities and on their perceptions that faculty and other
students may question their legitimacy as students (Sedlacek,
1999). For African American male college students, these experiences can be even more painful because of their internalization of
societal perceptions of them as marginal to the general campus
community. Many African American male college students harbor
self-doubt regarding their presence on campus, which often leads
to a high degree of unwillingness to immerse themselves in campus life. In addition, campuses with low numbers of African American students and a lack of African American university personnel
make these students feel even more isolated, which results in little
or no involvement in campus organizations or activities. Research
supports the idea that warm, nurturing, and supportive environments enhance an institution's ability to recruit, retain, and graduate minority students (Lavant, Anderson, & Tiggs, 1997; Astin,
1982). Receptive campus environments also encourage student
involvement and academic success. Such an environment is paramount to successful recruitment and matriculation of African
American college students. Thus, it becomes critical for university
officials, especially student affairs educators, to assist these students
to participate in the cocurriculum. Institutions—and student affairs
educators in particular—need to provide a campus environment
that welcomes and nurtures African American male college students; this is critical to helping these students believe that they
belong.

THE CASE STUDY

Although African American male college students struggle, overall, to connect to institutions in the face of stereotyping and negative perceptions, there are success stories among this population.
Some out-of-classroom activities, programs, and facilities appear to
be effective in helping them cope and matriculate successfully at
PWIs (Tracey & Sedlacek, 1985). To document this further, an
exploratory descriptive study using a qualitative research method
was conducted at a predominantly white public research university
to collect information and identify those out-of-class activities that

have a positive impact on the involvement of African American students in campus life. In addition, the study was conducted to add much-needed evidence on the academic and social adjustment required of this particular student population. Four focus groups, with the same African American male college students participating in each one, were used to gather information, which provided a means for students to share their campus experience. Collecting data with the focus group gave the researcher the opportunity to speak directly to the participants about their perception of how important campus involvement was to their social and academic adjustment. The individual interviews and focus group sessions also allowed participants to react and respond to their peers in the group.

PARTICIPANTS

The twenty-five African American males who participated in this study attended a research university in the South with an enrollment of 19,000. A purposeful sampling method (Merriam, 1998) was used to ensure that the students in the study provided vivid examples and information about social experiences, programs, activities, and facilities on campus that enabled them to successfully matriculate toward their degree. All twenty-five of the students in the study completed the demographic questionnaire. The group consisted of five freshmen, five sophomores, five juniors, and ten seniors. All twenty-five young men were full-time students in good academic standing. Fifteen of the students lived on campus and were involved in several student organizations and activities. There were five athletes and three fraternity members in the group.

PROCEDURE

The student participants in the study were all enrolled in African American studies courses. They were presented with the opportunity to participate in the study by their instructors. The students were introduced to the researchers who presented the purpose of the study. Each participant agreed to attend four focus groups and one individual session with the researcher. In the individual sessions the researcher focused on individual experiences that had a positive impact on the student's successful matriculation. The researchers served as the facilitator and note taker and used a tape recorder to ensure that valuable comments and opinions were not missed. The young men were asked open-ended questions to initiate interaction and discussion among the group participants. The recordings from the focus group were transcribed and used, along with the notes taken during group meetings and the individual interviews, to analyze the data qualitatively and to identify campus activities and programs that the students viewed as critical to creating a social climate that fosters positive matriculation for them and their peers. Notes and tapes from each of the focus groups were reviewed three times to check for accuracy of data interpretation.

Qualitative research methods were used in this study to collect potent information on those out-of-class campus activities and programs these students viewed as essential to creating a welcoming campus environment for African American male college students. Borg and Gall (1989) state that qualitative research methodology is appropriate to use when researchers try to record what individuals are experiencing at a certain point in their lives. Focus groups allow participants to share common academic and social experiences, and individual interviews permit the researchers to collect and analyze data on how participants interpret their environment (Merriam, 1998). This research allowed data to be collected on out-of-class activities that African American college students identify as critical to creating an environment that nurtures and fosters their academic success. However, it does not allow an in-depth understanding of why students identify certain out-of-class activities as ones that retain them. During the third focus group session, the researcher shared with the participants the findings gathered from the first two sessions and the individual sessions, to ensure reliability and to validate the participants' responses. From the notes and tapes, the researcher identified five noncognitive activities and facilities that were mentioned more frequently as having a positive impact on these students' adjustment to campus and their involvement in campus life programs. Participants were asked if the list was accurate and if others should be included. They agreed these were the ones they perceived as having the greatest impact on them and their peers. The final focus group session was the discussion of these five noncognitive items.

FINDINGS AND DISCUSSION

The group discussion began with the students being asked if they believed African American male students were viewed positively by most of the campus community. Most of the students believed that they were viewed negatively by faculty and their white peers. These African American males perceived that others viewed them as special admit students who probably should not be at the university. One student's comments summarized those of the group: "The stereotypes of African American males are enhanced by their portrayal in the media; often times I feel that we are shown as criminals and individuals exhibiting antisocial behavior. Last year an African American male hijacked a car on campus and I could feel people looking at me strangely, especially when I was the only African American among white students, especially women. I have learned to cope with this feeling by confronting individuals when they make subtle implications."

The feelings expressed by this student reflect Majors and Billson's (1992) premise that the media more often than not portray Black males negatively. Stereotypes about African American males are reinforced by the daily newscast reporting on crime statistics, and they become an ongoing issue for African American college males. As a result of these perceptions, these students believe that they cannot make the same mistakes as other students on campus because they will be dealt with more severely or treated differently. Other comments in the focus group indicate stereotypes of African American male college students based on physical characteristics. One of the freshman students shared the following: "Because I am six foot four, my white classmates assume I am a basketball player. During the first two weeks of class I was asked at least ten times if I were a basketball player. At the beginning of the semester I believed most of my professors thought I was an athlete. After I took my first exam and received a very good grade, I could tell the professor seemed surprised."

Dealing with such stereotypes can have a detrimental impact on both the academic and social development of these students. African American college men experience a higher degree of stress than their white counterparts because of the many negative images of them that they believe others have. Some students in this study coped with the stereotyping by participating in student organizations and activities. One student summarized some of the positive and negative aspects of participating in student activities or organizations:

> I try to show people that African American males are good people and have a strong sense of responsibility. I did this by joining organizations and seeking out leadership roles. I am a member of an African American fraternity, which allows me to participate in the campus Inter-Fraternity Council as well as the Residence Hall Association. I believe being active with these two predominately white groups has allowed me to diffuse some of the stereotypes. Being active with the fraternity and Black Student Union provides camaraderie. I am active in the church I attend, which provides opportunities to meet people outside of the university community.

Clearly these students have devised mechanisms to cope with the daily stereotyping by garnering support through their association with other African American students and getting involved rather than withdrawing in isolation or blaming themselves. Thompson and Fretz (1991) state that some Black students are able to cope better than others through strong relationships with other Black students or the external Black community surrounding the campus. But for many minority students attending PWIs located in less populated or rural areas, their interaction with other minorities is limited to the small number living in the campus community.

PERCEPTIONS OF CAMPUS SOCIAL NONACADEMIC ENVIRONMENT

The discussions of the campus social nonacademic environment produced some interesting findings. These students' comments focused more on their involvement in campus organizations and activities and the importance of such involvement to African American male college students. To stimulate the discussion, the participants were asked to agree on a list of five organizations, activities, facilities, programs, or events that made the campus environment more receptive, nurturing, and comfortable for them. A discussion on the extent of their involvement and participation followed. The students' list consisted of the Student Government

Association, intramural athletics and recreation, the student union, mentoring, and peer relationships.

STUDENT GOVERNMENT ASSOCIATION

The participants indicated that very few African American male students participated in the Student Government Association (SGA), but that they found many of the activities and events sponsored by this body were sometimes fun and entertaining. A majority expressed a negative perception of the SGA. They perceived it as an organization that had power, clout, and money to conduct campuswide activities. A majority of them had attended at least one event or activity sponsored by the SGA. The events attended by the students in this study were usually those pertaining to ethnic minority or multicultural activities. The students expressed a lack of trust in this particular organization but stated that African American males and females should be visible participants in the group. A sophomore's comments summarized a majority of the participants' responses to this organization: "I don't trust the leadership of the Student Government Association on this campus but because it has power and control of student fee dollars, I sought participation in the group. Until African Americans, especially males who are seen only as jocks, take an active role, it will not become sensitive to African American needs. Its leaders will continue to hold negative perceptions of minority students, especially African American male students."

Another student followed this student with this statement: "The Student Government Association is supposed to represent the student body and should include different student members and viewpoints but it has a difficult time dealing with conflicts and issues of race and diversity. On this campus, it is very difficult for African American males to get elected. Being one of a few who serves, I feel like I have to watch what I say and may be very guarded regarding who I debate an issue with. From my experience, it is easier for an African American female to become involved."

The comments of this student support the findings of Arminio et al. (2000) that students of color describe conflicts in predominantly white groups as more tedious, which is contrary to how most African American students prefer to deal with conflict. In addition, these students found that many African American students perceived white campus organizations as less honest and open, which creates frustration, tension, and anxiety. The students indicated that when they were members of these organizations they found themselves speaking less frequently, except to confront racist remarks or to act as a spokesperson for their racial group.

Recognizing that the SGA on this particular campus made decisions and controlled campus activities and programs through the budgetary process, a majority of the African American males in the group viewed this as a viable out-of-class learning experience. They recognized that the campus social climate was impacted tremendously by this group, and their interest, "although reluctant," implies that they understood that their involvement is critical and beneficial to their overall college experience (Sutton & Kimbrough, 2002).

The data gleaned from this discussion support how important it is for student affairs educators to create opportunities for African American males to become involved in organizations that they perceive as important to social development while matriculating on campus. In addition, student affairs educators must sensitize student leaders in campus organizations to the issues, concerns, and perceptions that African American male college students have regarding these organizations. Germane to this issue is the fact that minority students at PWIs do not attend many of the out-of-class activities, such as homecoming, concerts, and other social functions, and are also reluctant to join many heterogeneous student organizations because they are hesitant to cross cultural and racial lines (Brown, 1991; Nettles, 1988). This is especially true for African American males. Student affairs educators must develop strategies to encourage African American male students to become involved in organizations like the SGA, particularly if they feel such participation has value and can assist the students with developing lifelong coping skills beyond the college years.

INTRAMURAL ATHLETICS AND RECREATION

Participants felt that intramural athletics were very important to the campus social climate for them and most of their friends. Getting involved and participating in intramural athletics events was a way to feel comfortable at the university. Forming sports teams with their friends and participating in a wide range of intramural activities was good for their mental and physical health. The use of the recreation center was viewed as both a workout and social time. It provided them with the opportunity to meet other African American students, both male and female. A succinct explanation was given by one of the freshman participants: "Our numbers are small and we live in different areas on and off campus, so intramural sports and the recreation center is one of the primary social outlets for most of us. Also I use intramurals as a form of relaxation from the stress and strain I encounter as a student on the campus."

Many of the comments and opinions shared by the participants support the finding that Cuyjet (1997) extrapolated from the College Student Experience Questionnaire: African American men indicated greater participation in athletics and recreational activities than African American women. Cuyjet concluded that providing adequate recreational and athletic activities could be a vital component to creating welcoming environments for African American men. The welcoming environment allows these students to be communal, thus giving each other support and assistance. Student affairs educators must continue to provide opportunities for African American males to participate in intramural athletic programs and should understand how this activity creates comfort and enhances retention for the student population by providing social and personal outlets. Sedlacek (1987) found that African American student retention is enhanced when these students become involved in recreational and union board activities.

Student Union

The student union was listed as an important part of the group experience on this campus. Participants stated that it provided both a formal and an informal way to address campus cultural and social isolation, just as the recreational center provided opportunities for networking and socializing with other African Americans on campus. One athlete in the group had a very strong opinion regarding the student union:

> I visited the union because I like to play pool, table tennis, bowling and cards, and socializing with other men as well as African American women. It is the "hang out spot" because the frats and sororities

have offices and parties in the building. It is the focal point for campus activities for most minority students. It is also the "hang out hot spot," and serves as the living room for the campus because it provided me and many of my friends occasional opportunities to see the few African American faculty, staff, and administrators who worked on the campus. I visited the Union more frequently than the recreation center because it is a place for me to relax and get away from athletics-related activities.

One student indicated there were occasional problems with the staff. He reported that when a group of African American males are playing cards and become excited, the staff has been known to call public safety without first approaching the group and asking them to tone it down. To alleviate problems such as this, it was suggested by one student that African American males become part of the union programming board, which recommends and plans activities as well as reviews the facility operation policies and procedures. Only five of the twenty-five males in this group had any knowledge of this board and how its role impacted campus activities. Only 16 percent (four) of the participants knew the board was responsible, in coordination with the Student Government Association and college committees, for homecoming, speaker series, concerts, and other special events held on campus.

Even though the African American males in this group were active visitors to and users of the student union and saw it as a key facility in creating a welcoming environment, it was clear that only a very small number in the group knew how—or were encouraged—to seek membership on the union program board to provide more programs of interest to them and their peers. The students understood that positions on the board give students decision-making power. To encourage African American male involvement in these activities, it is imperative that student affairs educators take the lead in sensitizing other students to the importance of involving African American men by extending invitations to participate. Student affairs professionals can also identify African American male students and personally encourage their direct involvement. As Pascarella and Terenzini (1991) posit, active involvement in out-of-class activities and the nature and quality of students' social interaction with peers, faculty, staff, and administrators have a positive influence on persistence, educational aspiration, completion of their undergraduate degree, and subsequent enrollment in graduate school. Not only does the involvement and participation of African American males in student policy and decision-making positions enhance student organizational diversity, but it also enables them to become more comfortable in the campus environment.

MENTORING THAT ENCOURAGES COCURRICULAR INVOLVEMENT

The group overwhelmingly believed that having contact with African American faculty, staff, and administrators enhances the campus environment for African American males. A majority of the students in the group said they occasionally felt culturally and socially isolated. One student gave the example of being the only African American on his floor during his freshman year. There were times when he felt that he needed to talk with an African American adult but had no one to talk to about issues he confronted as a student on the campus. This student stated that "the presence of faculty and staff to talk with students outside of the classroom creates a level of comfort and provides nurturing for African American males." He further stated that "having access to African American male faculty and staff would be extremely helpful for [him] and many others because it would help to eliminate feelings of cultural and social isolation." Davis (1994) and others assert that African American students find their racial minority status salient and experience high degrees of alienation and isolation on white campuses, which explains why African American males who arrive on college campuses tend not to get involved to the same degree as other minority students. Thus, mentors can nurture and encourage these students to get involved.

As the discussion continued on this topic, two participants, one junior and one senior, shared how they, through their own initiative, had developed a relationship with an African American faculty member. Neither had taken a class with the professor, but they both identified him during their freshman summer orientation program when this particular faculty member served on a universitywide information panel. They both spoke with the professor about campus-related issues, as well as personal and family issues. The students stated they were guarded during their initial contact with the professor, but once they reached a level of comfort and trust, the faculty member became a mentor. This particular faculty member encouraged both students to stay focused on their academic goals but also to take advantage of everything the university had to offer. He encouraged them to get involved with campus activities and organizations as a way to develop personal and leadership skills. Because these two students sought out a faculty member to nurture and advise them, their college experience was enhanced and made more positive. Lavant, Anderson, and Tiggs (1997), Harris (1996), Woolbright (1989), Hughes (1987), Wright (1987), and Fleming (1984) assert that students who interact and become participants in mentoring relationships have a more enriching collegiate experience than those students who do not participate in positive mentoring programs. They cite other studies whose findings indicated that students participating in positive mentoring relationships express a high degree of satisfaction with their college experience. This is especially true for African American male students, who are less likely to become involved in campus activities (O'Brien, 1988).

Although two of the participants had developed relationships, it was clear that an overwhelming majority of the participants had not developed significant relationships with faculty and staff on this campus. It was also clear that the two participants who had developed a mentoring relationship sought involvement in out-of-class activities to supplement and support their classroom experience while developing personal, social, and leadership skills. This acknowledgment by these two students supports findings that suggest African American students at PWIs who performed better academically seemed to make a greater effort to interact with professors (Davis, 1994; Nettles, 1988; Tracey & Sedlacek, 1985).

PEER RELATIONS AND INVOLVEMENT

Students in this group said the lack of positive peer relationships could be detrimental to the successful matriculation of African American males on the college campuses. The group overwhelmingly agreed that bonding and having friendships with other African American males contributed greatly to their survival at this PWI. A student athlete stated, "Even though relationships with other African Americans are desired, it does not mean one cannot develop positive relationships with students of other races. However, it is more difficult because of the issue of race and the stereotypes that are often associated with us. If I were not an athlete, I would probably feel marginal or outside the mainstream of campus life."

It is important for these young men to foster relationships with other students similar to them. According to Harris (1996), the achievement of interpersonal relationships with same-sex peers is a significant determinant of individual interpersonal competences. She further states that students acquire skills in communication and in cooperating and managing relationships that extend to other situations. Thus, peer relationships among and between African American male college students can help to reinforce a sense of purpose, self-identity, and positive perception that fosters a more positive educational experience for these young men.

An interesting phenomenon was gleaned from the discussion on the importance of good peer relationships in the campus environment as it relates to these students. Several of the young men indicated a strong bond to friends who were not attending college and suggested that many of their non–college attending friends were regular visitors to the campus. These data support the need for student affairs educators to recognize and value the support system and peer network that exist between African American college students and their friends from high school who are not enrolled in higher education (Guiffrida, 2004). Because most of these students came from community high schools whose demographics were different from those of the university, it is reasonable to assume that their adjustment and campus involvement would be difficult. The relationship with their friends from high school provided support and strength that helped them transition into the university community (Lewis, 2002).

The discussions and examples shared by these students indicate that peer relationships support and encourage involvement. Having a fellow student with a similar background to interact with about academic and nonacademic issues increased the likelihood of these students becoming involved in campus activities and programs. Also, this study found that peer relationships with high school friends who were not enrolled at this university or who did not attend college had a positive impact on these students' involvement in campus life.

CONCLUSION

The student participants in this group were all successfully persisting toward graduation and were coping, better than most of their peers, with being an African American male college student at a PWI. Even though they faced challenges as they persisted, they perceived certain activities, facilities, programs, or relationships as critical to their social survival on the campus. Their identification of these five areas (Student Government Association, intramural athletics and recreation, student union, mentoring, and peer relationships) was not totally surprising, but the students' critical analysis of the issues related to their affiliation and participation was both insightful and beneficial. Their candor regarding stereotyping about them and their efforts to confront this problem indicate a need for more assistance and support from the campus community, especially from student affairs professionals. Although this study was limited to a small number of African American male college students, it reveals that many of these students want to be involved in campus organizations, as members and leaders as well as participants and consumers. Student affairs professionals must create more opportunities for them to become involved.

The study also revealed that, in order to facilitate such opportunities for cocurricular involvement, student affairs practitioners should assist these young men in their relationship development ability. Learning how to establish positive interpersonal relationships with African American male peers, with females, and with other males provides a medium for the communication by which leadership skills are transmitted. These interpersonal relationship skills are also critical to developing the connections with faculty and staff mentors that are often critical to successful matriculation.

The five noncognitive areas that these students perceived as essential to making this particular campus receptive and nurturing to African American male college students are reflective of earlier research pertaining to these issues. Student affairs professionals can use the findings from this study of one small group of African American male students (particularly their perceptions of noncognitive factors, such as attendance at programs, organization participation, and facilities use) to make the out-of-class campus environment supportive for these students. The following are specific actions that student affairs educators can take to create a campus environment that is perceived as receptive to African American college men.

1. Organize programs for African American male college students designed to introduce them to campus organizations and membership and leadership opportunities. This type of program is essential to integrating these students into the social fabric of the university. African American male students will benefit from an orientation program that advises, counsels, and helps them to negotiate a hostile climate. Even though the students in this study assigned some negative characteristics to the SGA and the Union Programming Board, they recognized and understood the role these two organizations played on campus. The SGA and Union Board activities were valuable to these students and made their lives more rewarding on this particular campus.

2. Provide opportunities for these students to become involved in campus organizations and to assume leadership roles by educating majority students about the plight of these students and the stereotypes they encounter on a daily basis. Teaching and educating the majority student leaders and faculty and staff about the needs and desires of African American male students is essential to creating a climate that makes them feel comfortable on campus. Special affairs educators should strongly encourage student organizations such as the Student Government Association, Residence Hall Association, and Union Programming Board to reach out to African American male college students on campus. If the members of these groups do not seem to know how to do this, student affairs professionals can serve as liaisons between the majority group leaders and individual African American men or the organizations to which they belong (such as fraternities).

3. Establish a mentoring program during new student orientation, encouraging African American faculty and staff to mentor African American male students. Train mentors to focus on assisting their protégés' cocurricular and social development

and not just their academic achievement. Make every effort to use African American male faculty and staff because research findings indicate that African American students do not look first to white faculty and staff as role models for their leadership (Hayward, 1985).

4. Because African American students in general tend to be more communal, create opportunities for African American male college students to build a sense of community. Using athletics and recreational opportunities is one way for these students to build a sense of community that helps support retention and a nurturing campus environment. Sedlacek (1987) found that African American students who use the campus gym and who were interested in activities sponsored by the student union had better retention than those who were not interested. Webster and Sedlacek (1982) found that the student union was central to African American students' community development. The comments of the students in the study cited here support that perception.

5. Provide opportunities for African American male college students to have meaningful relationships with their peers. One important way to accomplish this goal is to create and sponsor an ongoing support group for African American men, such as those profiled in Part Two of this book. To ensure the continued viability of such an organization, adequate resources—both human and fiscal—must be provided. Creating programs to match continuing students with new students should enhance retention and provide support for both groups of students.

The African American participants in this focus group shared their thoughts on out-of-class activities, programs, and facilities that can help to create a campus environment that is nurturing and comforting to them. The overwhelming majority of the African American males in this group believed they were viewed negatively by members of the campus community. However, they still felt they had opportunities to participate in a variety of campus activities, and they saw the need to partake in these opportunities. Because each of the twenty-five participants in this group had a 2.5 or higher grade point average, it could be assumed they all had made the transition from attendance at majority African American high schools to a PWI. One of the young men stated, "I have learned to negotiate the system for survival until graduation." The stereotyping of African American males will continue, so to help these students succeed in college it is prudent that we provide them with as much support as possible. College administrators, faculty, staff, and especially student affairs educators, must provide opportunities for African American males to become involved in out-of-class activities. Student affairs educators must create opportunities for African American males to meet their peers in formal and informal settings through structured activities and by creating a social environment that is inviting and comforting to all students. According to these twenty-five African American college students, the best mentoring program is one that has African American males matched with the students. One important word of caution—African American faculty, staff and administrators chosen for mentoring should be screened to ascertain their commitment to the mentoring tasks and then carefully matched with protégés sharing some similar ideas and interests. Simply because two individuals are both African American men does not guarantee they will prove to be a compatible mentoring pair. The importance of intramural sports programs, Greek life activities, student union, and student government participation expressed by these young men mirrors other studies that assert that students' involvement in campus-based programs increased their persistence and their eventual rate of graduation from college.

Even though this article was written from a conversation with twenty-five African American males discussing the social environment of one campus, the information collected from this informal setting reflects the current research that has focused on this crisis in higher education. It suggests that student affairs educators should use focus group discussions as an integral part of recruitment and retention program planning to find ways to make the campus environment one that invites these students to become involved and active.

References

Allen, W. R. (1992). The color of success: African American college student outcomes at predominantly White and historically Black public colleges and universities. *Harvard Educational Review, 6E,* 26–44.

Arminio, L. J., Carter, S., Jones, E. S., Kruger, K., Lucas, N., Washington, J., Young, N., & Scott, A. (2000). Leadership experiences of students of color. *NASPA Journal, 37,* 496–509.

Astin, A. W. (1982). *Minorities in higher education.* San Francisco: Jossey-Bass.

Borg, W., & Gall, M. (1989). Educational research (5th ed.). White Plains, NY: Longman.

Brown, C. (1991). Increasing minority access to college: Seven efforts for success. *NASPA Journal, 28*(3), 224–230.

Cuyjet, M. J. (1997). African American men on college campuses: Their needs and perceptions. In M. J. Cuyjet (Ed.), *Helping African American men succeed in college.* New Directions for Student Services, no. 80 (pp. 5–16). San Francisco: Jossey-Bass.

Davis, J. E. (1994). College in Black and White: Campus environment and academic achievement of African males. *Journal of Negro Education, 63*(4), 620–633.

Fleming, J. (1984). *Blacks in college: A comparison study of students' success in black and white institutions.* San Francisco: Jossey-Bass.

Guiffrida, D. A. (2004). Friends from home: Asset and liability to African American students attending a predominantly white institution. *National Association of Student Personnel Administrators, 41*(3), 693–708.

Harris, W. C. (1996, October 3). African American males in higher education: Reframing the issues. *Black Issues in Higher Education, 13,* 16, 92.

Hayward, S. L. (1985). Facilitating the educational development of Black students at predominantly White institutions. *Carolina View, 1,* 14–18.

Howard-Hamilton, M. (1997). Theory to practice: Applying developmental theories relevant to African American men. In M. J. Cuyjet (Ed.), *Helping African American men succeed in college.* New Directions for Student Services, no. 80 (pp.17–30). San Francisco: Jossey-Bass.

Hughes, M. (1987). Black students' participation in higher education. *Journal of College Student Personnel, 28,* 532.

Johnson, R. E. (1993). Factors in the academic success of African American college males. Unpublished doctoral dissertation, University of South Carolina.

Lavant, B. R., Anderson, J. L., & Tiggs, J. W. (1997). Retaining African American males through mentoring initiatives. In M. J. Cuyjet (Ed.), *Helping African American men succeed in college.* New Directions for Student Services, no. 80 (pp. 43–54). San Francisco: Jossey-Bass.

Lewis, R. (2002). Historical and institutional barriers to African American undergraduate students enrollment and initiatives for improving retention. *National Association of Student Affairs Professionals, 5*(1), 21–33.

Love, B. J. (1993). Issues and problems in the retention of Black students in predominantly white institutions of higher education. *Equity & Excellence in Education, 26*(1), 27–36.

Majors, R., & Billson, J. M. (1992). *Cool pose: The dilemmas of Black manhood in America.* San Francisco: New Lexington Press.

McEwen, M. K., Roper, L. D., Bryant, D. R., & Langa, M. J. (1996). Incorporating the development of African American students into psychosocial theories of student development. In F. D. Stage, G. L. Anaya, J. P. Bean, D. Hossler, & G. D. Kuh (Eds.), *College students: The evolving nature of research* (pp. 217–226). Needham Heights, MA: Simon & Schuster.

Merriam, S. B. (1998). *Qualitative research and case study applications in education.* San Francisco: Jossey-Bass.

Nettles, M. T. (1988). *Toward black undergraduate student equality in American higher education.* New York: Greenwood Press.

O'Brien, E. (1988). Dr. Charles Willis prescribes mentoring methodologies for minorities. *Black Issues in Higher Education, 5*(5), 15.

Pascarella, E. T., & Terenzini, P. T. (1991). *How college affects students: Insights from twenty years of research.* San Francisco: Jossey-Bass.

Sedlacek, W. E. (1987). Black students on white campuses: Twenty years of research. *Journal of College Student Personnel, 28,* 484–495.

Sedlacek, W. E. (1999). Black students on white colleges: 20 years of research. *Journal of College Student Development, 40*(5), 538–550.

Sutton, E. M., & Kimbrough, W. M. (2002). Trends in Black students, involvement. *NASPA Journal, 39*(1), 30–40.

Thompson, C., & Fretz, B. (1991). Predicting the adjustment of black students at predominantly white institutions. *Journal of Higher Education, 62*(4), 437–450.

Tracey, T., & Sedlacek, W. E. (1985). The relationship of noncognitive variables to academic success: A longitudinal comparison by race. *Journal of College Student Personnel, 26,* 405–410.

Webster, D. W., & Sedlacek, W. E. (1982). The differential impact of a university student union on campus subgroups. *NASPA Journal, 19*(2), 48–51.

Woolbright, C. (1989). *Valuing diversity on campus: A multicultural approach.* Bloomington, IN: Association of College Unions-International.

Wright, D. J. (1987). Minority students: Developmental beginnings. In D. J. Wright (Ed.), *Responding to the needs of today's minority students.* New Directions for Student Services, no. 38 (pp. 5–21). San Francisco: Jossey-Bass.

CHAPTER FOUR

ENHANCING AFRICAN AMERICAN MALE STUDENT OUTCOMES THROUGH LEADERSHIP AND ACTIVE INVOLVEMENT

Shaun R. Harper, The Pennsylvania State University

Amondo and Aaron are African American undergraduate men who attend a large predominantly White university in the Midwest. Both students are from the same hometown, attended the same high school, and are approaching the start of their junior year at the university. Amondo has a 3.7 grade point average in business; actively participates and holds leadership positions in multiple student organizations; has completed summer internships with Sony, Coca-Cola, and the New York Knicks; spent a portion of his sophomore year studying abroad in Ireland, Spain, and France; and has excellent relationships with his peers, faculty, staff, and key administrators at the institution, including the provost and university president. Although he constantly engages in cross-cultural exchanges with students from a variety of racial and ethnic backgrounds, Amondo is especially popular among African American undergraduates and is often called upon by administrators to represent the voices of the African American community on major university committees.

Aaron's profile is starkly different: he struggles academically; participates in no clubs, activities, or organizations; is recognized only by the faculty to whom he has petitioned for grade changes; and has few friends, all of whom are African American. Aaron spends his out-of-class time exercising, playing basketball, and pursuing romantic relationships with women. For quite some time, Aaron has felt disconnected from the campus and has repeatedly considered discontinuing his pursuit of the baccalaureate degree. However, he still contemplates returning to campus for the start of his junior year.

Interestingly, Amondo and Aaron's precollege academic profiles are nearly identical. Based on their high school GPAs and SAT scores, both students were predicted to excel in college. Participation in a summer program preceding the start of their first year of college was meant to address any deficiencies these two students and other racial or ethnic minorities brought to college, while exposing them to the campus-based resources that were available to ensure success. Apparently, Amondo and Aaron took different things from the summer program, made different decisions regarding the expenditure of their out-of-class time, and subsequently had drastically different academic and social experiences at the same institution.

Recent studies on African American male student involvement (for example, Cuyjet, 1997; Harper, 2003, 2004, 2005; Sutton & Terrell, 1997), coupled with the alarming retention and graduation trends reported throughout this book, suggest that Aaron's profile is actually representative of most African American undergraduate men, thereby making Amondo an anomaly. Involvement is central to the success of the African American male collegian, as he is highly likely to reap a return on the investments he makes in his experience. This chapter considers the gains and outcomes associated with African American male participation in out-of-class activities, particularly campus leadership experiences on college and university campuses. A review of existing research on the benefits that accrue when students make meaningful choices about the allocation of their out-of-class time is followed by a discussion of current involvement trends for African American men. Next, gains reported by highly involved African American male student leaders are described and discussed. The chapter concludes with recommendations for maximizing gains and outcomes and increasing African American male involvement in leadership experiences and student organizations.

How Involvement Affects Student Outcomes

Astin (1984) defined student involvement as "the amount of physical and psychological energy that the student devotes to the academic experience" (p. 297). The theory of student involvement is primarily concerned with how college students spend their time, the effort they devote to activities that are designed to produce desired gains and outcomes, and how various institutional resources and opportunities facilitate student development. Joining clubs and organizations, holding major leadership positions, spending time in campus facilities (such as the student union, residence halls, and the library), interacting with faculty in class and outside of the classroom, and socializing with peers about academic and nonacademic matters are all included in the definition of student involvement. Astin suggests that time is the most precious resource during the college years and that the way in which students spend that time affects what they learn and gain from college.

This theory and the gains and outcomes associated with student involvement in out-of-class activities have been widely studied and consistently documented by a host of researchers in higher education. In *How College Affects Students: Findings and Insights from Twenty Years of Research,* Pascarella and Terenzini conclude, "The greater the effort and personal investment a student makes [through involvement], the greater the likelihood of educational and personal returns on that investment across the spectrum of college student outcomes" (1991, p. 648). They also assert that active participation in out-of-class activities and the nature and quality of students' contacts with peers, faculty, and staff positively affect persistence, the development of educational aspirations, completion of a bachelor's degree, and subsequent enrollment in graduate school. In the second volume of *How College Affects Students* (2005), Pascarella and Terenzini add, "Also consistent with our 1991 synthesis, there is a substantial body of evidence suggesting that the nature of students' social and extracurricular involvement has a unique impact on learning" (p. 149).

Other researchers have found that involvement positively affects cognitive and intellectual skill development (Anaya, 1996; Baxter Magolda, 1992; Kuh, 1995; Ory & Braskamp, 1988; Pike, 2000), adjustment to college (Cabrera, Nora, Terenzini, Pascarella, & Hagedorn, 1999; Clarke & Tomlinson-Clarke, 1994; Delvin, 1996; Paul & Kelleher, 1995), moral and ethical development (Evans, 1987; Jones & Watt, 1999; Liddell & Davis, 1996; Rest, 1993), psychosocial development and positive images of self (Bandura, Peluso, Ortman, & Millard, 2000; Chickering & Reisser, 1993; Harper, 2004; Pascarella, Smart, Ethington, & Nettles, 1987; Taylor & Howard-Hamilton, 1995), and persistence rates (Berger & Milem, 1999; Braxton, Milem, & Sullivan, 2000; Fries-Britt, Gardner, Low, & Tinto, 2002; Milem & Berger, 1997; Peltier, Laden, & Matranga, 1999; Tinto, 1993).

Few would dispute that learning and the ability to apply what one has learned are the two most desired outcomes of college attendance. Those who spend four or more years on a college campus are expected to display signs of cognitive growth and to know more and be more intellectually curious than they were prior to enrollment. Much remains to be known and discovered about the processes and environments that best promote learning and cognitive development among contemporary undergraduate students. However, evidence clearly suggests that gains in cognitive complexity depend largely upon the extent to which students are able to connect their out-of-class experiences with what they learn inside the classroom. In fact, Kuh, Palmer, and Kish (2003) contend, "One thing about the college student experience is certain: students learn more when they are engaged at reasonably high levels in a variety of educationally purposeful activities, inside and outside of the classroom, over an extended period of time" (p. 1).

Participation in a variety of out-of-class activities has been shown to affect student learning and cognitive gains. Being a leader in student government, residing in an on-campus learning community, attending diversity workshops and cultural events, participating in academic honor societies and service organizations, and interacting with faculty and staff outside of the classroom have all been shown to have positive effects on the development of critical thinking and analytical problem-solving skills (Astin & Sax, 1998; Baxter Magolda, 1992; Kuh, 1995; Kuh & Lund, 1994; Pascarella, Palmer,

Moye, & Pierson, 2001; Villalpando, 2002), whereas participating in intercollegiate athletics and attending athletic events reportedly have negative effects on such development (Inmann & Pascarella, 1998; McBride & Reed, 1998). Many research studies have found that sorority and fraternity membership undermines the intellectual goals of college and stifles the learning process for White undergraduates, especially men. However, two recent studies (Pascarella, Edison, Whitt, Nora, Hagedorn, & Terenzini, 1996, and Pascarella, Flowers, & Whitt, 2001) found that fraternity membership positively influences cognitive development among African American male collegians. Harper, Byars, and Jelke (2005) maintain that Black Greek-letter organization membership "enhances students' integration into the life and social fabric of the university, thus improving their chances for retention and graduation" (p. 409).

Though some racial and ethnic minority students were included in the samples, most of the previously cited research studies examined gains and outcomes for undergraduate students in general. Specifically regarding involvement and African American undergraduates, Davis (1991) discovered that student organization members and leaders at predominantly White institutions (PWIs) were more satisfied with their undergraduate experiences and less likely to report that they had considered dropping out of school. Similarly, Jackson and Swan (1991) found that performance gains multiplied as African American students became increasingly involved on their campuses—their grades were higher, they were more alert in class and interested in learning, and they were more confident in themselves and their academic abilities. Sutton and Kimbrough (2001) assert that membership in minority student organizations—such as Black student unions, undergraduate NAACP chapters, and the historically African American sororities and fraternities—afford African American students a sense of mattering, cultural connections, and numerous opportunities to gain transferable leadership and communication skills. Furthermore, the participants in Guiffrida's (2003) study reported that involvement in Black student organizations afforded them the opportunity to connect comfortably with other African American students and faculty outside of class, give back to the African American community, and "feel safe enough to let their guards down and to be themselves without the fear of offending others or of perpetuating prejudicial stereotypes" (p. 315).

Unarguably, leadership experiences in student organizations prepare undergraduates for their postbaccalaureate educational, professional, political, civic, and social endeavors. In addition to reaping the benefits of involvement, student leaders significantly enhance their campus communities by serving as role models, peer advisors, guides, and confidants for their peers. Unfortunately, few African American undergraduate men choose to serve in these influential leadership capacities.

Involvement Trends Among African American Male Undergraduates

In spite of the well-noted impact of student involvement, Sutton and Terrell (1997) found that few African American students and even fewer African American men were actively involved in out-of-class activities on predominantly White campuses. According to Roach (2001), college and university administrators report that, as enrollment gaps widen between African American men and women, male students are increasingly withdrawing from campus leadership positions. These claims are repeatedly confirmed by student affairs professionals at national conferences, who describe the difficulty they experience in attempting to get more African American men involved in student organizations, engaged in structured university-sponsored activities, and interested in campus leadership positions. Based on an analysis of data from the College Student Experiences Questionnaire, Cuyjet (1997) found that African American men attended fewer campuswide programs, spent significantly less time looking in their campus newspapers for notices regarding involvement opportunities, and participated in clubs and organizations less frequently than their same-race female counterparts. Moreover, the female respondents served on more committees and assumed more leadership roles in student organizations than the men in the sample.

A 2003 study by Harper examined the impact of out-of-class involvement on the experiences of thirty-two African American undergraduate male student leaders at six large predominantly

White research universities. The sample comprised students who had made the most out of college—those who had earned cumulative grade point averages above 3.0, established lengthy records of leadership and involvement in multiple campus organizations, earned the admiration of their peers (as determined by peer elections to campus leadership positions), developed quality relationships with faculty and key campus administrators, participated in enriching educational experiences (such as study abroad programs, internships, and summer research programs), and earned numerous collegiate awards and honors. All student quotations in this chapter are from Harper's study, unless otherwise identified.

African American male student leaders in Harper's (2003) study also described the low involvement trends among their same-race male peers. Without exception, the thirty-two student leaders claimed that "the brothas aren't doing anything." The allocation of their out-of-class time was the most distinguishing factor between the student leaders and other African American men on their campuses. The participants reported that the majority of other African American male students were not involved in activities and organizations. Instead, they offered this list of ways in which their African American male peers spend their out-of-class time:

- In their residence hall rooms doing nothing
- Pursuing romantic endeavors with women
- Exercising in the campus fitness center
- Playing video games
- Playing basketball and other sports
- Trying to become rappers
- Showing off their material possessions (clothes, shoes, cars, and so on)
- Partying
- Hanging out informally with other African American men at designated spots on campus
- Studying alone in the library

The participants also called attention to the gender imbalance in leadership and involvement on their campuses, reporting that African American women were disproportionately more involved than men. One student, cited in Harper (2003), offered these remarks:

> There are not a lot of African American male leaders. On the contrary, there are a lot more African American female student leaders. You'll notice more African American women on this campus holding leadership positions. I see a lot more sistas than brothers at almost every leadership retreat or just about anything else that deals with the University outside of class. The president of NAACP, a sista . . . the president of Black Student Union, a sista . . . the majority of the presidents of all of the other minority student organizations are women. (pp. 133–134)

Harper and Wolley (2002) contend that African American males are underrepresented in student organizations and campus leadership positions at PWIs for the following reasons: (1) African American males do not see other African American males in student organizations and therefore conclude that involvement is abnormal and socially inexpedient; (2) men would rather assert proficiency through a more masculine array of activities, such as competitive sports, weightlifting, pursuing romantic endeavors with women, and video game play; (3) there is a lack of strategic outreach efforts from student organizations, as well as an absence of direct marketing to African American men; and (4) there is a poor assortment of activities and organizations that appeal to the unique social interests of African American men at PWIs. The African American male participants in Harper and McClure's (2002) study perceived mainstream student organizations and campus activities at PWIs to be "too White," culturally irrelevant, and unwelcoming of minority student participation, thus discouraging their involvement. It therefore appears that most African American male students miss out on the aforementioned gains and outcomes associated with involvement in out-of-class activities.

Self-Reported Gains for Highly Involved African American Men

To make leadership and involvement opportunities attractive to African American undergraduate men, it is first essential for higher education administrators to understand what these students may gain and the ways in which their college experiences can be enhanced. It is also important to develop viable ways to help make African American male students comprehend these gains and appreciate their positive consequences. Given the previously discussed low involvement rates among African American men on most campuses, the study sought to understand what it was like to be a highly involved African American male student leader at a PWI. In addition to describing their support sources, the impetus for their involvement, ways in which they were different from other African American men, the stressors of being high-profile student leaders, and their relationships with their universities, the thirty-two participants also discussed gains accrued in two major categories: (1) the acquisition of practical competencies and (2) the perks and privileges extended to them as a result of their leadership and active involvement in student organizations.

PRACTICAL COMPETENCIES

"Success during and after college requires practical competence—the ability to identify and solve problems, manage time effectively, and make good decisions" (Kuh et al., 2003, p. 19). Simply put, practical competencies are transferable skills gained in college that should be easily recalled and applied to other settings (for example, internships, jobs, graduate school). Participation and leadership in multiple student organizations added tremendous value to the African American male student leaders' skill sets throughout their time on their respective campuses. Many identified skills they had clearly acquired from specific experiences in student organizations and through interactions with their fellow student leaders, advisors, and administrators, and various external constituents. Some of these experiences were adversarial, but nonetheless helped the participants learn valuable life lessons that would help protect them from future failure. Although they may have had some of those talents and abilities before enrolling in college, the men were confident that their involvement had refined and enhanced those skills.

They noted how involvement had brought out different strengths they had not previously known they possessed. The student leaders believed these skills would be useful in their postgraduate studies and careers. Internships and summer research programs had offered many of them a glimpse of how useful these competencies would be in long-term employment situations. They felt prepared to enter and adapt to new situations that would afford them the opportunity to rely on the skills they gained through out-of-class involvement. Here are the six most frequently cited practical competencies: (1) working with people from different backgrounds, (2) prioritizing and effectively managing time, (3) contributing to and negotiating in teamwork settings, (4) communicating in small groups and large forums, (5) identifying talents in and delegating responsibilities to others, and (6) recognizing and successfully navigating highly political environments.

WORKING WITH THE CULTURALLY DIFFERENT

The ability to comfortably engage in cross-cultural communication was the most frequently cited practical competency. The participants said the student organizations with which they had been affiliated taught them how to work with people who were different in terms of race, ethnicity, nationality, sexual orientation, ability, socioeconomic status, and religious faith. They clearly understood that to be successful in college and beyond, they needed to be able to forge relationships with people from different backgrounds. The student leaders were cognizant of the fact that their college campuses were mere microcosms of the larger society. A junior premed student noted, "Interactions in clubs and student groups have introduced me to people of other cultures and have really prepared me to go into the world of medicine, where I'll be treating and constantly interacting with a lot of patients from different racial and cultural backgrounds."

Working with a diverse population of student leaders enabled them to learn about and fully appreciate the differences that people bring to different settings. In return, they were able to share their unique backgrounds, culture, and life histories with others. Although they all mentioned working with various cultures, significant emphasis was often placed upon "learning to deal with White people," which they deemed essential for future success. Many participants believed African American males who were not involved lacked this skill. "So many African Americans are miserable in college and in their jobs because they don't know how to deal with White people . . . they really aren't that hard to work with once you figure them out," one student commented.

TIME MANAGEMENT

Being actively involved in numerous organizations and activities required the participants to think carefully about their schedules and make conscious decisions regarding the allocation of their out-of-class time. Each student noted that involvement had taught him how to use his time well. None of the participants considered themselves "time wasters," but instead reported that they often made the most of every single waking hour of each day. With regard to prioritizing, the student leaders knew the more they got involved, the more tasks there would be to get done. "Time management is a big skill that comes with leadership because you have a role to play as a leader, a student, a social person, a mentor, and whatever else—you have to learn how to balance all of those things equally."

Despite the intensity of their schedules, the men unanimously confirmed that the time management skills they had gained would be extremely useful in their lives after college. One student used his multitasking skills in summer internships and quickly noticed how those skills would add value to his career: "One thing I learned from my internships is that you need to be able to multitask. So, I think I'm already a step ahead of someone who has never been involved in activities or held a leadership position. It's not like when I go to work I'm only going to have one thing to do. There are going to be things here, here, here, and here that need to be done all at once. Through being involved, I've learned to prioritize what's important."

Others noticed that all of the graduate students they knew were extremely busy juggling academic, assistantship, research, and familial commitments. Reportedly, involvement had taught them how to pursue similarly aggressive schedules, which would later lead to success in graduate school.

TEAMWORK

The ability to work collaboratively with others on a team was another skill the participants said they gained from their leadership and involvement in out-of-class activities. Establishing trust and credibility with peers was extremely important to the student leaders. They also saw the value in sitting down with fellow members and officers to brainstorm, agree upon a set of goals and objectives, consider multiple approaches and alternatives, and negotiate ideas—as one student expressed it, "Learning that just because I want to do it this way doesn't mean that's the only way to do it." They also figured out how to bring out the best in their group members and motivate them to achieve optimal results for the organization. Furthermore, they learned how to accept criticism from other team members without pouting or being upset. Above all, they were exposed to the art of working collaboratively with people with different personality types, learning styles, strengths, and weaknesses.

Teamwork experiences in student organizations enhanced the participants' ability to work effectively in groups in their classes. Most of the student leaders admitted that they strongly disliked group work and would have actually preferred to work alone on course assignments—this preference usually had a lot to do with their tight schedules, which were not really conducive to group meetings outside of class. Despite their feelings about class-related group work, they knew they were good at it because of their experiences in clubs and organizations. They were often appointed leaders on group projects in their classes because they were good at displaying the characteristics that are requisite for group success (mediation, flexibility, fairness, and the like). They knew these skills would serve them well in graduate school, as many post–baccalaureate degree programs tend to require collaboration and group assignments. Likewise, they were aware, for example, that most prosperous businesses depend on cross-functional teams, successful attorneys frequently have to collaborate with other attorneys on cases, and the best physicians usually work with others to achieve life-saving results.

Communication and Public Speaking

The study participants believed that their leadership experiences in student organizations—whether one on one, in small groups, or in front of large crowds—significantly enhanced their communication abilities. They talked about learning to listen to what other people had to say before crafting a response and the importance of thinking before speaking. They spoke of learning to form arguments and opinions quickly and to articulate their thoughts well in front of others. Their clubs and organizations were small, safe communication practice zones. Many participants admitted that their verbal communication skills were grossly underdeveloped before they became involved, but student organization membership helped them become more comfortable speaking in front of others. Predominantly African American and minority student organizations, as well as groups specifically designed for African American men, often provided culturally familiar "safe zones" for the participants to hone these skills.

Like their teamwork abilities, the communication skills the participants acquired through student groups also transferred nicely into their classes. For instance, a senior business major offered the following reflection: "My speaking abilities have really improved. I now can get up in front of a crowd of several hundred people and speak. I'm also not afraid to show it in class. We have group presentations for class and getting up in front of thirty students and a professor is nothing. I've learned how to speak in front of and communicate with people from leading meetings in my different student organizations."

Consistently, the participants called attention to their public speaking abilities and the confidence they had gained from the practice sessions in their student organizations. They had also mastered the skill of impromptu speaking, as many indicated that they had been unexpectedly asked to speak at a program or meeting without first having the opportunity to prepare formal remarks. This was something many participants believed they could not have done prior to getting involved.

The men also discussed the value of having a flexible communication style and being able to speak with anyone. "Sometimes we speak to large crowds of college students and sometimes we speak to small children, so you have to use different speaking styles for the audience you're speaking to." They mentioned how communicating with their university presidents and other top administrators was different from communicating with their peers. Even with one-on-one dialogue, the participants recalled how important it was to adjust their communication styles, without being intimidated. They knew this skill would be useful in their future careers, which would inevitably require countless conversations with people at different levels.

DELEGATING

"As a leader I have learned how to delegate things more and trust people. I have also learned that a good leader works to produce leaders." Through their involvement, the student leaders quickly mastered the skill of delegation. Realizing there was often too much work to be done by one person, they became more comfortable releasing things from their control and handing them over to other members. The participants admitted that they had not always been at ease giving people the "benefit of the doubt," and they previously subscribed to the notion, "if you want something done right, you better do it yourself." But as they grew in their organizations and their schedules became seemingly unbearable, they began to take risks by appointing only a select few members to carry out small, low-risk duties. Over time, they learned their fellow members could be trusted; therefore, they began to comfortably delegate larger, more important tasks to others.

Regarding skill transferability, the participants believed that delegating tasks and not trying to do all the work alone would serve them well in graduate school and in their future careers. They realized that effective managers, leaders, and administrators do not micromanage their employees or coworkers. "A CEO gives tasks to his [or her] vice presidents, leaves them alone and trusts they will do a good job," a sophomore participant indicated. Another student said his experiences as a student leader taught him how to motivate others to follow through and do their best on tasks they had been delegated.

POLITICAL ASTUTENESS

The participants repeatedly spoke of "the system" and how involvement had taught them how to work it, get around it, and manipulate it. In fact, one student commented, "Once you know the system, you can't necessarily beat it but you can manipulate it." A participant from one university said he learned how political games were played and how the rules were made on campus. This awareness prevented him from making a fool of himself and wasting his time trying to change things that were politically unchangeable. Conversely, his familiarity with the system enabled him to get things done quickly and push various agenda items forward without resistance from the administration.

Several other students talked about knowing the ins and outs of campus politics and being aware of how decisions were made from the closed-door meetings they had attended with campus administrators. Being the student representative on major campus committees provided the participants an excellent opportunity to witness interactions among senior-level decision makers, voice the opinions of their peers, and see how politics often clouded progress. Furthermore, the student leaders considered their political astuteness to be an invaluable addition to their skill sets. Apparently the same system that existed on their campuses also existed in businesses, hospitals, and courtrooms. The students were confident that they could successfully navigate different political environments by immediately identifying the major players and power brokers in any given organizational structure. Reportedly, they had learned how to "play the game."

The six gains reported herein are a direct result of the meaningful choices the thirty-two African American male student leaders made about how to spend their out-of-class time. Consequently, the investments they made in their educational and career development experiences in college will continue to accrue interest long after their student days are done. Moreover, many of the special benefits that were extended to them because of their leadership and active involvement will be treasured and long remembered. These memorable gains are discussed in the next section.

Perks and Privileges

Although the study participants did not seek leadership positions and involvement opportunities to enhance their resumes or receive accolades from their professors and administrators, they were handsomely compensated for their contributions to student life on their respective campuses, in the form of numerous perks. The four most frequently cited perks are described here.

Relationships with Key Administrators

Involvement afforded the student leaders access to the busiest person on campus—the president. In the interviews, these student leaders fondly recalled taking advantage of opportunities to dine at the president's home, sit in on meetings with the president, call the president's office and have their call put through without getting "the runaround," and solicit recommendation letters from the president for awards and graduate school. In addition to their relationship with the campus chief executive, they also spoke of those they had cultivated with other top administrators at their universities. "Having the opportunity to work side by side with the provost . . . not many students can say they've worked with the provost because you know provosts are usually very distant people," one student shared. Vice presidents, deans, associate deans, department chairpersons, and directors were among the key people from whom the student leaders regularly received support, mentoring, nominations, and recommendation letters. It appeared that since there were so few African American male student leaders on campus, administrators gave even greater attention to the study participants than to other student leaders.

Meeting Celebrities and Dignitaries

In addition to regularly interacting with campus-based high-profile administrators, the African American men in the sample were also afforded numerous opportunities to interact with a host of celebrities and dignitaries. Maya Angelou, Halle Berry, Spike Lee, Oprah Winfrey, Jesse Jackson, Hillary Rodham Clinton, Julian Bond, Nikki Giovanni, and Ray Charles were among the many famous people the student leaders had met. Because of their involvement in certain student organizations, they were often invited to dinner with major keynote speakers or given backstage passes to mingle with entertainers. Additionally, they sometimes attended national conferences where some of these famous people were speaking or performing. Regarding Maya Angelou's visit to his campus, one student noted, "Naturally, I would have been there with a ticket, but because of the positions I've held on campus,

I had the opportunity to go backstage to meet her." The students realized that they would not have had the chances to interact with these celebrities on campus or at conferences had they not been so actively involved.

SCHOLARSHIPS

"There have been certain scholarships that I couldn't have gotten. Like through the fraternity, I'm getting a $1,000 scholarship at a program tomorrow morning. I definitely couldn't have gotten that if I wasn't involved." Collectively, the thirty-two participants had been awarded more than $489,000 in merit-based scholarship awards. In their opinion, they would have been considerably less successful in awards competitions were it not for their leadership and active involvement on campus. They knew that more often than not, scholarship selection committees tended to view applications submitted by well-rounded students more favorably. When combined with their academic records, the participants' involvement lists usually made their applications for scholarships and awards stand out and be more competitive than other applicants'. Because of the relationships they had built with administrators and faculty, the student leaders said they had no trouble finding out about "exclusive" awards, receiving assistance in preparing essays for applications, and soliciting glowing recommendation letters. The relationships cultivated through involvement—not just the involvement record itself—tended to yield the most favorable results for the African American men as they went after different awards.

INTERNSHIPS

Several of the student leaders shared stories about how they had gotten summer internships and full-time employment opportunities. They reported that in employment interviews they would frequently refer to the lessons they had learned, conflicts they had resolved, and value they had added to their student organizations, which usually impressed company representatives. One participant, who had received six summer internship offers in one year, claimed his grades and his track record of leadership on campus were "a lethal combination that sealed the deal in all the interviews." Some participants indicated that their student involvement sometimes superseded and cancelled out things that have been traditionally deemed important in job and internship searches—such as courses taken, academic major, and previous field-related experiences. For instance, one English-major senior was offered a summer internship (which later led to a full-time job) in human resources at a leading pharmaceutical and nutrition company.

Many of the student organizations that participants were involved in, especially the academic clubs, were responsible for working with faculty to coordinate and host company visits, information sessions, and internship and job fairs. Of course, the officers of those organizations usually interacted most closely with company representatives throughout the program planning and coordinating stages and during their visits to campus. Consequently, they were often granted "first dibs" on job opportunities. The student leaders unanimously agreed that involvement had assisted them in getting their feet in doors that would have been closed to uninvolved students.

These four perks—access to administrators, the chance to meet celebrities, scholarships, and internships—will be forever remembered by these thirty-two African American men as they look back and reflect upon their undergraduate experiences. The skills they gained and benefits they accrued through involvement underscore the importance of finding ways to get more African American male collegians similarly engaged and exposed to the fruits of involvement and leadership in out-of-class activities.

Strategies for Increasing Out-of-Class Involvement and Leadership Participation

The following ten approaches to increasing African American male participation in out-of-class activities and leadership in student organizations are largely based on lessons offered by the student leaders on the six PWIs in Harper's (2003) study.

1. *Work with African American men who are already involved to recruit their uninvolved same-race male peers.* In most cases, African American male undergraduates seek membership in a student

organization because they are encouraged to do so by an older male student leader. No influence is greater than that of peer to peer. Student organization advisors should reach out to African American male student leaders who are involved and offer to partner with them to recruit more African American male members. These student leaders should be especially encouraged to reach out and get first-year male students involved before they establish patterns of disengagement and time-wasting.

2. *Systematically collect data from uninvolved African American men to determine how their out-of-class time is spent and why their participation in structured, university-sponsored activities and organizations is low.* Surveys, individual interviews, and focus groups would yield compelling insight into changes necessary for increasing involvement. For instance, African American male focus group participants may indicate that the extreme "Whiteness" of mainstream student organizations discourages their participation or that there are no perceivable activities that directly appeal to their unique cultural interests. Moreover, survey respondents may report a lack of knowledge about various involvement opportunities on campus. An absence of data will inevitably result in ineffective attempts to strengthen African American male involvement trends.

3. *Hold student organization leaders accountable for reaching out to underrepresented groups, including African American men.* Advisors should call attention to the disproportionate representation of nonminority students in clubs and organizations, and they should work with White student leaders to construct a recruitment plan to increase minority student participation. Likewise, student leaders who plan concerts, festivals, lecture series, and other campus programs must be held accountable for ensuring that African American student interests are taken into account. Otherwise, most will choose not to attend these events. An African American male student's first exposure to the campus activities board may be at a hip-hop concert sponsored by the board. He may subsequently choose to pursue membership in the organization because of the positive experience he had at the event. Conversely, if the board brings no African American musicians to campus, most African American men will conclude

that the organization is not intended for African American students or committed to African American interests.

4. *Provide financial and advisory support for minority student organizations, as they provide a much-needed involvement pipeline for African American men.* The most engaged African American male student leaders (such as student government presidents) almost always get their start in the Black student union, undergraduate NAACP chapters, the National Society of Black Engineers (NSBE), the five historically African American fraternities, and other minority student organizations. In addition to providing a pipeline to greater campuswide involvement, these minority student organizations offer a place where undergraduates can begin to understand—as the participants in Harper's (2003) study do—the personal benefits of involvement and leadership. On many campuses, these clubs are grossly underfunded and barely have the resources needed to effectively execute programming that positively impacts the wider African American and minority student communities. Furthermore, members and leaders of those groups often claim that increased African American faculty and staff advisory support is needed to help sustain effectiveness. Adding an African American male administrator to the advisory team of the Black student union, for example, may actually attract more African American male members to the organization.

5. *Create and support groups specifically for African American men.* Organizations that exist to uplift African American men play an important role on many campuses, as they provide a forum where interested students can gather to discuss race- and gender-specific issues, bond and build new friendships, and engage in programming that satisfies their unique needs and cultural interests. Although student ownership is key to the success of any undergraduate organization, groups for African American undergraduate men stand a better chance of survival with guidance and participation from African American male graduate students, faculty, and staff. Older men usually ensure continuity from year to year, offer suggestions for focused and purposeful programming, help lobby for financial support from the university, and serve as role models for the undergraduate members. Like other minority student organizations,

these groups usually serve as a catalyst for African American male involvement in other organizations and mainstream activities. If African American male faculty and staff are not available, other university employees who are genuinely committed to helping reverse the plight of the African American male collegian could be used in these advocacy and support roles.

6. *Encourage and support consciousness-raising programming, as it is likely to incite action.* Administrators often conclude that it is best to keep quiet reports of racist and discriminatory acts on campus, though most African American students have seen or personally encountered these for themselves at PWIs. Raising awareness about the issues that plague minority students, in a town hall meeting or some other program specifically for African American undergraduates, then using already involved African American male student leaders to plead for assistance in confronting those issues, could produce a larger cadre of men who become inspired to engage in initiatives to help improve conditions for other African Americans on their campuses. Also, groups specifically created to support and unify African American men (as suggested in recommendation five) can be enlisted to help programmatically facilitate consciousness-raising efforts.

7. *Persuade emerging African American male students to seek leadership positions in student organizations.* First-year students or African American male newcomers to student organizations should be strategically groomed by advisors to someday lead the groups in which they hold membership. The inadequate representation of African American male student leaders on most campuses poses an urgent need for advisors to give special attention to general members and help prepare them for leadership roles. Seeing an African American student government president would likely attract more African American men to the organization, and could even inspire previously uninvolved students to someday seek the presidency. If the larger body of African American males does not see its same-race male peers in high-profile leadership roles, most will conclude these positions are unattainable; thus the grooming of trendsetters is essential. At the same time, it is important to recognize that not everyone has the inclination or skills to attain a campus leadership position, so it is equally important to communicate to African American male

students that being a good active member of an organization still provides some of the important benefits that are extended to student leaders. Student organizations, minority and otherwise, need and thrive on the efforts of committed workers who are not always in leadership positions.

8. *Host an annual campus kickoff event for African American men.* A "Black Male Forum" or "Involvement Opportunities Fair for African American Men" will enable student leaders and advisors to attract a captive audience of African American men to whom they can promote the benefits of out-of-class involvement. The event should be widely marketed to all African American males on campus—students, faculty, and staff alike. One-on-one invitations, particularly through telephone calls or face-to-face contacts, are most effective in motivating otherwise reluctant African American male students to attend this type of program. Also, a high-ranking African American male administrator should be asked to address the attendees and challenge the students to reverse the low involvement trends, invest in themselves through leadership experiences, and leave their marks on the institution through involvement. Moreover, student leaders should be given time to reflect upon the gains and outcomes they have experienced, and advisors should note that employers and graduate schools tend to favor well-rounded applicants with quantifiable leadership experiences and good grades. The event should culminate with food and fellowship.

9. *Reach out to African American parents during new student orientation.* They should be made aware of the challenges that African American students—especially males—typically face at PWIs, and urged to recommend involvement in student organizations and out-of-class activities to their sons. African American parents should be told that involvement is one way for their sons to form meaningful relationships with administrators; compete successfully for scholarships, internships, and jobs; and gain practical competencies that can be easily transferred to other environments, including college classrooms. Above all, they should be told that their sons are less likely to discontinue their pursuit of the baccalaureate degree if they get actively involved in out-of-class activities. This form of parental outreach would be most effective in parent orientation programs sponsored by

Black culture centers or multicultural affairs offices. Occasionally sending a postcard that asks "How is your son spending his out-of-class time?" may also be effective.

10. *Form a coalition of collaborators who are interested in strengthening outcomes for African American undergraduate men.* This group should include, but not be limited to, the following: faculty, student affairs professionals (especially those from student unions, the residence halls, and student activities offices), Black culture center staff, athletics personnel, multicultural affairs professionals, and of course African American male undergraduates. The coalition must meet regularly to strategically plan ways to keep African American men involved and retained at the institution. Specific tasks and programs should be delegated to each stakeholder between meetings. This must be a highly visible group whose programmatic efforts confirm for African American men that their needs, issues, and outcomes are important and remain on the forefront of the coalition's agenda.

Conclusion

This chapter sought to explicate the powerful nexus linking involvement, leadership, gains, and outcomes—those who get involved are more likely to assume leadership roles that lead to many of the aforementioned gains, which positively affect the large body of outcomes documented in the student involvement research. Involvement indisputably makes the difference in African American men's short-term gains and long-term outcomes. It is clear that African American males who are actively involved in campus activities and hold leadership positions in student organizations have better experiences and gain more from college than their uninvolved same-race male peers. For instance, take Amondo and Aaron, the two African American undergraduates introduced at the beginning of this chapter. Aaron returned to the university for his junior year and continued to struggle. Unfortunately, he officially dropped out the following summer and returned to his hometown to work in a factory. Amondo graduated, secured a full-time job with a major television network in New York, and eventually enrolled in a top-ranked MBA program at Emory University.

College faculty, staff, and administrators are urged to take seriously the involvement trends that exist among African American undergraduate men, and to consistently encourage more male students to make meaningful choices about how they spend their out-of-class time. Consequently, retention rates will improve; students with profiles similar to Aaron's will become the anomaly; and African American male alumni like Amondo will help strengthen the institution's reputation and inspire younger African American male students to make smart choices, experience similar gains, and enjoy comparable outcomes accrued through leadership and active involvement.

References

Anaya, G. (1996). College experiences and student learning: The influence of active learning, college environments, and cocurricular activities. *Journal of College Student Development, 37*(6), 611–622.

Astin, A. W. (1984). Student involvement: A developmental theory for higher education. *Journal of College Student Personnel, 25*(2), 297–308.

Astin, A. W., & Sax, L. J. (1998). How undergraduates are affected by service participation. *Journal of College Student Development, 39*(3), 251–263.

Bandura, A., Peluso, E. A., Ortman, N., & Millard, M. (2000). Effects of peer education training on peer educators: Leadership, self-esteem, health knowledge, and health behaviors. *Journal of College Student Development, 41*(5), 471–478.

Baxter Magolda, M. B. (1992). Cocurricular influences on college students' intellectual development. *Journal of College Student Development, 33*, 203–213.

Berger, J. B., & Milem, J. F. (1999). The role of student involvement and perceptions of integration in a causal model of student persistence. *Research in Higher Education, 40*(6), 641–664.

Braxton, J. M., Milem, J. F., & Sullivan, A. S. (2000). The influence of active learning on the college departure process: Toward a revision of Tinto's theory. *The Journal of Higher Education, 71*(5), 569–590.

Cabrera, A. F., Nora, A., Terenzini, P. T., Pascarella, E. T., & Hagedorn, L. S. (1999). Campus racial climate and the adjustment of students to college: A comparison between White students and African American students. *Journal of Higher Education, 70*(2), 134–202.

Chickering, A. W., & Reisser, L. (1993). *Education and identity* (2nd ed.). San Francisco: Jossey-Bass.

Clarke, D., & Tomlinson-Clarke, S. (1994). Predicting social adjustment and academic achievement for college women with and without pre-college leadership. *Journal of College Student Development, 35*(2), 120–124.

Cuyjet, M. J. (1997). African American men on college campuses: Their needs and their perceptions. In M. J. Cuyjet (Ed.), *Helping African American men succeed in college.* New Directions for Student Services, no. 80 (pp. 5–16). San Francisco: Jossey-Bass.

Davis, R. (1991). Social support networks and undergraduate student academic-success-related outcomes: A comparison of Black students on Black and White campuses. In W. R. Allen, E. G. Epps, & N. Z. Haniff (Eds.), *College in black and white: African-American students in predominantly White and in historically Black public universities.* Albany, NY: SUNY Press.

Delvin, A. S. (1996). Survival skills training during freshman orientation: Its role in college adjustment. *Journal of College Student Development, 37*(3), 324–334.

Evans, N. J. (1987). A framework for assisting student affairs staff in fostering moral development. *Journal of Counseling and Development, 66,* 191–193.

Fries-Britt, S., Gardner, J. N., Low, L., & Tinto, V. (2002, March). *Retaining students: New questions and fresh perspectives* (video teleconference print resource packet). Columbia, SC: University of South Carolina, National Resource Center for the First-Year Experience and Students in Transition.

Guiffrida, D. A. (2003). African American student organizations as agents of social integration. *Journal of College Student Development, 44*(3), 304–319.

Harper, S. R. (2003). *Most likely to succeed: The self-perceived impact of involvement on the experiences of high-achieving African American undergraduate men at predominantly White universities.* Unpublished doctoral dissertation, Indiana University, Bloomington.

Harper, S. R. (2004). The measure of a man: Conceptualizations of masculinity among high-achieving African American male college students. *Berkeley Journal of Sociology, 48*(1), 89–107.

Harper, S. R. (2005). Leading the way: Inside the experiences of high-achieving African American male students. *About Campus, 10*(1), 8–15.

Harper, S. R., Byars, L. F., & Jelke, T. B. (2005). How membership affects college adjustment and African American undergraduate student outcomes. In T. L. Brown, G. S. Parks, & C. M. Phillips (Eds.), *African American fraternities and sororities: The legacy and the vision* (pp. 393–416). Lexington, KY: University Press of Kentucky.

Harper, S. R., & McClure, M. L. (2002). *Black students' perceptions of and reactions to largely White physical spaces and activities at a predominantly White institution.* Paper presented at the annual conference of the National Association of Student Personnel Administrators, Boston, MA.

Harper, S. R., & Wolley, M. A. (2002). Becoming an "involving college" for African American undergraduate men: Strategies for increasing African American male participation in campus activities. *Association of College Unions International Bulletin, 70*(3), 16–24.

Inmann, P., & Pascarella, E .T. (1998). The impact of college residence on the development of critical thinking skills in college freshmen. *Journal of College Student Development, 39*(6), 557–568.

Jackson, K. W., & Swan, L. A. (1991). Institutional and individual factors affecting black undergraduate student performance: Campus race and student gender. In W. R. Allen, E. G. Epps, & N. Z. Haniff (Eds.), *College in black and white: African American students in predominantly white and in historically black public universities* (pp. 127-141). Albany, NY: State University of New York.

Jones, C. E., & Watt, J. D. (1999). Psychosocial development and moral orientation among traditional-aged college students. *Journal of College Student Development, 40,* 125–132.

Kuh, G. D. (1995). The other curriculum: Out-of-class experiences associated with student learning and personal development. *Journal of Higher Education, 66*(2), 123–155.

Kuh, G. D., & Lund, J. P. (1994). What students gain from participation in student government. In M. Terrell & M. J. Cuyjet (Eds.), *Developing student government leadership.* New Directions for Student Services, no. 66 (pp. 5–17). San Francisco: Jossey-Bass.

Kuh, G. D., Palmer, M., & Kish, K. (2003). The value of educationally purposeful out-of-class experiences. In T. L. Skipper & R. Argo (Eds.), *Involvement in campus activities and the retention of first-year college students,* The First-Year Experience Monograph Series, No. 36 (pp. 19–34). Columbia, SC: University of South Carolina, National Resource Center for the First-Year Experience and Students in Transition.

Liddell, D. L., & Davis, T. L. (1996). The measure of moral orientation: Reliability and validity evidence. *Journal of College Student Development, 37*(5), 485–493.

McBride, R. E., & Reed, J. (1998). Thinking and college athletes—are they predisposed to critical thinking? *College Student Journal, 32*(3), 443–450.

Milem, J. F., & Berger, J. B. (1997). A modified model of college student persistence: Exploring the relationship between Astin's theory of involvement and Tinto's theory of student departure. *Journal of College Student Development, 38*(4), 387–400.

Ory, J., & Braskamp, L. (1988). Involvement and growth of students in three academic programs. *Research in Higher Education, 28,* 116–129.

Pascarella, E. T., Edison, M., Whitt, E. J., Nora, A., Hagedorn, L. S., & Terenzini, P. T. (1996). Cognitive effects of Greek membership during the first-year of college. *NASPA Journal, 33,* 254–259.

Pascarella, E. T., Flowers, L., & Whitt, E. J. (2001). Cognitive effects of Greek affiliation in college: Additional evidence. *NASPA Journal, 38*(3), 280–301.

Pascarella, E. T., Palmer, B., Moye, M., & Pierson, C. T. (2001). Do diversity experiences influence the development of critical thinking? *Journal of College Student Development, 42*(3), 257–271.

Pascarella, E. T., Smart, J., Ethington, C., & Nettles, M. (1987). The influence of college on self-concept: A consideration of race and gender differences. *American Educational Research Journal, 24,* 49–77.

Pascarella, E. T., & Terenzini, P. T. (1991). *How college affects students: Findings and insights from twenty years of research.* San Francisco: Jossey-Bass.

Pascarella, E. T., & Terenzini, P. T. (2005). *How college affects students, volume 2: A third decade of research.* San Francisco: Jossey-Bass.

Paul, E. L., & Kelleher, M. (1995). Precollege concerns about losing and making friends in college: Implications for friendship satisfaction and self-esteem during the college transition. *Journal of College Student Development, 36*(6), 513–521.

Peltier, G. L., Laden, R., & Matranga, M. (1999). Student persistence in college: A review of research. *Journal of College Student Retention, 1*(4), 357–375.

Pike, G. R. (2000). The influence of fraternity or sorority membership on students' college experiences and cognitive development. *Research in Higher Education, 41,* 117–139.

Rest, J. R. (1993). Research on moral judgment in college students. In A. Garrod (Ed.), *Approaches to moral development* (pp. 201–213). New York: Teachers College Press.

Roach, R. (2001). Where are the Black men on campus? *Black Issues in Higher Education, 18*(6), 18–24.

Sutton, E. M., & Kimbrough, W. M. (2001). Trends in Black student involvement. *NASPA Journal, 39*(1), 30–40.

Sutton, E. M., & Terrell, M. C. (1997). Identifying and developing leadership opportunities for African American men. In M. J. Cuyjet (Ed.), *Helping African American men succeed in college.* New Directions for Student Services, no. 80 (pp. 55–64). San Francisco: Jossey-Bass.

Taylor, C. M., & Howard-Hamilton, M. F. (1995). Student involvement and racial identity attitudes among African American males. *Journal of College Student Development, 36*(4), 330–336.

Tinto, V. (1993). Leaving college: Rethinking the causes and cures of student attrition (2nd ed.). Chicago: University of Chicago Press.

Villalpando, O. (2002). The impact of diversity and multiculturalism on all students: Findings from a national study. *NASPA Journal, 40*(1), 124–144.

CHAPTER FIVE

DEVELOPMENTAL MENTORING OF AFRICAN AMERICAN COLLEGE MEN

E. Michael Sutton, Winston-Salem State University

Mentoring programs enrich the careers of education and business professionals as well as the welfare of minority youth. Although the primary objective of much private sector and educational mentoring is to empower the protégé's skills to advance within the organization or to enlarge the protégé's sphere of influence, those created for adolescents emphasize the positive development of the protégé's affective characteristics of self-esteem and confidence—this emphasis is a primary characteristic of faith community and ethnic mentoring programs (Kessler, 1999). In particular, African American communities have integrated various mentoring programs to confront the social maladies that are common in these communities. For example, Hill (1998) reports that through participating in such a mentoring program, protégés gain a greater appreciation of financial matters as well as issues that pertain to marriage and family. The composition of most minority mentoring programs is coeducational, but a growing number of mentoring programs are evolving specifically for African American men, to address the critical issues surrounding their academic welfare. As noted by Hall (1996), such mentoring programs are desperately needed because African American men are likely to encounter many challenges in adjusting to the traditional educational system.

Although the majority of mentoring programs involving African American men have positively influenced the academic and social success of this student subculture, one limitation of such programs is that their format and content is characterized as highly instructional rather than developmentally stimulating for the protégé.

This chapter will define and analyze mentoring from the instructional and the developmental perspective and illustrate how the Student African American Brotherhood (SAAB) program has incorporated the latter approach to provide a more enriching mentoring experience for African American men. In addition, a brief yet descriptive analysis explores how environmental factors at both historically Black and predominantly White campuses impact the mentoring experiences of these men. The chapter concludes with recommendations for practitioners to consider when implementing a mentoring program for their campuses.

Instructional Mentoring and Developmental Mentoring: Two Different Approaches

As mentoring programs have evolved, so have the objectives and methods to address the specific professional and social needs of participants. This is clearly illustrated in both educational and corporate arenas, in which neophyte professionals are no longer simply introduced to the customs and policies of their new environments. Today they are also provided important moral support by a seasoned counterpart and advised on navigating the political aspects of the agency or institution. Another important recent development is a focus on guidance, nurturing, and support of individuals perceived to be disenfranchised by gender, skill, or ethnicity; these are common elements of most mentoring programs (Fong, 2000; Tallerico, 2000; Shandley, 1989; Moore & Salimbene, 1981). The literature provides several examples illustrating how instructional mentoring programs can positively shape the behavior of protégés in the areas of educational and social issues. Hill (1998) suggests that African American adolescents who participated in community mentoring programs experienced greater knowledge and appreciation of their culture than those who did not. In addition, mentoring programs sponsored by faith communities not only emphasize pertinent skills for educational and personal survival but, more important, affirm the participant's self-esteem and confidence, as previously stated by Kessler (1999). As a result of these positive outcomes, the popularity of mentoring programs has flourished in higher education settings. Specifically, the success of mentoring programs in the public school system as well as institutions of higher education has produced significant retention results among participants who are "academically at risk" or minority group members (Jackson & Matthews, 1999; Terrell, Hassell, & Duggar, 1992; Pope, 2002). These programs continue to meet a need both in the general community and in educational environments. Despite the positive outcomes of the majority of established mentoring programs, some suggest that the typical one-dimensional "instructional" format not only encourages the protégé to become more dependent upon the mentor but, of greater concern, retards the protégé's learning from a developmental perspective.

Such mentoring relationships, according to Johnsrud (1991), remain hierarchical in nature because of the protégé's need for affirmation and continued guidance and the protégé's desire to please the mentor. As a result, such relationships are likely not only to remain dependent but also to fail to mature beyond that of teacher and student. This is often a major concern in cross-gender mentoring programs. Although the female protégé is likely to benefit from such a relationship, Kanter (1977) cautions that women are more likely to become highly dependent on the future advice of their male mentors than to become empowered by them. Cross-race mentoring also poses challenges: according to Patton and Harper (2003), African American female graduate students overwhelmingly perceived that a mentoring relationship with an African American female mentor is the optimal experience, largely due to their ability to help them understand the complex intersection of race and gender issues within the academy as well as to provide friendly advice to help them avoid professional pitfalls.

Regardless of the mentor's gender or ethnicity, it is imperative that the mentoring experience of the protégé foster learning from an active rather than a passive mode. Mentoring programs that are developmentally focused are more likely to achieve this objective.

The developmental concept of learning is not foreign to student affairs professionals. In fact, many theorists, such as Chickering (1969), Cross (1991), and Helms (1993), have formulated their own theories purporting that as students traverse through various stages they are likely to mature developmentally. The significance of this observation is that it means mentors should be fluid in their roles, adapting to the diverse stages of the protégé's learning. According to R. Taibbi (personal communication, May 16, 2002), the four distinct developmental roles a mentor should play are (1) supervisor as teacher, (2) supervisor as guide, (3) supervisor as gatekeeper, and finally (4) supervisor as consultant. This is best illustrated in a graduate mentoring program by Selke & Wong (1993). In essence, the model encourages the faculty mentor not to provide a convenient solution for the protégé but rather to use the personal and professional challenges experienced by the protégé, affirming successes and assisting the protégé to examine alternative suggestions or opportunities that the protégé may not have considered. Such experiences, according to Jarvis (1992), not only challenge the protégé to engage in self-reflection to resolve his or her own problems but also to grasp the concepts that undergird the practice. Interestingly, this format can be found in many contemporary mentoring programs for minority students. For example, the Arranged Mentor for Instructional Guidance and Organizational (or Other) Support (AMIGOS) program (Stromei, 2000) is an excellent mentoring model, integrating both formal and developmental components, that encourages interaction between the mentor and protégé. Such models may have significant implications for mentoring programs for African American men in that the combination of previous social, cultural, and economic forces has historically kept these individuals from mastering vital developmental tasks such as establishing positive self-esteem, control of emotions, positive interpersonal relationships with women, appreciation for academic success, and basic interaction skills during their childhood and adolescent years (Staples, 1982). Another programmatic example, the African American male mentoring component of the SAAB program, is a truly comprehensive mentoring paradigm that is developmental in nature.

THE SAAB MENTORING PROGRAM

As described in the profile in Chapter Thirteen, the SAAB program was founded in 1990 on the campus of Georgia Southwestern University. The organization emphasizes mentoring African American men from a developmental approach by enhancing their understanding of their responsibilities as United States citizens. Although the overriding objective of the program is to assist each participant in clarifying his purpose and life goals, leadership development and training are also salient issues of this mentoring program.

The context of the program includes various facets that encourage the protégé's development beyond that of one-on-one interaction with the mentor. Such an approach coincides with Ianni's (1990) findings that mentoring should be an exchange relationship between the protégé and the mentor that involves mutual nurturing, caring, and exchange of resources—rather than simply a form of "giving" by the mentor. According to Bledsoe (personal communication, May 20, 2002), the SAAB mentoring objective is accomplished in three dimensions: (1) student-to-student at the collegiate level, (2) Project ACE collegiate Black males mentoring high school Black males; and (3) advisor-to-student mentoring at both K–12 and collegiate levels. Although these components of the program certainly address mentoring from a conventional standpoint, the significance of the student-to-student aspect of the program provides the greatest opportunity for participants to grow developmentally. Specifically, protégés are philosophically challenged to embrace the program's core values through the model's mentoring perspectives: proactive leadership, principles of accountability, self-discipline, and intellectual development. It is interesting to note that the personal development perspective encourages collaboration with the institution's student support services, to maximize the academic performance of the participants. Bledsoe proudly states that significant developmental growth of the participants is observed as a result of their involvement with the mentoring perspectives.

Student-to-student mentoring relationships make up one of the three dimensions of the SAAB program. Researchers such as Bowman, Bowman, and Delucia (1990) as well as O'Brien (1989) have indicated the significance and value of peer mentoring. Peer mentoring—according to Allen, Russell, and Maetzke (1997) as well as Grant and Ensher (2000)—is the process of introducing the inexperienced student to the mores and traditions of the campus culture while informally performing similar functions as the adult mentor in areas of information sharing, emotional support, and friendship.

These relationships are beneficial for a number of reasons. First, in the absence of available adult mentor candidates, potential peer mentors are generally more abundant. Thus, with appropriate training, these young men are able to provide some of the benefits of mentoring relationships for each other. Second, peers are more easily empathetic. Although not all young African American men have the same or similar experiences, it is often much easier for them to relate to the day-to-day events in each other's lives than for adult males of a different generation. Third, it is likely that peer mentor programs increase the accountability of participants to each other as well as the goals of the mentoring program. This is usually evident in academic achievement as well as service to the community at large. Student affairs professionals seeking to provide mentoring opportunities to African American college men are advised to include a peer mentor component as a complement to the contemporary adult mentor program or to develop such a program in the absence of a viable adult-youth program.

Similar to other African American male mentoring programs, the mentors selected for the SAAB program are not only expected to establish a one-on-one relationship with individual protégés but also encouraged to sustain a relationship with all program participants throughout the college years and beyond. Such relationships are formulated and enhanced through focus groups. The emphasis of these groups certainly underscores the developmental aspect of the program in that they provide a unique opportunity for the protégé to discuss how the experience has augmented his attitudes toward himself and others as a result of each mentoring perspective. An additional observed difference between conventional mentoring programs and the SAAB model is the intricate involvement of each protégé in his own behavior modification through creating a Personal Action and Leadership Plan.

Each protégé completes the personal action plan when he enters the SAAB program. The objective is to encourage him to develop his own personal mission statement that coincides with his specific collegiate goals. Both the adult mentor and the protégé attempt to create specific goals around the general goals of graduation from college, setting personal and professional goals, determining his own motivation, developing a sense of identity with the home institution, and establishing a sense of purpose. This personal action plan serves as the protégé's map for the next five years. Bledsoe (personal communication, May 20, 2002) strongly emphasizes that the young man, not the mentor, assumes ownership of his plan. Even more important and significant than the development of a personal action plan, the SAAB model also assists protégés to identify negative attitudinal behaviors that may impede their future efforts to attain leadership roles within the greater campus community.

The research by Lee (1991) and Kunjufu (1986) certainly indicates that African American men are likely to encounter many negative stereotypes from society as a whole. Consequently, for the African American male mentoring experience to be successful, it is imperative that the mentoring programs provide venues for these men to identify and discuss these emotions. Committed to addressing the holistic development of each participant, the SAAB mentoring model attempts to rectify negative perceptions through the Leadership Development Plan. This instrument encourages male participants to identify negative self-images or programs internalized during early childhood or early adolescence. This coincides with Lee's (1991) conjectures suggesting that African American male mentoring programs should empower them by transforming cultural dimensions that are conventionally perceived as negative into positive developmental experiences. By identifying and tracing (with the assistance of the mentor) such behaviors to their origin, these men become aware that negative behaviors such as poor motivation, the paucity of organizational skills, and the desire to give up are not innate, but learned behaviors that can be changed. Another hallmark of this program worth mentioning is the commitment of each participant to teach and hold each other accountable throughout the peer mentoring process. This concept is also expressed by Selke & Wong (1993), suggesting that individuals can implement mentoring behaviors without being mentors in the traditional sense of the term.

The infrastructure described in this model clearly gives the practitioner an alternative to conventional mentoring programs for African American men. To summarize, although most conventional mentoring paradigms have yielded positive results, the design of such programs remains intrusive and attempts to modify participants' antagonistic behaviors without accentuating their developmental needs. Further, the process of instruction is content-oriented in that the mentor assumes the role of power by transmitting the knowledge to the protégé. On the other hand, in the SAAB model, although there is some degree of hierarchy between the mentor and protégé, it occurs primarily during the initial relationship; the remainder of the program emphasizes the protégé developmental growth in conjunction with the mentor, in which nurturing and sharing of goals and progress of both parties are mutually defined and developed. With awareness of the diverse academic and social needs of African American males, it is salient that the program mentors exercise care in designing an experience that specifically addresses the unique and personal developmental needs of the individuals involved, rather than creating one that conforms to the overall goals of the mentoring program. As a result, the mentoring experience is likely to developmentally benefit both the protégé and the mentor.

CAMPUS ENVIRONMENTAL FACTORS THAT INFLUENCE MENTORING

A commentary on African American male mentoring programs would be incomplete without analyzing how the developmental growth of the protégé is impacted by the campus climate or environment. Although Gerber (as cited in Kuh, Schuh, & Whitt, 1991) generally defines campus environment as physical properties such as size and location of facilities and the use of open space, Green (1989) more succinctly addresses the concept from the aspect of influential factors such as culture, habits, decisions, practices, and policies. This latter definition encompasses several of the significant factors that distinguish mentoring programs at historically Black colleges and universities (HBCUs) from those at predominantly White institutions (PWIs).

Historically, HBCUs are known for their remarkable ability to transform students with marginal academic performance into scholars. This success is attributed in large part to the institution's nurturing and empowering environment, which enables students to overcome their previous post-secondary academic experiences. Despite the high academic standards found at these institutions (Cole, as cited in O'Brien, 1989), students who were perceived as academically marginal find themselves succeeding as a result of the intrusive yet nonthreatening environment provided by faculty and staff. Not surprisingly, such a supportive environment, serving in loco parentis, fosters opportunities for formal and informal mentoring relationships between professional staff members and students to succeed. For example, it is highly likely that mentoring experiences between faculty and students may foster collaborative research opportunities, and mentoring relationships with campus administrators provide encouragement and support for protégés who may wish to pursue career paths similar to those of their mentor. If minority students, particularly African American men, are to have similar mentoring opportunities and experiences at PWIs as meaningful as those of their counterparts at HBCUs, it is essential that faculty and administrators at PWIs also exhibit strong personal sentiments of interest and caring toward these students. Despite the efforts made by the majority of faculty and staff at PWIs to create a welcoming and safe learning environment as well as positive mentoring experiences for minority students, the research provides several reasons why mentoring relationships within these environments are often intermittent at best (Sutton & Kimbrough, 2001).

One major impediment that continues to obstruct positive mentoring experiences between white faculty and minority students is the negative perception white faculty members have regarding African-American students' academic performance in the classroom (Ponterotto, 1990). As cited in O'Brien (1989), Cole indicates that some white faculty members subtly implied that the presence of African American students in the classroom is a direct result of affirmative action and further suggesting that these students are not expected to achieve at the same level as their white counterparts. These disturbing indications also have direct implications for African American men as reflected in Allen's (1987) findings that some white faculty members subconsciously assume that African American male students are academically inferior, underachieving, and poorly motivated. Moreover, such sentiments are indicative of systemic dominant group values that embrace the tenets of competition and individual achievement. As a result, faculty and staff who serve as mentors for minority students in this environment continue to perpetuate the conventional one-dimension model of mentoring: sharing their expertise with the academically and socially disenfranchised. If PWIs are to enjoy the same mentoring success stories as their HBCU counterparts, it is essential that campus stakeholders and student affairs practitioners begin to inform their faculty and staff colleagues that mentoring is more than providing academic and social remediation for a particular student subculture. It should be an experience designed to empower protégés rather than foster dependency. A successful developmental program will match undergraduate African American male students with a suitable mentor—professional or nonprofessional, Black or White, male or female—who not only provides guidance but also assists the students in setting their own priorities and developing other relationships that are likely to contribute positively to their success (Abercrombie, as cited in Morgan, 1996). White institutions should assume a proactive posture in changing the campus conditions by educating faculty and motivating them to adopt this approach to their mentoring activities. Certainly, although such a mentoring program can fill the academic and social void for African American males at PWIs, the presence of more African American male faculty and staff at PWI campuses will significantly enrich the campus climate even more, as well as provide additional potential mentors for African American male students.

Summary and Recommendations

Mentoring is a viable practice that enables as well as empowers its participants. Numerous mentoring programs exist in the business and educational arenas, but those that are targeted to enrich the welfare of minority youth in urban areas appear to have significant results. Although these programs produce positive outcomes among their participants, the one-dimensional, instructional format that characterizes the majority of mentoring programs may be inadequate for providing a holistic learning experience for both the protégé and the mentor. In comparison, those mentoring programs whose goals and programs are developmentally grounded will likely observe a permanent rather than an intermittent transformation of the protégé's behavior. Many student development practitioners have the professional expertise to ensure that mentoring programs in general—and particularly those identified for African American men—reflect this emphasis. This is not surprising, as these professionals are familiar with a variety of theoretical developmental paradigms that can assist them in constructing educational and social programs that foster identity development among students.

Generally speaking, mentoring from a developmental perspective considers the protégé's individual stage of developmental learning as the protégé traverses through the various academic and social episodes of the mentoring experience. As a result of the collaborative goals and objectives established by the mentor and the protégé at the beginning of the experience, the mentor becomes acutely aware of the appropriate role to assume, depending on the protégé's circumstances. Consequently, the protégé not only is able to obtain valuable skills but, more important, also can learn essential problem-solving skills and self-confidence to effectively resolve subsequent challenges as a result of the less intrusive involvement of the mentor. Such interactions are likely to become more enriching to both parties as greater dialogue is increased and the relationship becomes more parallel rather than hierarchical. A parallel relationship is particularly important to cultivate in mentoring across ethnic and gender lines, as these protégés are unfortunately more likely to become dependent upon the guidance and the advice of the mentor. Such an outcome, typical of the instructional approach, should be avoided by using the developmental approach.

Even more striking is how different campus environments have been found to validate mentoring from a developmental perspective. As previously stated, the nurturing and warm campus environment characteristic of many HBCUs certainly implies that African American men at HBCUs are more likely to have a positive experience of being mentored than their counterparts attending PWIs. The preponderance of the research attributes this to the fact that the professional staff at HBCUs perceive student growth along a continuum and assume various roles as surrogate parents, educators, counselors, and friends to these students during and after their collegiate experience. For African American men to have similar mentoring experiences on PWIs, it is suggested that these institutions continue not only to increase the recruitment and retention of African American faculty and staff but also to establish means to sensitize White mentors to the cultural and social characteristics of African American men. In addition, student affairs practitioners should be more demonstrative in their commitment to shepherding African American male leaders of ethnic organizations to assume leadership roles within campuswide organizations.

The following are specific recommendations to complement this model of mentoring for African American men.

1. COMPREHENSIVE TRAINING FOR SELECTED MENTORS

A comprehensive orientation session introduces selected mentors to mentoring from a developmental aspect and educates them to emphasize this. Such an orientation could be facilitated by African American male student affairs practitioners who are familiar with the diverse theoretical paradigms that address how students make meaning of various challenges and experiences. To broaden selected mentors' understanding of the significance of mentoring from a developmental paradigm, it is suggested that facilitators encourage them to reflect how specific challenging professional and personal experiences enhanced their own learning developmentally.

2. FINANCIAL SUPPORT OF AFRICAN AMERICAN MALE MENTORING PROGRAMS

Although many predominantly white and historically Black institutions may be interested in sponsoring a mentor program for African American males, it is unlikely that such programs will ever materialize, because of shrinking institutional budgets. However, it is possible that many community organizations, such as the Urban League or the local YMCA, as well as specific organizations, such as 100 Black Men or the graduate chapters of African American fraternities, may be viable alternative resources. These organizations, functioning either independently or collaboratively with university administrators and staff, may serve as viable sponsors for such mentoring programs for African American men.

3. Utilize Multiple Mentoring Experiences

As stated throughout this chapter, a major benefit associated with developmental mentoring is the creation of greater opportunities for fluid exchange between the protégé and the mentor. In addition, the developmental approach to mentoring is characterized by various or multiple mentoring experiences. This concept, according to Pope (2002), suggests that the protégé should be provided opportunities to learn and interact from several mentors instead of one. Consequently, institutions not only should consider designing mentoring programs that will validate Pope's assumption, but also should create activities within the mentoring experience that will allow learning from other protégés throughout the learning experience, as reflected in the SAAB Mentoring Program.

4. Develop Intercampus Mentoring Symposia

It is likely that African American men enrolled at rural PWIs who seek mentoring may encounter greater challenges, for various reasons—primarily the paucity of African American faculty and staff professionals as well as professionals of color in the community at large. However, student affairs practitioners can offset such deficiencies by sponsoring mentoring symposia or by collaborating with sister institutions experiencing similar challenges in the state or region. The format of such a program could be conducted on a weekend once a semester to bring together the young male protégés and their selected mentors and promote camaraderie and community among them. Despite its unconventional and abbreviated weekend format, if the program is carefully designed it is quite possible that both the mentor and the protégé can achieve similar outcomes developmentally as their counterparts who interact with their mentors more frequently. One strategy to achieve this goal is for the protégé to use electronic mail to interact individually with the mentor to discuss his progress in relation to the stated learning objectives. In addition, the protégés from the various isolated campuses can use distance education technology to peer mentor one another as they discuss their challenges and successes throughout the mentoring experience. Such cyberspace interactions can be viable and useful alternatives when conventional mentoring opportunities are nonexistent.

5. ENCOURAGE DEVELOPMENTAL MENTORING EXPERIENCES WITHIN CAMPUSWIDE ACTIVITIES

This chapter has focused on developmental mentoring from the perspective of self-awareness and the enrichment of African American men. The concept also has significant implications for preparing these men to assume leadership roles in campuswide organizations. In contrast to their leadership roles in ethnic campus and fraternal organizations, leadership provided by African American men in campuswide organizations is marginal at best. Although negligible participation by the majority of African American men can be attributed to incompatible organizational goals or lack of interest, there are some men who likely will become involved and have much to contribute as future leaders. Consequently, student affairs practitioners should identify and solicit the involvement of these men and encourage them to develop their latent leadership potential in committee leadership roles by mentoring them developmentally. Such opportunities are an excellent learning laboratory for the mentor to assume diverse developmental roles as coach, advisor, or friend to these men, depending on the various operational and programmatic situations they encounter. Furthermore, such experiences not only clarify and strengthen the leadership skills of these men but, more important, also increase their self-esteem, confidence, and capabilities to pursue additional leadership opportunities campuswide.

6. INSTITUTIONAL AFFIRMATION AND CELEBRATION OF AFRICAN AMERICAN MALE CONTRIBUTIONS

Campus administrators and student affairs professionals should not only affirm the mentoring efforts of African American men philosophically but also validate their efforts campuswide with tangible rewards at public events such as the annual campus Awards Day program. Although most informal mentoring activities may occur outside of the campus, many African American men use their talents not only to mentor academically but also to coach and encourage active involvement within student committees among their peers. The criteria used for affirming such mentoring efforts by these men within the campus and larger community should be inclusive, to reflect the values of minority students as well as the African American community at large. Such institutional recognition reinforces for these men that the institution values inclusion, fairness, and sharing of power.

Conclusion

This chapter addresses how mentoring from the developmental perspective can be an enriched learning experience for African American men. It is not intended to criticize the format or efforts of most conventional models, rather to inform the practitioner that conventional models of mentoring can be enhanced by allowing the protégé to become proactive in identifying and developing educational goals or experiences without totally relying on the mentor's guidance and advice. Although this concept has produced excellent results—as evidenced in the AMIGOS and SAAB formal mentoring programs—it can be used also to enrich informal mentoring experiences, such as volunteering in professional organizations and networking. The definition of the term *networking* is broad, but Reesor (1998) simply defines the concept as an informal way to meet new colleagues that is usually characterized as collaborative and collegial. Batchelor (1993) suggests that prior to the initiation of any mentoring relationship developing from a networking experience, potential protégés should first identify the goals and skills they wish to learn and then select the appropriate mentor to explicitly refine them. When the developmental approach is thoroughly integrated into the majority of mentoring programs, it is likely that both mentor and protégé alike will perceive the experience not as give and take but rather as collaborative, benefiting and enriching the learning experience of both.

References

Allen, T. D., Russell, J.E.A., & Maetzke, S. B. (December, 1997). Formal peer mentoring: Factors related to protégés' satisfaction and willingness to mentor others. *Group and Organization Management, 22*(4), 488–507.

Allen, W. E. (1987, May/June). Black colleges vs. White colleges: The fork in the road for Black students. *Change, 19*(3), 28–31.

Batchelor, S. W. (1993). Mentoring and self directed learning. In M. J. Barr and Associates, *The handbook of student affairs administration* (378–389). San Francisco: Jossey-Bass.

Bowman, R. L., Bowman, V. E., & Delucia, J. L. (1990, September). Mentoring in a graduate counseling program: Students helping students. *Counselor Education and Supervision, 30*, 58–65.

Chickering, A. W. (1969). *Education and identity.* San Francisco: Jossey-Bass.

Cross, Jr., W. E. (1991). *Shades of Black: Diversity in African American identity.* Philadelphia: Temple University Press.

Fong, B. (2000, Fall). Toto, I think we're still in Kansas: Supporting and mentoring faculty and administrators. *Liberal Education, 86*(4), 56–60.

Grant, E. J., & Ensher, E. (2000, November-December). Effects of peer mentoring on types of mentor support, program satisfaction and graduate school success: A dyadic perspective. *Journal of College Student Development, 41*(6), 637–642.

Green, M. F. (Ed.). (1989). *Minorities on campus: A handbook for enhancing diversity.* Washington, DC: American Council on Education.

Hall, D. T. (Ed.). (1996). *The career is dead, long live the career: A relational approach to careers.* San Francisco: Jossey-Bass.

Helms, J. E. (1993).Toward a model of white racial identity development. In J. E. Helms (Ed.), *Black and white racial identity: Theory, research and practice* (pp. 49–66). Westport, CT: Prager.

Hill, P. (1998, Fall). Afro-centric rites of passage: Nurturing the next generation. *Reaching Today's Youth, 3*(1), 9–13.

Ianni, F.A.J. (1990). Social, cultural, and behavioral contexts of mentoring. New York, NY: Institute for Urban and Minority Education. ERIC Document Reproduction Service No. ED354294.

Jackson, J.F.L., & Matthews, J. G. (1999). *An evaluation of the target success mentor group program.* ERIC Document Reproduction Services No. ED434881.

Johnsrud, L. K. (1991). Mentoring between academic women: The capacity for interdependence. *Initiatives, 4*(3), 7–17.

Kanter, R. M. (1977). *Men and women of the corporation.* New York: Basic Books.

Kessler, R. (1999, December). The call to initiation. *Educational Leadership, 57*(4), 30–33.

Kuh, G. D., Schuh, J. H., & Whitt, E. J. (1991). *Involving colleges.* San Francisco: Jossey-Bass.

Kunjufu, J. (1986). *Countering the conspiracy to destroy Black boys.* Chicago, IL: African American Images.

Lee, C. C. (1991, December). *Empowering young Black males.* ERIC Document Reproduction Services No. ED341887.

Moore, K. M., & Salimbene, A. M. (1981). The dynamics of the mentor-protégé relationship in developing women as academic leaders. *Journal for Educational Equity and Leadership, 2*(1), 1–64.

Morgan, J. (1996, October 12). Reaching out to young Black men. *Black Issues in Higher Education, 13*(16), 16–19.

O'Brien, E. M. (1989, October 12). HBCUs promise and deliver success to their students, officials say. *Black Issues in Higher Education, 5*(1), 3–5.

Patton, L. D., & Harper, S. R. (2003, Winter). Mentoring relationships among African American women in graduate and professional school. In M. H. Hamilton (Ed.), *Meeting the needs of African American women* (pp. 67–79). San Francisco: Jossey-Bass.

Ponterotto, J. G. (1990, Winter). Racial/ethnic minority and women students in higher education: A status report. In J. G. Ponterotto, D. E. Lewis, & R. Bullington (Eds.), Affirmative action on campus. *New Directions in Student Services,* no. 52 (pp. 45–59). San Francisco: Jossey-Bass.

Pope, M. L. (2002). Community college mentoring: Minority student perception. *Community College Review, 30*(3), 31–45.

Reesor, L. M. (1998). Making professional connections. In M. J. Amey & L. M. Reesor (Eds.), *Beginning your journey: A guide for new professionals in student affairs* (pp. 53–66). NASPA Monograph 21.

Selke, M. J., & Wong, T. D. (1993, April). *The mentoring empowered model: Facilitating communication in graduate advisement.* ERIC Document Reproduction Services No. ED380889.

Shandley, T. C. (1989). The use of mentors for leadership development. *NASPA Journal, 27*(1), 59–66.

Staples, R. (1982). *Black masculinity.* San Francisco: Black Scholar Press.

Stromei, L. K. (2000). Increasing retention and success through mentoring. In S. R. Aragon (Ed.), *Beyond access: Methods and models for increasing retention and learning among minority students* (pp. 55–62). San Francisco: Jossey-Bass.

Sutton, E. M., & Kimbrough, W. M. (2001, Fall). *Trends in Black student involvement. NASPA Journal, 39*(1), 30–40.

Tallerico, M. (2000, November). Why don't they apply? Encouraging women and minorities to seek administrative positions. *American School Board Journal, 187*(11), 56–58.

Terrell, M. C., Hassell, R. K., & Duggar, M. (1992, Spring). Mentoring programs: A blueprint for personal growth and academic development. *NASPA Journal, 29*(3) 199–205.

CHAPTER SIX

THE ROLE OF SPIRITUALITY AND RELIGION IN THE EXPERIENCES OF AFRICAN AMERICAN MALE COLLEGE STUDENTS

Lemuel W. Watson, Northern Illinois University

When it comes to African American college men, we know very little about the spiritual aspect of their lives and how it affects their college experiences. Spirituality is a complex subject to deconstruct in regard to how African Americans might choose to view the term. For the purpose of this chapter, we must first provide working definitions for the terms spirituality and religion for African Americans. By examining these interrelated concepts, we may discover that for a significant number of African Americans, the two are tightly intertwined.

These two distinct words—*religion* and *spirituality*—are often used to mean the same thing (similarly, many professionals in higher education assume that *diversity* and *multicultural* initiatives are the same thing). Therefore, I will try to clarify exactly what is meant by the term *spirituality* in this chapter. The *American Heritage College Dictionary,* 3rd edition (2000), defines spirituality as "The state, quality, manner, or fact of being spiritual [of relating to, consisting of, or having the nature of spirit; not tangible or material]"

(p. 1313). However, going to the root word *spirit* as a more appropriate word for this chapter, we find it defined as "The vital principle of animating force within living beings; incorporeal consciousness; The Holy Spirit; A supernatural being as an angel or demon; The part of a human being associated with the mind, will, and feelings; with us in spirit" (page 1313).

The same source defines *religion* as "Belief in and reverence for a supernatural power or powers regarded as creator and governor of the universe; A system grounded in such belief and worship; The life or condition of a person in a religious order; A set of beliefs, values, practices based on the teachings of a spiritual leader; A cause, a principle, or an activity pursued with zeal or conscientious devotion" (p. 1153). Parks (2000) also described spirit as the animating essence at the core of life, because all humans are in a search for wholeness, purpose, and the apprehension of spirit. Succinctly stated, for the purpose of this chapter, spirituality is a belief in some external, animating force, whereas religion is the adherence to an established system of beliefs and practices grounded in spirituality.

Constantine, Wilton, Gainor, and Lewis (2002) purport that some literature bases use spirituality and religion as a single theoretical construct. Therefore, in this chapter spirituality and religion will have a similar construct for the population being addressed. And although the religious faith of many African Americans is one of the branches of Christianity, the references to religion herein embrace all faiths and beliefs in spirituality.

College agents must therefore understand how African American students' actions and their perceptions of their responsibilities are guided by spiritual and religious influences. Considering the strong historical context of spirituality in the general African American culture, it must not be conceptualized in a vacuum. For many African Americans, whether Christian or not, religion is often viewed as subsuming spirituality, and it reflects the manifestations of formal theological beliefs and activities as well as cultural rituals and, historically, the adoption of Western philosophy into African-centered practices for many who share a group identity. Thus the central focus of this chapter is to identify first, where spirituality fits within the lives of African American males in college, and second, how spirituality contributes to their identity and survival techniques in the college experience.

Spirituality and the notion of freedom are tightly intertwined for African Americans. This expression of freedom is evident through their efforts to create practices that preserve the inner spiritual self and to cultivate imagination and creativity as idioms of survival—an important dimension of African ideas of freedom. "Freedom, then, is not predicated on external conditions or milieu alone, but on the capacity of individuals to create and to respond to life on sovereign terms according to the spirit of God, the creator. It is this premise that is the key to Black wholeness, vitality, and well-being and may be the key to human freedom in general" (Stewart, 1999, p. 11).

In other words, the ability to be engaged in spiritual and religious worship as a manifestation of their relationship to God is the first freedom of African people. Awareness of this freedom and the consequent personal relationship individuals develop with God on a daily basis are powerful concepts. They are transformed to mean that, however oppressive external social political conditions are, the African spirit is never completely constrained because one is always free, regardless of place, time, or circumstance, to be in relationship with the Almighty God, who encompasses freedom, prosperity, and power. This freedom is the penultimate locus of African consciousness, destiny, and identity.

SEVERAL PERSPECTIVES ON SPIRITUALITY

Stewart (1999) gives us two perspectives to consider from the spiritual kaleidoscope: creative soul force and resistant soul force. Creative soul force is an element of spirituality that creates cultural nuances that assist African Americans in adapting, transforming, and transcending reality through the creative construction of Black culture. Resistant soul force, on the other hand, enables one to deal with barriers and constraints that enforce complete domestication of one's values, processes, behaviors, and beliefs for purposes of subjugation, domination, and annihilation. Resistant soul force allows individuals to overcome human oppression through creating, transforming, and transcending, so one's spirit can survive and thrive. Let us examine how these concepts and corresponding spiritual frameworks reveal themselves in the lives of African American college students' daily activities.

On college campuses, African Americans and other minority students use their creative soul forces to interject their unique culture into every part of the collegiate experience. This is similar to "cool pose," the ritualized form of masculinity described by Majors and Billson (1992) that allows African American male adolescents to cope and survive in an environment of social oppression and racism. They project a front of emotionlessness, fearlessness, and aloofness that counters their inner pain from damaged pride, poor self-confidence, and fragile social competence that stem from being a member of a subjugated group. When African American college men find that they cannot interject their unique cultural values or that the mainstream culture does not want to accept or acknowledge them, they begin to use resistant soul force to create separate organizations to affirm their identity, spirit, and values. For example, Black fraternities and Black student organizations at White institutions exist because there is a need for African American students to express their unique experiences and issues in a platform that will be taken seriously. Hence, resistant soul force exists because of the need for survival and commitment to one's self and one's people.

Another perspective on spirituality, identity, and the college experience can be obtained from Erikson's (1964) research, which identified religion (spirituality) as an important domain of identity in the process of self-discovery. Perhaps, for African American males, spirituality may be more important to their development and life aspirations than some might believe. Like Stewart, Erikson defined spirituality and religion as a belief system that provides the internal person with a framework for moral reasoning, values, and sense of purpose. Therefore, African American spirituality is a socially functional process or praxis that creates an ethos and culture whereby Black people encounter, interpret, adopt, adapt, integrate, transform, and transcend human experience through the creative appropriation of divine spirit for self-empowerment and survival. The daily practice of African American spirituality is the catalyst to consciousness, identity formation, and destiny both individually and collectively and is manifested in various forms of Black culture, creating a unique ontology. Therefore "this spirit permeates black life and instills in African-American people a will to survive; a desire to confront and surmount all threats to their being and existence while creating idioms of life and culture which provide them with adaptive mechanisms that reinforce their sanity, affirm their wholeness, and establish their spiritual and ontological location in American society" (Stewart 1999, p. 3).

Scholars have suggested that for many students, the college years can be a period of decline for religiosity (Astin, 1993; Bowen, 1997; Dalton, 2001). Student experiences indicate they tend to be less favorable toward worship services, less convinced of the reality of God, less favorable toward the observance of the Sabbath, less fundamental, and less conservative. Roof and Hadaway (1988) confirm that college attendance is a leading predictor of religious decline, and their findings are typical of other noted scholars in the field. However, the young men in the study described in the next section of this chapter gave responses that are in stark contrast to what is portrayed in the literature. The overall theme from the research is that most of the young men have a very personal form of spirituality, which is connected to God through either creative soul force or resistant soul force, in line with Stewart's perspective. The majority of the young men in this study affirm some higher power in their lives regarding their individual purpose in life. In addition, they are all generally involved in worship of some kind and have woven spirituality throughout their daily lives.

A RESEARCH STUDY

The phenomenon of spirituality and religion in the lives of college students often permits them to share their unique and very personal perspectives with others in that collegiate community. The students in this study took the time to share their innermost beliefs about their personal survival techniques and coping mechanisms as young African American men, so the significance of their statements as a group is well worth our investment of time and effort to try to understand them. Hence, the significance of the study is that they are able to share with us their voices about the role of spirituality and religion in their college experience.

The study was conducted at three private, historically Black colleges in the southeastern United States, all within two hundred miles of each other. One is located in a large city, the remaining two in small towns. As all the colleges are located in the Bible Belt and each is affiliated with a religious denomination, the influence of religion and spirituality is part of the culture at all three institutions.

METHODOLOGY

The population for this study was ninety-seven first- and second-year African American college males enrolled in the spring semester of 2002 at the three colleges. Students from a teacher mentoring program were used for the study because the author was a research associate with the mentoring program and worked with the director on assessing the outcomes of the students' experiences. Students were asked to complete the instrument with a series of other information given during a spring workshop on each campus. Students were given the option at the end of the workshop to participate or not. Participation was strictly on a volunteer basis. From the ninety-seven surveys distributed in the workshop, forty-six of the students completed some parts of the instrument in the study.

A simple twenty-three-item instrument, comprising twenty questions with a Likert scale and three essay questions, was used to gather information about the students' educational experiences in general and their spiritual and religious beliefs and practices as they related to survival and success. For questions relating to practice and beliefs, students could select one of four possible answers: 1 = Never, 2 = Occasionally, 3 = Often, 4 = Very Often. The open-ended essay questions asked students to discuss their perceptions of and rationale for their success prior to college attendance and in their current academic enrollment. To exemplify their attitudes, this study extracted some of the written responses from the survival questions; examples are presented in the following sections.

FINDINGS

The findings reveal that spirituality through religious activities is important to the young men and their purpose in life. The African American college men in this study are committed to holding onto the value of spirituality and religion as they struggle through their college experiences and strive to obtain their goals. The life force of the spirit is undeniably present in their identity as college students and African American men. Table 6.1 presents the students' answers related to spiritual and religious activities. Various questions had different numbers of respondents, as some questions were not answered by all participants. The number of respondents to the questions ranged from thirty-seven to forty-six. The statement "I feel proud to be an African American male" had the highest mean score (M = 3.81) and appears to be directly related to identity, cultural heritage, and masculinity in the scope of American life. Although most of the students responded that they "very often" were proud to be African American (M = 3.81), one may wonder why every respondent did not give the highest response, such that the mean would be 4.00. The response to this question may be explained in two ways. First, it is normal for students to begin to question all aspects of their life. Students are compelled to think about their purpose and what road they will travel based on their race and background. Second, the students in this study are attending institutions where they are a part of the dominant race on campus. Depending on the student's social and cultural background and level of racial identity development, this environment could be either empowering or more challenging with regard to race and personal identity.

The next highest mean was M = 3.54, for the statement "I take time to meditate, pray, or sit and reflect on life experiences." This was followed by "Attend a workshop service at a church, mosque, or temple," with a mean of M = 3.16, which is in total contrast to the actual level of religious activities among college age students found by some studies. Most of the students also reported that they often "Participate in religious activities off campus," with a mean of M = 3.08. The lowest mean, M = 2.68, represents that students "occasionally" or "often" attend religious activities on campus.

The students' answers to the open-ended question, "When times are difficult whom do you turn to for support in order to survive?" were sorted into three categories. After briefly introducing these categories, we provide more detailed discussions of each and a sampling of representative responses.

The first category, Individual Identity and External Power Reference, seems to support the belief that students depend on themselves or other people in their lives to find their strength. This category of responses does not necessarily mean that the participants

TABLE 6.1. AFRICAN AMERICAN MALE RESPONSES TO SPIRITUAL
AND RELIGIOUS ACTIVITIES.

Responses to Questions	Valid N	Mean	SD
Attend a workshop service at a church, mosque, or temple	37	3.16	1.014
Talk with a minister, friend, or other persons about spiritual issues	37	2.97	.866
Participate in religious activities on campus	37	2.68	1.056
Participate in religious activities off campus	37	3.08	.954
Take time to meditate, pray, or sit and reflect on life experiences	37	3.54	.836
Feel proud to be an African American male	37	3.81	.569
Believe African American men in the classroom will make a difference in our society and educational system	37	3.03	.440
Had serious discussions with students whose religious beliefs were very different from mine	46	2.91	1.007
Care about social issues such as peace, justice, human rights, equality, race relations	44	3.05	.914

Note: Ranges of score for questions are 1=Never; 2=Occasionally; 3=Often; 4=Very Often

do not believe in a higher being, only that they did not articulate such a belief. The second category, A Higher Being, represents those students who gave affirmation of how spirituality and a higher being fit into their lives for their survival. The third category, representing another form of spirituality—which supports Stewart's (1999) concept of African spirituality—we call Resistant Soul Force and Power. It is manifested in the commitment to overcome and survive due to constraints and challenges. Responses in this category shed light on students' undying spirit to conquer and beat all odds.

External Power Reference

Most of the students recognized some important person in their lives as a component of their survival. The examples of participant responses that follow speak to some of the personal resources they had used for surviving their precollege years, getting to college, and surviving while there.

"The setting of a place can be a distraction. Before I came to college, I had a made up mind that I was going to get my lesson no matter what people say about me. I was once told to get what I came to get out of college; that is an education. The choice is mine to receive a good education or just sit back and do nothing toward earning a degree."

"My beliefs and reasons for my survival and success through my high school and college experience are because I had the right leadership. When I say leadership I mean people to look up to and want to be like. My grandmother is one leader, I saw in her the ability to go on and do more. My grandfather also helped to know that I can do more with my life."

"My reasons for survival and success through high school and college are to have friends who want the same as you and try to be the top of your class by making good grades and studying hard every night."

"I believed in myself and others believed in me also. I also set a goal for my self to be better than my siblings. For example, my parents both received their college degree and my sister is working on her doctorate, so I have to meet her standards or go beyond her."

"The reason why I have succeeded was by having positive role models in my life. Also, having people that served as mentors for me."

"My parents are very supportive of me and that means much to me. I believe that if a person wants to be successful and overcome, he can."

One important conclusion we may infer from these students' comments is that they have positive self-images due to family role models and expectations. Most refer to people from their immediate family who have influenced them and who have helped them in developing a positive self construct of their purpose in life and personal identity. The African American male who, with the help of significant others, develops a healthy and positive self-concept may find himself on a different and often lonely road. This may mean ignoring peer pressures to shrink from personal academic success; it may mean overcoming unsupportive teachers and administrators who have prescribed certain negative behavior characteristics to them due to their skin color and or race.

A Higher Being

The students' responses in this category, a few of which follow, seem to reveal that regardless of what comes their way, they can handle it through the grace of a higher being:

"I thank God for the program because it has helped me to prepare for the work force and preparation to pass the Praxis test."

"There are many reasons why my success is important. Certainly, this process of achieving a degree in Education is simply because I have learned that I am here not by accident nor by chance, but there is a Divine Calling that has been placed upon my life."

"My strong conviction in the Lord has helped me endure racism, discrimination and downfalls."

"Upon reflection, I attribute my survival and success to what I believe to be God's purpose for my life."

"The reason for my survival and success through high school and college is having Christ apart from other support."

"The only belief that I have is what I was taught. I was taught by my mother to always put God first. I have, and it has helped me achieve many goals in life. My suggestion is to tell any young brother to follow those words closely and keep the faith."

"First and foremost, I was kept throughout my high school because I chose to serve the Lord."

If those of us in the collegiate environment fail to recognize spirituality—demonstrated by a belief in a higher being—as an important element in the educational process, we are ignoring a very important factor and characteristic that affects African American males' educational outcomes at all levels. A central theme in Fowler's (1981) research in faith development is that the individual is able to reflect on his or her own existence and process of development and begin to self-define and self-construct roles and relationships with ideas and people. Holistic development in the African American man is facilitated by the ability to go into a place of consciousness where he can find strength to deal with the stresses of life. As the study revealed, the answers for this survival very often rest with these students' belief, trust, and faith in God, as demonstrated in the students' comments.

Stewart's (1999) notion of creative soul force also seems to mesh with the responses of these students who are deeply rooted in spirituality. For example, their statements reference and acknowledge God as the source of their strength and well-being. These students believe that regardless of what comes their way they can handle it through their faith in and connection to God. Many times, because of family situations, there is no one else to whom these males can turn for help in coping with their particular struggles in higher education, which may be exacerbated by racism and the negative stereotyping of African American males. Thus, this notion of spirituality and affirmation of faith can be very culturally specific to the development of African American college men.

Resistant Soul Force

Some of the statements made by men in this study (examples of which follow) revealed the challenge of being an African American and male. They exemplify Stewart's concept of resistant soul force: that which enables one to handle those barriers and constraints that enforce complete domestication of one's values, processes, behaviors, and beliefs; that enables one to overcome human oppression through creating, transforming, and transcending, so one's spirit can survive and thrive. "Resistant soul force, on the other hand, enables one to deal with barriers and constraints that enforce complete domestication of one's values, processes, behaviors, and beliefs for purposes of subjugation, domination, and annihilation. Resistant soul force allows individuals to overcome human oppression through creating, transforming, and transcending, so one's spirit can survive and thrive."

"To be black means survival. We have come so far and still we must go farther. My reason for survival is that I never give up. No matter how hard life gets, I know how to hang in there."

"I feel that people are always harder on African American men because they have us stereotyped to be a certain way. Yes, there are a lot of black men in jail but every black man is not the same. Through high school and even now, I don't give anyone the chance to stereotype me because I always try to stay on top of things. If you do what's right and do the best you can in all you do, then you don't have to worry about people saying things they shouldn't about you. They won't have a choice but to say something positive."

"With all the negativity that I face as an African American male, this has been my motivation for a long time. The stereotype that we are only good in sports has been my motivation. At the same time, I have dreams to make us equal."

"I believe that African American men seem to be plagued with a host of negative claims about their survival in academic settings because some of the males didn't have a positive role model in the home. Some African American men also don't perform well because they don't set goals for themselves, and if you don't stand for something, you will fall for anything."

"Survival is not something that I wish to do, SURVIVAL, is something that I MUST do."

"The African American man has been robbed of many things. The world only wants us to kill each other with various types of weapons. The average black male educated or not can read, write, and count. See he is a very skillful man but, the white or better yet society will not give him or us a chance."

"In responding to the African American men, the problem is not whether Black Men wish to become successful but this claim however denotes that African American men are able to perform. However, society has placed into the minds of our Black Brothers, that they are not capable of performing up [to] standard."

These statements demonstrate that identity formation and changes in perceptions of the surrounding environment are inextricably linked. Mead (1962) explained the self and its development as arising from social experiences. Like Stewart, Cushman (1995) explained that interpretations of the world require a "cultural matrix," which enables individuals to conceive of their world and their place in it, as well as the rules, relations, and responsibilities that govern their choices and behaviors. Alford, McKenry, and Gavazzi (2001) state that "Black male youth in many western societies live in an atmosphere where racism is pervasive. Countless Black males are socially stifled by their experiences of racism" (p. 142). African American males are certainly aware of how people respond to them in multiple environments. Coping with racism is not an easy task for most young African American men. African American men are subjected to a certain amount of environmental stress from racism with regard to organizational practices, faculty attitudes, and other activities in their collegiate experiences. Along with belief in a higher being, an awareness of their "Blackness" completes the sense of spirituality these African American male students use to sustain themselves in the college environment.

CONCLUSION

Given the culture of most institutions of higher education, spirituality and religious notions are not affirmed in today's secular environments. Except at institutions affiliated with religious denominations, they are often shunned or looked down upon. In addition, students are sometimes stigmatized for showing this important attribute of their lives. Yet, as this study reveals, the ability to affirm his spirituality is an essential part of the African American man's identity development.

The results of this study represent how the social construct of spirituality affects one's ability to focus on collegiate experiences. Erikson's (1965) views of identity explained the impact of the social context on the inner self. One of his stages for identity development is identity versus identity diffusion. Erikson viewed individuals' development as a process in which they must confront and overcome a series of challenges in the environment. Observing the issues, policies, and practices of multiculturalism and diversity leads to the conclusion that religion and spirituality have not been readily addressed from a culturally specific perspective for individuals.

Nevertheless, if we are to expend efforts on racial, ethnic, sexual orientation, and disability concerns, it seems to me that we should also welcome to the table other important cultural characteristics that would enhance the educational outcomes of those who could benefit from the consideration.

Ignoring the spiritual component of the individual is not a beneficial practice for the development of African American college students. As educators, we need to think about how we can interweave assistance in their developmental maturation into students' lives and be flexible in providing for the social, psychological, physical, and spiritual needs of all of our students, particularly African American men. As we begin to develop and assess existing programs, we need to think about how we can, both in and out of class environments, maximize our students' development. If we are to improve the conditions of African American male students, we must understand what is salient to their learning conditions and development during late adolescence and early adulthood. Failure to provide a nurturing environment that facilitates opportunities to bring spirituality openly into every component of their lives does a disservice to the authenticity of the cultural identity of African American males.

It is very important that practitioners who are committed to holistic student development notions understand how spirituality affects the college experiences of African American men and other students. Perhaps educators do not know how to incorporate spirituality into the educational environment. Love and Talbot (1999) suggested that college and university professionals needed to

- Reflect on their own spirituality
- Be open to the various notions of spirituality that students bring to campus
- Acknowledge that some students are deeply emotionally invested in the spiritual element of their lives
- Admit the need for training to equip them to deal with the spiritual development of the student

Dalton (2001) states that students who maintain their spiritual development throughout college incorporate their deepest values and beliefs with career and life plans. They are also better able to make the transition from college to work and a life of satisfaction and success. Covey (1995) also states that individuals who live according to their spiritual convictions are able to be successful in their professional and social lives because of their integrity and respect for others in society. Therefore, professionals may wish to encourage students to find a quiet place to meditate and to pray. The campus community should be flexible enough to embrace the inclusion of spirituality within its diversity and multiculturalism discussions. Although overt support of religious activities may be somewhat restricted at public institutions of higher education because of the constitutional mandate for separation between church and state, at private institutions, which generally operate under less restrictive guidelines, professionals need to make sure that discussions around spirituality and religion are given the attention they need to allow students to develop in all categories of their lives. Ignoring this most salient aspect of the student's life is not the answer. Student affairs professionals, in considering their support for African American men, also need to recognize that spirituality is tightly intertwined within the historical cultural nuances of the African American life experience. College and university professionals need to understand that the spiritual component of the African American male's life often helps him define his life purpose as well as provide for his survival. To ignore this aspect is likely to do harm.

References

Alford, K. A., McKenry, P. C., & Gavazzi, S. M. (2001). Enhancing achievement in Black adolescent males: The rites of passage link. In R. Majors (Ed.), *Educating our Black children,* (pp. 141–156). London: Routledge/Falmer.

American Heritage College Dictionary (3rd ed.). (2000). Boston: Houghton Mifflin Company.

Astin, A. (1993). *What matters in college? Four critical years revisited.* San Francisco: Jossey-Bass.

Bowen, H. (1997). *Investment in learning: The individual and social value of American higher education.* Baltimore: Johns Hopkins University Press.

Constantine, M. G., Wilton, L., Gainor, K. A., & Lewis, E. L. (2002). Religious participation, spirituality, and coping among African American college students. *Journal of College Student Development, 43*(5), 605–13.

Covey, S. (1995). *The seven habits of highly effective people.* New York: Simon and Schuster.

Cushman, P. (1995). *Constructing the self: Constructing America.* Reading, MA: Addison-Wesley.

Dalton, J. C. (2001). Career and calling: Finding a place for the spirit in work and community. In M. A. Jablonski (Ed.), *The implications of student spirituality for student affairs practice.* New Directions for Student Services, no. 95 (pp. 17–25). San Francisco: Jossey-Bass.

Erikson, E. H. (1964). *Insight and responsibility.* New York: Norton.

Erikson, E. H. (1965). *The challenge of youth.* New York: Doubleday.

Fowler, J. W. (1981). *Stages of faith: The psychology of human development and the quest for meaning.* San Francisco: Harper San Francisco.

Love, P., & Talbot, D. (1999). Defining spiritual development: A missing consideration for student affairs. *NASPA Journal, 37*(1), 361–375.

Majors, R., & Billson, J. (1992). *Cool pose: The dilemmas of Black manhood in America.* San Francisco: New Lexington Press.

Mead, G. (1962). *Mind, self, and society.* Chicago: University of Chicago Press.

Parks, S. D. (2000). *Big questions, worthy dreams: Mentoring young adults in their search for meaning, purpose, and faith.* San Francisco: Jossey-Bass.

Roof, W., & Hadaway, C. (1988). Apostasy in American churches. In D. G. Bromley (Ed.), *Falling from the faith.* Thousand Oaks, CA: Sage.

Stewart III, C. F. (1999). *Black spirituality and Black consciousness soul force, culture, and freedom in the African-American experience.* Trenton, NJ: Africa World Press.

CHAPTER SEVEN

THE ROLE OF BLACK FRATERNITIES IN THE AFRICAN AMERICAN MALE UNDERGRADUATE EXPERIENCE

Shaun R. Harper, The Pennsylvania State University

Frank Harris III, University of Southern California

A thirteen-year-old African American boy in a small segregated town in southern Georgia was raised by his mother in a single-parent home. Most of his same-age peers and neighborhood play-mates were girls; thus, his interactions with other African American boys were confined almost exclusively to school. Prior to eighth grade, all of his teachers were female; most were White. Though there was clearly something special about him, his potential remained untapped and his academic performance was marginal, as evidenced by the many C's and occasional failing marks he received on elementary and middle school report cards.

His first African American male teacher, who was active in a local Black fraternity, reached out to the eighth-grade student and ignited his interest in academic success. In that same year he was elected president of the student council, the boy's first-ever leadership position in school, which his same-race male teacher highly encouraged. When he transitioned to ninth grade, his high school guidance counselor immediately detected the young man's potential and invited him to participate in a fraternity-sponsored leadership development league for African American male teens.

Participation in the program exposed the student to a cadre of powerful, accomplished, and professional African American men, which included the town's mayor, business leaders, and several school administrators. These men invested significantly in the development of young African American male high school students—they met with them weekly, took them on field trips, helped with their homework, engaged them in community service projects, and often spent one-on-one fathering time with those who were from single-parent homes. The aforementioned teen especially benefited from the program, as he was personally mentored by the program's chairperson, who groomed him to assume the presidency of the group, taught him how to effectively lead meetings, and coached him on public speaking and self-presentation. Consequently, his confidence, self-esteem, and high school academic performance simultaneously increased. As a high school senior, he competed in the fraternity's regional and national high school student of the year competitions and won first place. This honor was accompanied by a lucrative scholarship that offset the costs associated with his college attendance. Few would have predicted that a previously low-performing elementary and middle school student would benefit so profoundly from participation in this high school program sponsored by the alumni chapter of a Black fraternity.

It came as no surprise to anyone that this young man entered college with a strong desire to join the undergraduate chapter of the fraternity on his campus. Like the men in his hometown, the undergraduate fraternity members displayed achievement in multiple endeavors and were actively engaged in several community service projects. Moreover, they were extremely poised and popular. The aspirant worked hard to make himself eligible for induction into the fraternity. He had been told by his high school mentors that active involvement in undergraduate clubs and organizations, a solid academic record, and a reputation for leadership inside and outside of the classroom would strengthen his chances for membership. After earning a 3.6 cumulative grade point average, serving as editor-in-chief of the university's student newspaper, assuming high-profile leadership positions in multiple campus organizations, and being elected president of the student body, the young man achieved his dream of becoming a member of the fraternity. The eighteen other high-achieving African American male undergraduates with whom he pledged offered something to the young man that had been lacking since his childhood—opportunities for brotherly bonding and meaningful friendships with other African American males his age. They encouraged and applauded his success, elected him president of the chapter, and extended to him the perpetual branch of brotherhood. When he left for graduate school, the eighteen brothers gathered for an emotionally memorable sendoff.

When he arrived at graduate school, in a small, predominantly White college town in the Midwest, he was immediately welcomed by undergraduate members of the fraternity there, as well as alumni brothers who resided in a nearby city. The latter group instantly became his closest friends, as they made his transition seamless and enjoyable. Meaningful friendships also solidified with other fraternity brothers who were pursuing post-baccalaureate degrees at the university. He later developed mentoring relationships with many of the undergraduate members, became the faculty advisor for the undergraduate chapter, and was subsequently honored at a Greek leadership conference with the National Advisor of the Year Award. In his doctoral dissertation, he devoted a page of acknowledgments to the fraternity brothers who had supported and encouraged his pursuit of the doctoral degree. To say that fraternity affiliation changed this young man's life would be a gross understatement.

For nearly a hundred years, Black Greek-letter organizations (BGLOs) have played similarly significant roles in the lives and college experiences of thousands of African American undergraduates. The effects of fraternity membership on African American male students are reported and discussed in this chapter. Although membership tends to be a lifetime commitment for most people who join BGLOs, emphasis here is placed almost exclusively on the role of Black fraternities in the African American male experience during the college years. A brief overview of the historical context out of which these groups emerged is followed by a description of

Cleveland Avenue Branch
404-762-4116
www.afpls.org

patron's name:ALLEN, JAMIE EDWARD

title:Black college student's s
author:Kunjufu, Jawanza.
item id:R0106918147
due:2/25/2011,23:59

title:Helping African American
author:Cuyjet, Michael J.
item id:R0087364469
due:2/25/2011,23:59

title:African American men in c
author:Cuyjet, Michael J.
item id:R0109748842
due:2/25/2011,23:59

the positive outcomes and benefits commonly associated with undergraduate membership. Contemporary issues and explanations for the reasons why some rightfully question the value of Black fraternities are presented later in the chapter, as are implications for college and university administrators who seek to enhance the African American male undergraduate experience.

BLACK FRATERNITIES IN A HISTORICAL CONTEXT

The early 1900s marked a period in which higher education was largely inaccessible to African Americans. Alienation, prejudice, and intolerance were harsh realities for the few African Americans who were permitted to matriculate at almost exclusively White colleges and universities. During this era, a group of African American men at Cornell University organized themselves in pursuit of two stated purposes. First, given the hostile racial climate on campus, they desired greater contact with each other beyond what was offered through their classes (Wesley, 1981). With this purpose as a primary motive, they established a social studies club that was used as a vehicle to support their pursuit of the Cornell degree—an accomplishment that had been reached by few African Americans. A second stated purpose was to organize what would become the nation's first continuous Black college fraternity (Kimbrough, 2003; Wesley, 1981).

Secret societies served as important social networks for Cornell students, yet these organizations were off limits to African Americans (Ross, 2000). Hence, seven African American men deemed it necessary to establish their own group out of a need to combat the isolation, hostile campus environment, and socially debilitating conditions in which African American men were expected to learn. These purposes were realized on December 4, 1906, when Alpha Phi Alpha was officially founded. Kimbrough (2003) notes that the organization was started forty years after the White fraternity movement began at Cornell. Several founders of the new African American men's group worked as laborers in Cornell's White fraternity houses to support themselves financially, and they witnessed firsthand the benefits that came with membership in such an organization.

The influence of Alpha Phi Alpha quickly spread. By 1910, just four years after its founding, the fraternity had established chapters on twelve different college campuses and ignited a movement that would birth four other national Greek-letter organizations for African American male collegians.

In the wake of racial hostility, ten academically successful African American undergraduate men at Indiana University sought to create a support system for each another by starting a social fraternity. In 1911, Kappa Alpha Psi, the second BGLO in the country, was founded on the predominantly White campus with "achievement in every field of human endeavor" as its aim (Crump, 1991). Nine of the ten founders graduated from Indiana and subsequently assumed important roles as leaders in their communities and achievers in their professions. Little is known about how these African American men perceived the impact of fraternity involvement on their overall college experiences. However, Crump confirms that membership in Kappa afforded these students the opportunity to build something previously lacking on the Indiana campus—relationships with other African American men. He claims: "Black men were almost completely ignored by White students. To make matters worse, one Black student might be on campus for weeks without seeing another. Under these circumstances, assimilation into the life of the school was impossible. The administration maintained an attitude of indifference as Blacks were slowly matriculated and swiftly forgotten . . . the members [of Kappa Alpha Psi] sought one another's company between classes and dropped by one another's lodging place to discuss a new approach to an old problem. The depressing isolation earlier experienced was relieved as new friendships solidified" (p. 3).

Unlike their predecessors, which were founded on predominantly White campuses, Omega Psi Phi and Phi Beta Sigma were started at Howard University, a historically Black institution, in 1911 and 1914, respectively. The founding of these two fraternities, coupled with the establishment of a chapter of Alpha Phi Alpha in 1907 and the founding of Alpha Kappa Alpha Sorority in 1908 and Delta Sigma Theta Sorority in 1913, made Howard the center of Black Greek life in the early 1900s. "Howard University could be referred to as the 'cradle of Black Greek civilization,' in that five of the first eight collegiate organizations that went on to exist continuously were founded on that campus" (Kimbrough, 2003, p. 32). The influence of these organizations was felt across the nation shortly after they were founded, as new chapters were chartered at hundreds of post-secondary institutions and members increasingly became involved in a wide array of important sociopolitical endeavors.

Iota Phi Theta, the fifth national Black fraternity, was founded in 1963 at Morgan State University. The fraternity's motto, "Building on a Tradition, Not Resting on One," characterizes the spirit in which the organization was created. Its founding members were unwilling to settle for the perceived social complacency displayed by the four preexisting Black fraternities, especially during the height of the civil rights movement of the 1960s (Ross, 2000). They also believed the other groups were divisive during a critical time when African Americans needed to unite. Today, Iota Phi Theta continues to pride itself on the foundational principles that originally distinguished it from the other four national Black fraternities.

In spite of the differences that characterized their origins, these groups share philosophical commitments to brotherhood, scholarship, and service. With membership in each fraternity comes the expectation that brothers will offer lifelong service to the organization and unconditional support to each other. Academic excellence has always been and continues to be a value espoused by each organization (Harper, Byars, & Jelke, 2005). Furthermore, members of the five Black fraternities collectively embrace the belief that volunteerism and service to one's campus, community, church, and profession are both necessary and spiritually rewarding. These organizations continue to enhance the African American male undergraduate experience and fulfill many of their original purposes, as evidenced through the gains and positive outcomes discussed in the following section.

WHAT AFRICAN AMERICAN MEN GAIN THROUGH FRATERNITY MEMBERSHIP

The positive effects of fraternity and sorority affiliation on African American undergraduates have been well-documented by a host of scholars. For instance, Patton and Bonner II (2001), as well as Schuh, Triponey, Heim, and Nishimura (1992) and Harper et al. (2005) contended that BGLOs have historically served and continue to serve as valuable social support outlets for African American students, especially at predominantly White institutions

(PWIs). Sutton and Terrell (1997) suggest that this support is especially valuable for African American male collegians, as undergraduate fraternities encourage unity among members and offer early opportunities for leadership, which increases retention. Harper and Wolley (2002) also called attention to the role of Black fraternities in increasing African American male participation in campus activities and acknowledged how these groups typically require aspiring members to demonstrate academic excellence, active out-of-class engagement, and leadership potential.

Furthermore, Sutton and Kimbrough (2001) found that predominantly Black student organizations, including BGLOs, afford African American students a sense of belonging, cultural connections, and numerous opportunities to gain transferable leadership and communication skills. Harper et al. (2005) considered the various ways in which Black sororities and fraternities affect the college adjustment of African American students. Accordingly, BGLOs often assume responsibility for providing social programming that otherwise would not exist for African American students on predominantly White campuses, thus leading to increased social engagement and satisfaction. "As colleges and universities become more focused on improving their retention and graduation rates, particularly in closing the gaps between White and African American students, they cannot overlook the important roles that BGLOs play in African American students' adjustment and success" (Harper et al., 2005, p. 410).

Finally, Hayek, Carini, O'Day, and Kuh (2002) found that sorority and fraternity members were just as engaged as their unaffiliated peers—or sometimes even more engaged—in academic preparation and studying, active learning, interactions with faculty both inside and outside of the classroom, community service, and diversity-related activities. Thus, members were significantly more satisfied with their undergraduate experiences.

Students who belong to Greek-letter organizations do not fare worse and in many cases fare better than other students in terms of their levels of engagement in educationally effective practices. This was true almost across the board—from the amount of effort they put forth inside and outside of the classroom (including experiences with and exposure to diversity), to self-reported gains in educational and personal growth areas, to perceptions of the campus environments (p. 657). (It should be noted that Hayek et al.'s assertions are based on data from the National Survey of Student Engagement, and the sample included some African American sorority and fraternity members.)

A wide range of gains and outcomes associated with African American male involvement in campus activities and leadership in student organizations are described in Chapters Three and Four of this book. Existing published evidence suggests the following are strongly tied to fraternity membership: (1) racial identity development, (2) leadership development, (3) the development of practical competence, and (4) cognitive development. Gains and outcomes in these four areas are explained in detail in the following sections.

RACIAL IDENTITY DEVELOPMENT

Racial and ethnic identity development theories provide insight into how "individuals come to understand the implications of their ethnicity and make decisions about its role in their lives" (Phinney, 1990, p. 64). Helms (1990) suggests that one's racial identity is based on perceptions of racial collectivism and the belief that she or he shares a common racial heritage with others. Regarding Black identity development, the Cross Model of Psychological Nigrescence is most widely cited. William Cross introduced this five-stage sequential model in 1971 to explain Nigrescence, which he later reduced to the following four stages: (1) Preencounter, (2) Encounter, (3) Immersion-Emersion, and (4) Internalization. At the heart of this model is the process whereby African Americans come to terms with their Blackness and the ways in which they situate their identities among others from different racial or ethnic backgrounds. Cross describes Nigrescence as a "resocializing experience" in which a preexisting identity is transformed from non-Africentrism to Africentrism to multiculturalism.

Parham and Helms (1985) found that African American students exhibiting high self-esteem often displayed development in line with the latter stages of Cross's model. Thus, these students typically held positive perceptions of other African Americans, recognized disparities in the social conditions of marginalized groups, and interacted comfortably with people from other racial and ethnic backgrounds, thereby developing strong racial identities (Evans, Forney, & Guido-DiBrito, 1998). Branch (2001) asserts that African American men "see the fraternal system as a means of reconnecting with their African social and cultural identity" (p. 125). This and other documented evidence suggests that Black fraternities have a significant positive effect on the racial identity development of African American men because of the emphasis they place on social and cultural awareness and collectivism.

In examining the relationship between racial identity and membership in student organizations, Taylor and Howard-Hamilton (1995) collected data from undergraduate students at ten PWIs. Their study revealed that higher levels of out-of-class involvement contributed to stronger Black identities. Using Cross's model, highly involved students tended to be at the Immersion-Emersion and Internalization stages, while less-involved participants reported higher levels of Preencounter attitudes. Moreover, when compared to their nonaffiliated peers, fraternity members in the sample showed significantly higher levels of Immersion-Emersion and Internalization attitudes (Taylor & Howard-Hamilton, 1995). These findings supported Taylor and Howard-Hamilton's hypothesis that BGLO members were more involved in student organizations. Thus, they offered the following conclusion: "Regarding fraternity involvement, these findings suggest that African American males who participate in Greek-letter organizations tend to embrace a stronger, more positive sense of self-esteem and racial identity than their non-Greek counterparts" (p. 334).

Black fraternities also afford African American men the opportunity to build meaningful relationships with other African Americans. The service and volunteer efforts of these organizations are aimed primarily at eradicating the socioeconomic and sociopolitical challenges faced by African Americans in institutions of higher education and in society at large. Additionally, participating in and cosponsoring events with other, more mainstream clubs and organizations affords members the opportunity to engage in working relationships and purposeful cross-cultural interactions with peers from other racial and ethnic backgrounds. These cross-cultural exchanges enable African American men to negotiate relationships with the culturally different, while remaining attuned to their own identities and committed to Black issues, which are consistent with attitudes held by those at the Immersion-Emersion and Internalization stages of Cross's model.

LEADERSHIP DEVELOPMENT

It is not at all coincidental that many of the most celebrated and influential African American male leaders—Dr. Martin Luther King, Jr., Jesse Jackson, Johnnie Cochran, Tavis Smiley, W.E.B. DuBois, and Cornel West, to name a few—have been affiliated with one of the five Black Greek-letter fraternities. This legacy of leadership and success is described by Branch (2001), who writes, "he [the undergraduate Black fraternity member] is no longer a single African American male struggling to survive on a college campus. Rather, he has become part of a legacy of leadership and success" (p. 55). At PWIs, the Black fraternity remains the most popular venue for African American male leadership and involvement (Harper et al., 2005; Sutton & Terrell, 1997). Harper and Wolley (2002) contend that initial displays of leadership potential are usually requisite for fraternity membership; that is, aspiring members are expected to be involved in other clubs, organizations, and activities on campus before seeking membership in a Black fraternity. Prospective members with qualities that will enhance a chapter's stature on campus—including, but not limited to having made a reputation for oneself as a leader—are often most desirable.

Once these students join, they help nurture each other's leadership abilities and benefit from their previous collective experiences in other organizations. Representation in different circles on campus is extremely important to most undergraduate chapters. For example, friendly competition among two Black fraternities can result in members from the two chapters competing against each other for high-profile campus leadership positions, such as Black Student Union president or an executive role in student government. Such representation strengthens the image of both chapters and increases the likelihood that other students will see the fraternities as attractive outlets for leadership development. More important, fraternity members' assumptions of leadership positions in other groups serve the greater good by equipping them with additional transferable skills and experiences that are personally rewarding, as well as adding value to the chapter. Connections with other student leaders, access to financial resources and collaborative programming opportunities, and meaningful relationships with important university administrators are additional ways in which Black fraternities benefit from member involvement and leadership in other student organizations.

Kimbrough and Hutcheson's (1998) study revealed that BGLO members were more involved in campus activities and organizations, and generally had more confidence in their abilities to perform several leadership-related tasks than unaffiliated African American students. Two-thirds of the Black fraternity men in Kimbrough's (1995) study reported that fraternity involvement enhanced their leadership skills. Furthermore, his research reports that BGLO members are more likely than unaffiliated African American students to hold membership and multiple leadership positions in other campus clubs, including mainstream student organizations. Leadership experiences in BGLOs and other predominantly Black groups also connect African American students to their same-race peers, thereby solidifying their efforts to provide leadership to the African American student communities on their campuses.

PRACTICAL COMPETENCE

Practical competence refers to the portfolio of transferable skills acquired through a variety of in-class and out-of-class experiences that can be used in educational and career experiences beyond the college years. These skills are required for success both during and after college (Kuh, Palmer, & Kish, 2003). For example, the African American undergraduates in Harper's (2005) study—43 percent of whom held membership in Black fraternities—identified time management, the ability to work collaboratively with people from different backgrounds, persuasion and negotiation tactics, multitasking and delegating, and improved communication skills as some of the competencies they acquired through their membership in student organizations. These competencies not only allow college graduates to compete successfully for jobs and admission to top graduate and professional schools, but also equip them with the proficiency and understanding required for success and leadership in a wide array of post-undergraduate roles.

Fraternities also offer African American men a platform on which to acquire the practical competencies that are requisite for entry into progressive social and professional circles; members not only gain access, but often assume leadership roles. Examples of practical competencies gained through fraternal affiliation are:

- Acquiring skills in marketing and sales through planning, promoting, and selling tickets for step shows, parties, and formal events
- Learning to be effective in political situations through debating and voting on important issues at chapter meetings and regional and national conventions
- Recognizing and cultivating talent in others through recruitment and membership intake activities
- Balancing multiple commitments simultaneously, such as studying and preparing for class, attending chapter meetings, planning and executing programs, and remaining involved in other aspects of campus life

Anyone who has ever attended graduate school or served in a busy management-level capacity will confirm the necessity and usefulness of these skills.

Although these skills may be acquired in a variety of campus organizations, fraternities are the primary organizations with which African American men are involved. Thus, one can logically conclude that they are the venues in which most African American men gain practical competency and supplement their classroom learning experiences. Holding a leadership position or simply being a general member who participates actively in chapter-related activities gives fraternity members a set of transferable skills and experiences to utilize in their post-undergraduate endeavors and professional work environments. These practical competencies typically serve them well for the rest of their lives.

COGNITIVE DEVELOPMENT

Many of the activities in which Black fraternity members participate positively affect cognitive development. Pascarella, Edison, Whitt, Nora, Hagedorn, and Terenzini (1996) found that Black fraternity membership had a slightly positive effect on some areas of cognitive development, specifically mathematical reasoning, critical thinking, composite scores on tests, and reading comprehension. These findings are supported by the work of Kuh, Douglas, Lund, and Ramin-Gyurnek (1994), which showed that Black fraternity membership led to positive gains in cognitive complexity, knowledge acquisition, and knowledge application for African American men.

Academic success—a valuable outcome of cognitive development—is often measured by grade point average, an index by which, ironically, African American men do not seem to perform as well as African American women, Whites in general, or the institutional averages (Harper, 2000). However, other academic achievement indicators might include being elected to honor societies, qualifying for scholarships, or being admitted to graduate programs. Unfortunately, limited data are available to verify how Black fraternity members rank on these dimensions. An indirect link can be made between leadership development, membership in Black fraternities, and cognitive development. Leadership responsibilities have been connected to growth in cognitive complexity as well as other factors, such as practical competence and interpersonal gains (Kuh, 1995).

Moreover, existing published evidence clearly confirms that active student engagement, both inside and outside of the classroom, produces a profound set of learning outcomes and cognitive gains among college students. Simply put, those who are more engaged learn more in college. As previously mentioned, African American male fraternity members, in comparison with their unaffiliated same-race male peers, hold more campus leadership positions and are more engaged in clubs, organizations, and activities. Thus, it is plausible that they learn more.

Participants in a recent study noted that their fraternity affiliation actually led to higher levels of class participation and engagement in predominantly White classroom environments (see Harper, in press). Members were cognizant of the fact that their academic performance affected the chapter's overall academic standing and believed it was important to serve as academic role models for younger, unaffiliated African American peers in their classes. They were committed to debunking stereotypes their White instructors and classmates held about African Americans, and they wanted to offer intelligent and unique cultural perspectives on various course topics. These convictions inspired them to participate more actively in their classes. The 131 participants consistently noted that their in-class engagement increased dramatically after they became members of their respective fraternities and sororities, as suddenly they not only were representing themselves in their classes but also were serving as ambassadors of their chapters.

Furthermore, a set of gains and cognitive outcomes—including higher grades, heightened academic self-concept, goals to attend graduate school, and increases in general and disciplinary knowledge—also accrues from participation in community service and structured service learning activities (Astin & Sax, 1998). Black fraternities pride themselves on their civic contributions and community service endeavors, thus many members enjoy the benefits associated with engagement in these activities.

Despite the positive ways in which fraternity membership affects African American male student outcomes and provides a vehicle through which they can improve their campuses and communities, there are some risks and areas of concern, which are discussed in the next section.

CONTEMPORARY ISSUES AND NEGATIVE ASPECTS OF BLACK FRATERNITIES

Several factors have contributed to the diminishment of the luster and prestige that previously distinguished Black fraternities from other organizations. Some chapters have struggled to maintain a critical mass of active members—especially those on predominantly White campuses, where African American male enrollments are woefully low. Other chapters lack adequate support and accountability from Greek Life offices, chapter advisors, alumni chapters, and national headquarters. Budget cuts in higher education have resulted in limited funding for student organizations. When funds are limited, fraternities and sororities are less likely to receive financial support from the institution, as administrators often believe those organizations are more capable than other student groups to raise their own funds. While there are many reasons that some question the value of Black fraternities, perhaps none raises more concern than the practice of illegal hazing, which has caused serious injuries and, in a few cases, death; often leads to legal trouble; and frequently dissuades potentially good candidates from pursuing membership. Along with hazing, low academic achievement and the increasingly negative public image of Black fraternities are discussed in this section.

Hazing

The practice of hazing in Black fraternities is an unintended consequence that emerged from the once sanctioned act of pledging. As a result, there is much confusion regarding what distinguishes the two practices. Broadly defined, pledging entails solidifying a lifelong commitment to the ideals of a fraternal organization and typically involves learning and reciting the organization's history, bonding with the other new initiates, and being groomed for induction into a chapter (DeSousa, Gordon, & Kimbrough, 2004). Hazing, on the other hand, is simply characterized by "activities that go beyond what any civil person would cast as within the dignity of an adult seeking membership in a reputable organization" (DeSousa et al., 2004, p. 106). Over the years, such activities were secretly incorporated into the pledging process. Typical acts of hazing include extortion of money or favors, paddling, sleep deprivation, public humiliation, psychological abuse, exposure to harmful elements and conditions, forced calisthenics, forced consumption of alcohol and gross substances, and physical punishment (Sutton, Letzring, Terrell, & Poats, 2000). Fraternities (BGLOs and predominantly White chapters, alike) have been indicted for engaging in some of the most ridiculous and damaging hazing activities.

Although numerous anecdotal accounts suggest that elements of hazing have always been part of the pledge process, the practice began receiving considerable attention following a string of serious injuries to and deaths of prospective members who participated in pledging activities. The 1989 hazing-induced death of Joel Harris, a Morehouse College student pledging Alpha Phi Alpha, made clear the urgent need for change (Jones, 2004; Kimbrough, 1997). In response to this tragic incident and other compelling evidence of the detrimental aspects of hazing, the National Pan-Hellenic Council (NPHC), the body that governs the nine historically Black Greek-letter organizations, prohibited the act of pledging as a condition for membership (Jones, 2004; Kimbrough, 1997, 2003). In 1990, pledging was replaced with a "membership intake process" (MIP), a series of intensive classroom-oriented sessions in which new members were formally indoctrinated into the organization and their respective chapters. However, MIP has been largely ineffective in curtailing hazing activities in most undergraduate chapters. In fact, some would contend that it led to the unmonitored "underground" pledging process in which initiates are subjected to acts of hazing even more intense and brutal than those that occurred in the past. Prior to the incorporation of MIP, pledge processes were monitored by persons of authority such as a chapter advisor or alumni chapter members. Today, such activities take place secretly, without the guidance and supervision of older members. Thus, the act of pledging has now become synonymous with hazing (DeSousa et al., 2004; Jones, 2004; Kimbrough, 1997, 2003).

Kimbrough (1997) explains why undergraduate student support for and adherence to the MIP is woefully low. Student input was not solicited as national presidents of the BGLOs unilaterally made a significant policy decision that would dramatically alter the culture, customs, and practices that undergraduate chapters had long embraced. "Pledges would no longer walk together in a single file line, dress alike, or shout loud greetings for 'big sisters' and 'big brothers.' Phrases like 'on line' and 'pledgee' would no longer be used" (Kimbrough, 1997, p. 233). Many BGLO undergraduate chapters, especially the fraternities, have continually engaged in practices that mirror aspects of pre-1990 pledge practices, because students are yet to be afforded a voice in designing a mutually agreeable MIP. In fact, Kimbrough describes how undergraduate members who attended national fraternity conferences shortly after the new policy was introduced felt "outranked and outvoted." The survey of BGLO members upon which Williams' (1992) study was based confirmed that undergraduates disagreed with the new MIP and believed it lacked meaningful opportunities for bonding among members. He came to a number of conclusions concerning how BGLO members felt:

• The MIP policy was enacted too quickly with little input from members at large.
• Hazing definitions were too broad.

- Insufficient time was allowed by MIP to teach the history of the organizations.
- Bonding is lost.
- Lifelong commitment is jeopardized.
- The policy promotes disunity in chapter ranks.
- New members feel they get no respect and acceptance from older members.

Williams' findings indicate that MIP is shunned by many BGLO members. Given that "above ground" pledging was no longer permissible, many chapters created dangerous underground pledge processes that proved to be more destructive. Unfortunately, underground hazing has led to the death of multiple African American male undergraduates who were seeking membership in Black fraternities.

In his book *Black Haze,* Ricky Jones provides what unarguably stands as the most comprehensive consideration of pledging and hazing practices among BGLOs. Although Jones's treatment of the shift from pledging to membership intake, as well as his provision of multiple sociocultural explanations for the persistence of hazing, are both admirable and exemplary, his description of the student deaths and injuries that have ensued as a result of blatant disregard for the MIP provides a powerful illumination of the seriousness of this problem. Among them is the 1994 death of Michael Davis, a student at Southeast Missouri State University, who was killed by members of Kappa Alpha Psi fraternity during a hazing ritual. Jones (2004) describes several other brutal incidents (though not leading to death) that have occurred on college and university campuses across the nation since 1990; for example:

- A Michigan State University student suffered kidney damage after being paddled by Phi Beta Sigma members.
- Twenty-four Omega Psi Phi members were arrested and charged after brutally hazing six pledges at the University of Maryland, College Park.
- A Lincoln University student was hospitalized after being hazed by Alpha Phi Alpha members from another campus.
- At the University of Pittsburgh, Kappa Alpha Psi members were charged with aggravated assault, reckless endangerment, and conspiracy after beating aspiring members.

Jones chronicles these and dozens of other disturbing incidents in the appendix of *Black Haze.*

Beyond the unfortunate deaths and physical injuries, the prevalence of hazing has also created rifts both within and between Black fraternities. Members are no longer judged solely on the merits of their credentials (e.g., grade point average, campus involvement, community service, and character). Instead, the amount of hazing they endure during their pledge processes is a significant factor. Members often brag and boast about the duration and intensity of their pledge processes. Jones (2004) argues that African American men conceptualize, negotiate, and validate their manhood by proving that they can withstand physical abuse during the fraternity pledge process. Hazing rituals become internalized components of individual and group masculine identities. That is, the toughest men and the purportedly "ultra-masculine" chapters usually earn their reputations and garner respect through survival of the most brutal physical challenges during membership intake. These values are unfortunately passed on during the new member socialization period.

There are some who pursue fraternity membership and choose not to participate in illegal and unsanctioned pledging activities. However, doing so does not come without consequences. These men often face intense scrutiny, harassment, threats of violence, property damage, and social alienation. Fraternity members who did participate in hazing activities prior to joining the organization derisively refer to those who choose not to engage in the hazing process as "paper" brothers, implying that although they have the certification of membership, they are not "real" brothers. In many cases, they are not allowed to participate in chapter events, wear organizational paraphernalia, visit brothers in chapters at other universities, or claim membership in the fraternity. This can be an especially troubling experience that, for some, has led to temporary leaves of absences, transfers to another institution, or permanent withdrawal from higher education—all of which are counterproductive to the retention of African American male undergraduates.

Scholars have attributed the continued practice of hazing to several factors. For example, Kimbrough (1997, 2003) contends that the practice endures because of the BGLO national leaders' continued refusal to incorporate input from undergraduate student members into the revised MIP. Sweet (2004) offers a theoretical

explanation, contending that hazing is simply the product of complex group-interaction processes that satisfy students' needs for peer
approval and group acceptance. In addition to the aforementioned
masculine intra- and inter-group dynamics, Jones (2004) also links
this violent behavior to larger sociopolitical dynamics that hinder
African American men's advancement. Yet regardless of the reasons
to which one attributes the ongoing practice of hazing, at times it
negatively affects the college experiences of men who choose to join
Black fraternities. Thus, hazing remains a critical issue on college
campuses and threatens the foreseeable future of Black undergraduate chapters.

ACADEMIC MEDIOCRITY

Although all Black fraternities identify academic excellence as a core
value, claims that membership improves academic performance may
be overstated. In spite of reportedly high levels of in-class engagement (Harper, in press), African American male fraternity members'
cumulative grade point averages frequently contradict their
espoused commitments to academic achievement—that is, members
somehow fail to connect active participation to quantifiable evidence
of success in the college classroom. As is the case with most college
Greek-letter organizations, the academic performance of Black fraternities is reported in the post-semester academic standings reports
produced by Greek Life offices and departments of institutional
research on most campuses. These reports provide the chapters and
the institution an indication of how they are doing in comparison
with other Greek-letter organizations on campus by displaying the
average end-of-semester grades for all active and new members in
a given chapter. Accordingly, "semester grade reports validate
perceptions—be they positive or negative—about the impact
fraternity/sorority involvement has on student scholastic achievement" (Harper, 2000, p. 14).

Harper (2000) found that BGLOs typically fell in the bottom
tier of all sororities and fraternities listed on official academic standings reports retrieved from multiple PWIs in different parts of the
country. Upon analyzing data from 24 institutions and 119 BGLO
undergraduate chapters, he discovered that nearly 92 percent of all
the BGLO chapters had GPAs well below the all-Greek averages,

which included all social fraternities and sororities (not just BGLOs) on the campuses. Only seven percent of the BGLOs had GPAs either at or above the universitywide or all-undergraduate averages. The mean GPAs for the BGLO sororities and fraternities in his study were 2.54 and 2.43, respectively. Harper offered several explanations that may account for the meager academic performance of BGLO members, including excessive programming and chapter commitments, extreme involvement in other organizations, too much time devoted to step-show preparation, hazing, a lack of organization-specific resources offered by national headquarters, and poor advising from Greek Life offices.

Such issues, combined with the typical challenges faced by non-affiliated African American students at PWIs, contribute to the less-than-stellar academic performance of Black fraternity members. Participation in a sorority or fraternity does not, unfortunately, ensure African American students immunity from acts of racial insensitivity at PWIs or feelings of underrepresentation and isolation in classroom environments that lack racial or ethnic diversity. Hence, they too are vulnerable to academic and social disengagement, which also leads to below-average academic performance.

These low-grade trends obviously contradict the degrees of active engagement reported by the participants in Harper's (in press) study. As mentioned in the cognitive development section of this chapter, the 131 BGLO members in the sample indicated that their participation and in-class engagement increased once they joined their respective sororities and fraternities. Why such engagement—whether perceived, actual, or exaggerated—does not yield quantifiable gains in GPAs merits further study.

DIMINISHED PUBLIC PERCEPTION

Some question the continued necessity of undergraduate chapters in the five national Black fraternities. There is growing skepticism among college men regarding the extent to which fraternities add value to their college experience. Social conditions and campus climates have improved dramatically for African Americans since the early 1900s. In the past, fraternal membership was essential to retention and overall success, as it provided the sole source of social support for African American college men. Today's men have a wider range of social networks from which to choose. Organizations such as 100 Black Men, the Student African American Brotherhood (SAAB), and the Black Man's Think Tank, as well as other local grassroots initiatives, provide viable alternatives for African American men without forcing them to participate in potentially brutal hazing activities or putting their academic performance at risk.

Black fraternities have also been charged with splintering African American communities rather than building them on college and university campuses. For instance, some chapters invest significant resources in exclusive "Greek-only" activities that could be beneficial to the larger African American student population on campus but are enjoyed only by members. In addition, it is not uncommon for some fraternity members to limit their peer interactions to brothers within their respective chapters, which leads to social stratification among African American men on campus.

Black fraternities and sororities are also criticized for their exclusionary member selection processes. Patton and Bonner II (2001) offer the following: "The current malaise involving historically Black Greek-letter organizations and the public's perception involves their selection of organizational members based on group image. Terms such as 'pretty boy,' 'pretty girl,' and 'dog' are but a few of the names associated with select organizations. As a result, groups often choose members who they perceive will uphold the images they have established . . . students interested in membership feel they must buy into the stereotype associated with these groups in order to be accepted, often times to the detriment of their individual identity development" (p. 24).

Maisel (1990) further illustrates this point by claiming that "fraternities and sororities are exclusionary by practice, sexist in nature, and gender specific by design" (p. 8). Furthermore, members are reportedly too arrogant to actively recruit students who would add value to the organization, believing that aspirants should go above and beyond to make their interests known. Dwindling numbers and small chapter sizes at the undergraduate level are byproducts of these image issues. Simply put, BGLOs, especially fraternities, are not as popular as they once were because of declining public perceptions regarding their usefulness and effectiveness at fulfilling stated purposes.

CONCLUSION

Since their origination in the early 1900s, Black fraternities have affected the lives and college experiences of more than one million men. These organizations emerged at a time when institutions cared little about the success of African American male students, as administrators reinforced the racial segregation that existed outside of the academy and traditional campus social networks were established exclusively for White students. Today, published research suggests that Black fraternities continue to enrich outcomes for African American male undergraduates. Racial identity development, leadership development, practical competence, and cognitive development have all been linked to membership. In addition, these organizations play a positive role in improving the quality of campus life for African American students, as they provide much-needed outlets for cross-cultural engagement, community service, civic participation, campus politics, and social support.

Despite their prominence on college and university campuses, the reputation of Black fraternities has been called into question. Scholars have identified several factors that threaten their existence. The practices of illegal pledging and hazing have created warranted concern. And although academic excellence is a core principle for each of the five Black fraternities, their members' performance in the classroom has been average at best—especially when compared to chapters in other Greek councils. As a result, the public perception of Black fraternities has declined steadily, thereby leading potential aspirants to pursue membership in alternative Black male social networks.

The experience of the African American male fraternity member described at the beginning of this chapter is not an isolated occurrence; many Black fraternity members tell similar stories. To produce similar gains and outcomes, college and university administrators should acquaint themselves with the histories, traditions, and national programs of the five Black fraternities; invite undergraduate members to serve as student representatives on campus boards and committees; partner with chapter advisors to make certain that organizational policies are consistent with the institution's policies (especially as they relate to the recruitment and initiation of new members); and provide BGLOs with adequate funding and access to campus resources and facilities. Likewise, leaders and national headquarters staff of the five Black fraternities must ensure that chapter advisors are equipped to guide members in their psychosocial development and academic endeavors; are intentional in reinforcing campus leadership and academic achievement as core organizational values; solicit and actually incorporate undergraduate students' ideas for a more effective, mutually satisfactory, and less dangerous MIP; and publicly recognize members who display outstanding campus leadership and academic success. Furthermore, it appears that national headquarters staff and chapter advisors should partner with university professionals to offer more structured academic resources (study guides, handbooks, programs and workshops, tutors, and so on) that will aid BGLO members in improving their academic standing.

Perhaps most important, those who are already members—undergraduates and alumni brothers alike—should publicly reflect on the value that fraternity affiliation has added to their experiences; continue to serve as powerful and dependable sources of social support to fellow African American men; lead by example; reach out to younger African American men who show potential for leadership; and consistently enact the espoused values of brotherhood, scholarship, and service.

References

Astin, A. W., & Sax, L. J. (1998). How undergraduates are affected by service participation. *Journal of College Student Development, 39*(3), 251–263.

Branch, C. D. (2001). *Stepping through these hallowed halls: Performance in African American fraternities.* Unpublished doctoral dissertation, University of California at Los Angeles.

Cross, W. E., Jr. (1971). The Negro to black conversion experience: Toward a psychology of black liberation. *Black World, 20*(9), 13–27.

Crump, W. L. (1991). *The story of Kappa Alpha Psi: A history of the beginning and development of a college Greek letter organization* (4th ed.). Philadelphia: Kappa Alpha Psi Fraternity International Headquarters.

Davis, R. B. (1991). Social support networks and undergraduate student academic-success-related outcomes: A comparison of Black students on Black and White campuses. In W. R. Allen, E. G. Epps, & N. Z. Haniff (Eds.), *College in Black and White* (pp. 143–157). Albany: State University of New York.

DeSousa, D. J., Gordon, M.V.W., & Kimbrough, W. M. (2004). Pledging and hazing in African-American fraternities and sororities. In H. Nuwer (Ed.), *The hazing reader* (pp. 106–109). Bloomington: Indiana University Press.

Evans, N. J., Forney, D. S., & Guido-DiBrito, F. (1998). *Student development in college: Theory, research, and practice.* San Francisco: Jossey-Bass.

Harper, S. R. (2000, Fall). The academic standings report: Helping NPHC chapters make the grade. *Association of Fraternity Advisors Perspectives,* 14–17.

Harper, S. R. (2005). Leading the way: Inside the experiences of high-achieving African American male students. *About Campus, 10*(1), 8–15.

Harper, S. R. (In press). The effects of sorority and fraternity membership on class participation and African American student engagement in predominantly White classroom environments. *College Student Affairs Journal.*

Harper, S. R., Byars, L. F., & Jelke, T. B. (2005). How membership affects college adjustment and African American undergraduate student outcomes. In T. L. Brown, G. S. Parks, & C. M. Phillips (Eds.), *African American fraternities and sororities: The legacy and the vision* (pp. 393–416). Lexington: University Press of Kentucky.

Harper, S. R., & Wolley, M. A. (2002, May). Becoming an "involving college" for African American men: Strategies for increasing African American male participation in campus activities. *Association of College Unions International Bulletin, 70,* 16–24.

Hayek, J. H., Carini, R. M., O'Day, P. T., & Kuh, G. D. (2002). Triumph or tragedy: Comparing student engagement levels of members of Greek-letter organizations and other students. *Journal of College Student Development, 43,* 643–663.

Helms, J. E. (Ed.). (1990). *Black and White racial identity: Theory, research, and practice.* Westport, CT: Greenwood Press.

Jones, R. L. (2004). *Black haze: Violence, sacrifice, and manhood in Black Greek-letter fraternities.* Albany: State University of New York Press.

Kimbrough, W. M. (1995). Self-assessment, participation, and value of leadership skill, activities, and experiences for Black students relative to their membership in historically Black fraternities and sororities. *Journal of Negro Education, 64*(1), 63–74.

Kimbrough, W. M. (1997). The membership intake movement of historically Black Greek-letter organizations. *NASPA Journal, 34*(3), 229–239.

Kimbrough, W. M. (2003). *Black Greek 101: The culture, customs, and challenges of Black fraternities and sororities.* Madison, NJ: Fairleigh Dickinson University Press.

Kimbrough, W. M., & Hutcheson, P. A. (1998). The impact of membership in Black Greek-letter organizations on Black students' involvement in college activities and their development of leadership skills.
Journal of Negro Education, 67, 96–105.

Kuh, G. D. (1995). The other curriculum: Out-of-class experiences associated with student learning and personal development. *Journal of
Higher Education, 66,* 123–155.

Kuh, G. D., Douglas, K. B., Lund, J. P., & Ramin-Gyurnek, J. (1994). *Stu-
dent learning outside of the classroom: Transcending artificial boundaries.*
ASHE-ERIC Higher Education Report, no. 8. Washington, DC:
George Washington University Graduate School of Education.

Kuh, G. D., Palmer, M., & Kish, K. (2003). The value of educationally purposeful out-of-class experiences. In T. L. Skipper & R. Argo (Eds.),
*Involvement in campus activities and the retention of first-year college stu-
dents* (pp. 1–18). Columbia: University of South Carolina.

Maisel, J. M. (1990). Social fraternities and sororities are not conducive
to the educational process. *NASPA Journal, 28*(1), 8–12.

Parham, T. A., & Helms, J. E. (1985). Relation of racial identity attitudes
to self actualization and affective states of Black students. *Journal of
Counseling Psychology, 32,* 431–440.

Pascarella, E. T., Edison, M., Whitt, E. J, Nora, A., Hagedorn, L. S., &
Terenzini, P. T. (1996). Cognitive effects of Greek membership during the first year of college. *NASPA Journal, 33,* 254–259.

Patton, L. D., & Bonner II, F. A. (2001). Advising the historically Black
Greek letter organization (HBGLO): A reason for angst or eupho-
ria? *NASPA Journal, 4*(1), 17–30.

Phinney, J. S. (1990). Ethnic identity in adolescents and adults: Review of
research. *Psychological Bulletin, 108,* 499–514.

Ross, L. C. (2000). *The divine nine: The history of African American fraternities
and sororities.* New York: Kensington Publishing.

Schuh, J. H., Triponey, V. L., Heim, L. L., & Nishimura, K. (1992). Student involvement in historically Black Greek-letter organizations.
NASPA Journal, 29(4), 169–177.

Sutton, E. M., & Kimbrough, W. M. (2001). Trends in Black student
involvement. *NASPA Journal, 39*(1), 30–40.

Sutton, E. M., Letzring, T., Terrell, M. C., & Poats, L. (2000). Hazing as a
form of campus violence. *NASPA Journal, 3*(1), 35–45.

Sutton, E. M., & Terrell, M. C. (1997). Identifying and developing leadership opportunities for African American men. In M. J. Cuyjet
(Ed.), *Helping African American men succeed in college.* New Directions
for Student Services, no. 80 (pp. 55–64). San Francisco: Jossey-Bass.

Sweet, S. (2004). Understanding fraternity hazing. In H. Nuwer (Ed.), *The hazing reader* (pp. 1–13). Bloomington: Indiana University Press.

Taylor, C. M., & Howard-Hamilton, M. F. (1995). Student involvement and racial identity attitudes among African American males. *Journal of College Student Development, 36*(4), 330–335.

Wesley, C. H. (1981). *The history of Alpha Phi Alpha: A development in college life.* Chicago: Foundation Publishers.

Williams, J. A. (1992). Perceptions of the no-pledge policy for new member intake by undergraduate members of predominantly Black fraternities and sororities. Doctoral dissertation, Kansas State University, Manhattan. *Dissertation Abstracts International, 53*(09), 3111.

CHAPTER EIGHT

AFRICAN AMERICAN MALE COLLEGE ATHLETES

Kenya LeNoir Messer, Teachers College, Columbia University

Dr. Henry Louis Gates states in Schulman and Bowen (2001) that "the blind pursuit of attainment in sport is having a devastating effect on the Black community" in that many students feel the road to wealth and fame is through extreme competition and perfection in sports and not in the classroom. Gates adds that too many Black kids treat the playing field as an alternative classroom and take on the attitude that it is okay not to excel academically as long as one is excelling athletically.

Dr. Gates's point is further illustrated by the inordinate amount of time and attention that student athletes must give to practicing, conditioning, and traveling to compete in athletic contests. This appears to have a tangible, negative effect on these students; for example, of the sixteen schools in the final rounds of the NCAA Division I men's basketball tournament in March 2004, only four had graduated more than half of their male basketball players. (Campbell, 2004). The Institute for Diversity and Ethics in Sport at the University of Central Florida's (UCF) analysis of the 2004 NCAA Graduation Rates Report states that thirty-nine of the fifty-six football teams that played bowl games graduated fewer than half of their players (Institute, 2004). Dr. Richard Lapchick, the Institute's director, believes that it is necessary to look at race, because although rates for African American male football have improved, the gap between the rates for African American football players and Whites has grown wider (Towers, 2004).

These cases illustrate that the numbers of African American male student athletes graduating from predominantly white institutions (PWIs) are low, particularly among those in the revenue-generating sports of football and basketball. In 2003, the graduation rate for African American male student athletes was only 48 percent (NCAA, 2004). The NCAA graduation rates report shows that over a five-year period the rate has increased for African American male student athletes (AAMSAs), from 40 percent five years ago to 48 percent today; nevertheless, the numbers still indicate that less than half of this population completes a degree. In general, African American males have the highest dropout rate among college athletes, and academic variables have most often been cited as the contributing factor (Brice, 1992). The graduation rate for AAMSAs is low at 48 percent, compared to a 62.5 percent graduation rate for White student athletes, which is actually higher than the 59 percent graduation rate for the student body in general (NCAA, 2004).

Given the consistently low rates over time, it becomes clear that this population cannot be perceived as particularly successful in graduating from college. On the other hand, because a small but consistent number have graduated over time, we may want to examine those strategies being used by African American male student athletes to complete their degrees successfully. Hyatt (2001) found that mandated degree requirements and certain noncognitive variables, such as personal accountability, accounted for persistence among African American male student athletes that she studied. On average, African American male student athletes graduated at a higher rate than African American male students who did not participate in athletics. The African American student athletes' graduation rate was 48 percent compared to a 36 percent graduation rate for African American nonathletes. Nonetheless, any population consistently graduating fewer than half of its members has a serious problem, and institutions must make a concentrated effort to assist them in improving their situation. We need to identify the factors that may be impeding these student athletes' ability to be successful. In addition, an examination of factors that aid in the success of African American male student athletes should provide much-needed insight into assisting this population. Therefore, this chapter will address several factors that may aid or inhibit African American male student athletes' progress toward degree completion. In addressing this issue, we may identify successful strategies and supports, programs, and services in place for African American male student athletes that can be modified for African American male students in general.

Review of the Literature

An examination of the literature about African American male student athletes and the literature on retention and persistence in higher education is an important first step to increasing the graduation rates for this population. This chapter begins with such a review by giving a brief description of African American male student athletes and their history in higher education. Next, the chapter explores some of the literature on persistence and retention in higher education and devotes special attention to studies that examined retention and persistence among African American male students in general and African American male student athletes in particular. Then the chapter reviews the common themes in the literature that provide insight into factors that may or may not aid or inhibit success for this population. The chapter ends with some recommendations for programs and methods that may facilitate persistence, with examples of programs and program components that have helped this population to be successful in college.

Description of African American Male Student Athletes on Campus

The literature has provided a great deal of information about the history of student athletes in American higher education (Adler & Adler, 1991; Pascarella & Smart, 1991; Greene & Greene, 2001; Gerdy, 1994, 2000; Clark & Parette, 2002; Snyder, 1996; Arno, 1990; Murray, 1997; Hale, 1999; Rivas-Quinones, 2003; Ridpath, 2002; Lapchick, 1988; Schulman & Bowen, 2001; Bowen & Levin, 2003;

Sperber, 2000; Hoberman, 1997). Covering everything from the creation of the Ivy League to the formation of the Knight Commission aimed at combating the abuses in athletic programs, the literature gives a good overview of student athletes' evolution in higher education.

Within this body of literature we can also find some insight into the African American male athlete's experiences on campus. The literature specific to the history of African American male student athletes in higher education (Sperber, 2000; Barbalias, 2004; American Institutes for Research, 1989; Hawkins, 1995; Gaston, 2003; Wiggins, 1991, 1998; Walter, 1996; Berry, 2002) covers a wide range of topics, from discussions about exploitation by coaches and the myth of the "dumb black jock" to the more recent discussion surrounding student athletes' unrealistic emphasis on a career in professional athletics.

The National Collegiate Athletic Association (NCAA) was formed in 1905, in response to the increasingly intense physical and often dangerous play in college football. It initially formed to provide oversight for football programs, but quickly began to provide oversight for the whole of intercollegiate athletics. Throughout the 1970s, 1980s, and 1990s the NCAA enacted a number of propositions aimed at improving standards of eligibility for student athletes. Several of these legislative actions have had a particular impact on African American male athletes, especially in men's football and basketball. Propositions 48 and 16 were intended to provide stricter academic standards of eligibility for student athletes, in hopes of enrolling a more academically prepared student. At the 2005 meeting of the NCAA new legislation was introduced that will require at least a 50 percent graduation rate per team. If a team fails to meet the 50 percent graduation rate they could face loss of academic scholarships for players, be eliminated from post season, and eventually lose their membership in the NCAA (Suggs, 2005). This latest ruling has the potential to significantly impact colleges and the student athletes they serve, specifically in areas in which student athletes may be coming to institutions underprepared to meet the academic challenges ahead. Unfortunately, too many African American male student athletes arrive on campus underprepared academically and socially (Clark & Parette, 2002).

RESEARCH STUDY OF AFRICAN AMERICAN MALE STUDENT ATHLETES

In 1989, the NCAA produced the findings from a research study conducted by the American Institutes for Research entitled "The Experiences of Black Intercollegiate Athletes at NCAA Division I Institutions" (American Institutes, 1989). Though the study may seem somewhat dated, it is still significant because it is the most comprehensive study of African American male student athletes at NCAA Division I institutions to date and its findings give good insight into the population. The study revealed that nearly one-half of all black football players and basketball players came from the lowest socioeconomic quartile, in which the mean annual income was $17,500 dollars. For these students the head of household was most likely a female and the median level of parental education was the eleventh grade. Most parental occupations were unskilled labor or clerical. These data also reflected a high first-generation college student population. Although this study was conducted in 1989 it is still relevant today because many of the issues still hold true.

Academically, the 1989 research study showed that nearly 60 percent of black student athletes scored in the lowest quartile of the ACT and SAT standardized tests; 6 percent scored in the highest quartile. Black male athletes in the study made up 48 percent of the lowest quartile for high school grades and 61 percent of the lowest quartile for college grade point average, with the mean grade point average being 2.16. Because athletes spend so much of their time with athletics-related activities, they tend to spend less time with other endeavors. The study showed that, on average, Black male student athletes spent twenty-eight hours preparing for and participating in their sport and twenty-three hours preparing for class, and on average would miss two classes per week during the season and one class during the off-season. Edwards (cited in Sperber, 2000) states that some student athletes spend upwards of forty hours a week on their sport, and when they are done practicing or playing they are often in pain from the intense physical activity or a combination of mental, physical, and emotional exhaustion, so the motivation to study their course work lost priority over getting rest.

The majority of Black male student athletes in the 1989 study were not majoring in physical education, as was generally assumed, but reported a major in business administration. The survey indicated that although the Black male athlete placed a high priority on completing his degree, education was not his primary goal. The data revealed that had these young men not been recruited for athletics, many would not have attended college at all. Hyatt (2001) summarizes the African American male student athletes' experience as a paradox because they are provided an opportunity to attend college that many of them would not have had if it was not for their athletic ability, but, given their commitment to and involvement in athletics, they do not have the time to integrate into the total life of the campus. This often proves problematic, as research has shown that integration is a key factor in student persistence in college (Tinto, 1987).

FACTORS THAT IMPACT AFRICAN AMERICAN MALE STUDENT ATHLETES

The literature on retention and persistence for African American male student athletes revealed several variables that factor into their ability to be successful and complete college. Endecavage (2000) found that social support was an important factor in college success for African American male student athletes. Dixon (1999) identified academic integration, social support and integration, financial assistance, and family background as key variables that influenced African American male student persistence in college. Hyatt (2001) studied the nature of the goal commitment and institutional commitment of African American male football and basketball players and discovered a number of factors that were common to that population's persistence in college, among them academic readiness, academic integration, self-motivation or personal accountability, career maturity, and institutional social integration (Hyatt, 2001). Okinaka (1991) noted the importance of social networks and relationships to the student athlete's performance in college. Person and LeNoir (1997) found that financial support, mentoring, and academic advising programs were some of the factors that African American male student athletes reported as helping them succeed in college.

Although the literature cited here identifies several barriers to persistence that are frequently the cause of students leaving college, it also presents various modes of support that assist students in persisting to the completion of their degrees (Tinto, 1993). Therefore it is important to examine the common themes or factors that were identified throughout the literature as having an impact on the retention and persistence of African American male student athletes.

Academic Support

Academic and financial support emerged as one of the most common themes in helping African American male student athletes persist in college. Comprehensive academic support programs that begin with an extensive orientation to academics and student life are the first steps on the road to success for these students (Clark & Parette, 2002; Gaston, 2003). Comprehensive support programs in general are programs that are designed to meet the needs of the "whole student." The emphasis must be shifted to emphasize the "student" in student athlete. Programs that help orient the student to academics—through interactions with faculty, campus life, and the history and traditions of the institution—and are coordinated with the academic advising and support that the student athlete receives in the athletic department provide the student athlete with a good foundation for success. Research reveals that in addition to an early orientation to academics and their roles as students, ongoing scholastic support has a positive impact on athletes' academic success. Carr (1992) examined fourth-semester persistence rates of Black male athletes and investigated the effects of athletic and academic support programs on persistence. The study showed that 100 percent of the Black male athletes involved in a highly supported basketball program persisted for four semesters.

Still relevant is Roper and McKenzie's (1988) comprehensive academic advising model for black student athletes, adapted from Douglas Heath's theoretical model of maturity. A sample of several of the initiatives suggested by the authors in their comprehensive model include ongoing assessment in years one through four, with goal setting and collaborative decision making in year one; group discussions, career counseling, and career discussion in year two; community service, independent study, and public speaking in year three; and updating of goals, leading of group discussions, internships, and living transition programs in year four. This model would provide the holistic support needed to assist the population because it outlines interventions aimed to promote student success in each academic year. The consistent academic and cocurricular support given to students throughout their career should provide them with the balance needed to complete their degrees.

Academic support can also come in the form of mentors and opportunities for peer support through study groups and collaborative learning outlets. Faculty and coaches serving as mentors can positively impact African American male student athletes' persistence (Hill, 1997). Taylor (cited in Hayes, 1996) writes that attentive instruction, high expectations, and collaborative student study have proved beneficial to students and led more of them to complete their degrees. Faculty are a very important source of academic support. Steele (cited in Hayes, 1996) suggested that one of the keys to successfully retaining students is convincing them that their instructors are allies. If students believe that they are working in partnership with their instructors and that their instructors are genuinely interested in their progress they are more likely to succeed.

Hayes (1996) described Georgetown University's high success in retaining and graduating minority students; he stated that Georgetown has an overall 92-percent graduation rate for students of color because the students were serious minded and knew that support was readily available if they needed it. John Thompson, coach at Georgetown, had a 97-percent graduation rate with his African American male student athletes, having graduated sixty-eight out of seventy students in his years as coach. Hayes attributes Thompson's success to effectively mentoring, advocating for students, helping the students to negotiate the bureaucracy, and successfully integrating the African American male student athletes into the campus without special benefits. New student athlete orientation, comprehensive academic support programs, and grade monitoring are some examples of how to begin assisting student athletes to be successful. The orientation program is important because it provides the students with an opportunity to meet their advisors early on so the advisors can outline resources to help the students be successful and can explain the students' own responsibilities in this process.

Family and Community Support

College administrators know how beneficial parental involvement and support can be to students in college. A 1997 study of African American male scholars at University of Maryland, Baltimore, reported that nearly all of the participants in the study identified the support of their mothers and other family members as instrumental in their success in college (Hrabowski, Maton, & Greif, 1998). Often the feelings of pride and encouragement from the family members give the student athletes a heightened sense of self-confidence once they arrive on campus (Figler & Figler, 1991; Gerdy, 1994). Research shows that parental encouragement has an impact on students' belief that they can attend and succeed in college. Parents actively involved in attending college fairs, going on campus visits, and engaging with coaches and school officials often help students feel more comfortable in making decisions. Ultimately this support from home can help students to be successful in college (Hyatt, 2001).

Unfortunately, the family and community can also create undue amounts of stress for the African American male student athlete by emphasizing the importance of a professional career in sports. African American male student athletes often develop unrealistic expectations about sports careers after college. Families place undue pressure on students to compete, and this is compounded by the overemphasis that coaches and schools sometimes place on these students' participation in sports (Gerdy, 2000). Edwards (1984), Funk (1991), and Harris (1989) discussed the emphasis that Black youth, along with their families, place on sports. A UCLA study found that Black families are four times as likely as White families to view their children's involvement in athletics as something that may lead to a professional sports career (Funk, 1991). Edwards (cited in Sperber, 2000) stated that the myths and stereotypes about the likelihood of success in professional sports created by the media and enhanced by the students' home experiences are often further supported by the educational system. This creates in the students a false sense of security in the anticipation of their possible career in professional sports.

Academic and Social Integration

Integration, both academically and socially, can be difficult for most first-time college students, and the added responsibility student athletes face on entering college can often be overwhelming, for a number of reasons. Yet integration is a key component in student success. There always will be student athletes who come to college academically underprepared (Clark & Partette, 2002, Leach & Conners, 1984). Lapchick (1989) discusses the inordinate amount of attention given to student athletes. Socially, the frequent isolation of student athletes at study tables, especially in high-profile sports, compounds the problems of integrating them into the campus academic community. Also, many African American male student athletes are shocked when they arrive on campus. Because they have been superstars in high school, many are surprised to find that their professors, administrators, and peers see them as "dumb jocks," which leaves them with feelings of deflated self-esteem, abandonment, and isolation (Funk, 1991). In sum, the student athlete is encouraged to perfect the athlete half of the student athlete equation while the student half suffers, leading to poor grades and a less than average academic performance. Many of these students come to campus less confident academically than their nonathlete counterparts, and the continuation of poor performance off the field just lowers their self-worth in that arena even more.

African American student athletes attending PWIs arrive on campus and see that, on average, only seven percent of the student body, three percent of the faculty, and less than five percent of the top athletics administrators and coaches look like them (Lapchick, 2001). This means limited opportunities for African American male student athletes to participate in mentorship and advisory relationships with people from similar racial backgrounds. In such an environment, they also have the same difficulty as other African American students in forming social and academic interactions with peers. However, because of the typically close relationship athletes have with other athletes and with their coaches, the lack of persons of color in those roles is particularly devastating. The athletic department and student affairs agencies need to continue to provide opportunities for student athletes to become more integrated into the life of the campus. Unfortunately, there are often obstacles that make it more difficult for African American male student athletes to become integrated into the life of the campus.

Race, Class, and Stereotypes

In addition to the many demands on their time that limit the opportunities for interaction with nonathletes, issues of race, discrimination, stress, and striving to meet unrealistic expectations make the college experience particularly difficult for many African American male student athletes and can affect their ability to interface with other students, faculty, and administrators. Tracey and Sedlacek (1985) and Fleming (1984) regarded racist experiences in college as one of the main explanatory variables accounting for differences in academic performance, social and psychological adjustment, and levels of involvement between minorities and non-minorities on college campuses. The detrimental effects of race and class issues for many student athletes heighten their sense of disillusionment and isolation on campus. In the worst case, student athletes stop out or drop out of school completely because of their inability to withstand the pressure of how they are perceived racially (Berry, 2002). Smedley, Meyers, and Harrell (1993) regarded experiences of racism and discrimination on campus as psychological and sociocultural stressors, which could lead to the maladjustment of minority students.

In addition to dealing with the psychological and sociocultural stressors, African American male student athletes have to combat the myths and stereotypes commonly held by members of the campus community that they are less intelligent, more violent, and poor. Lapchick (2001) states that the media is persistent in portraying basketball and football players, many of whom are African American, as more violent than student athletes in other sports or in society as a whole. The author states that most of the stories written about athletes who are violent in general or violent toward women in particular are about African American athletes and that reinforces the racial stereotypes so prevalent in society.

In Lapchick (2001), a former quarterback for Syracuse University recounted instances in which he encountered racial stereotypes as an African American male student athlete. He stated that most students assumed that he was poor and that football was going to make him rich; however, like many other Blacks on campus, he was middle class and the child of two professionals. He stated that although he played football at a time when being a Black quarterback was more acceptable, the stereotypes still remained: as a player, people still remembered him as a great runner and very athletic, but not as a great strategist or thinker as most people characterize White quarterbacks. The reality of his background and his leadership accomplishments had not altered their image of the physical rather than intelligent Black athlete.

Hill (1997) states that there is a relationship between successful mentoring and the racial background of coaches and their players. However, because of the racism prevalent in hiring practices and what he terms "the old boy network," the possibility of there being more Black coaches is still slim because they do not get the coaching jobs. Therefore, hiring practices also begin to indirectly affect African American male student athletes, because mentoring—a means of support that has been proven effective in aiding retention—is not actualized for them.

These are examples of a wide variety of factors that may aid or inhibit African American male student athletes' persistence in college. This population has a diversity of needs to be met. Because of their participation in sports they appear to be involved in the life of the college at a higher rate than other students, yet they face many of the aforementioned obstacles, which may impair their ability to be successful. Therefore, it is necessary to identify and implement programs and services aimed at retaining this population.

EXAMPLES OF BENEFICIAL PROGRAMS AND PRACTICES

Comprehensive programs to assist in acclimation to the campus community and to make appropriate adjustments academically, socially, and programmatically provide all students with the tools that can be used to be successful in college. Initiatives specific to student athletes with regards to orientation, advising, and community building are provided to give examples of beneficial programs and practices for working with this population.

COMPREHENSIVE ADVISING AND ORIENTATION PROGRAMS

Comprehensive orientation and advising programs introduce student athletes to the resources and personnel on campus in and out of the athletic department. Successful programs give student athletes the opportunity to meet their peers and faculty and successfully merge their academic and athletic worlds. These programs have the potential to be most successful when the student affairs staff and athletic department staff work collaboratively in design and implementation. The Challenging Athletes' Minds for Personal Success (CHAMPS) program is an example of a program aimed at retaining student athletes. Started in 1991, the program's goals are to support the intellectual growth of each student athlete and to promote life skills and personal success. The CHAMPS program has been instituted at 127 NCAA Division 1 institutions and has reportedly had some positive impact on student success in college. CHAMPS has been successful and will continue to have relevancy because of the program's emphasis on supporting the growth and development of the whole student. The goals of academic excellence, career development, respect for diversity, and involvement in community service as well as athletic excellence provide the students with the holistic foundation to persist in college.

Fairfield University in Connecticut offers its student athletes a comprehensive support program focusing on academics. In addition to the traditional academic support components, such as grade monitoring, tutoring, and study hall, they offer the Skills To Achieve Growth and Success (STAGS) program, to provide opportunities for personal and social development through community service experiences and career exploration. The program focuses on helping student athletes to be successful through the use of time management and organizational techniques, as well as providing them with exposure to methods of note taking, test taking, critical thinking, research, technology, and career development.

Another example of a successful intervention is Florida State University's multi-tiered support program for their student athletes. The program provides academic support, including a tutorial program, a dedicated study hall, a mentoring program, and an academic honors and awards component.

All in all, providing comprehensive support programs can aid in the retention of student athletes. Therefore, programs that emphasize early intervention, comprehensive orientation, mentoring, and academic support should help them persist.

Building Community: Sharing Best Practices

Another method for developing programs and services to increase African American male student athletes' persistence in college is to model programs and services that have aided other populations. We know there are issues unique to this population, but this should not stop practitioners from trying to adapt aspects of successful programs when working with this population. Benton (2001) suggests that staff at PWIs look to historically Black colleges and universities (HBCUs) for best practices in retaining students of color. There are aspects of some retention programs in place at HBCUs that can be generalized and implemented at PWIs. Program components that are transferable to students at PWIs include mentoring models, student events, and social outlets, and the creation of connections with the African American community near the institution. Some examples of community outreach programs that take HBCU students into nearby African American communities are Benedict College in South Carolina, Grambling State University in Louisiana, and North Carolina Central University in North Carolina; each partnered with the Technology Opportunities program, providing opportunities for their students to go into the surrounding communities and bring technological equipment, expertise, and training to the area residents. The program provides important technological resources to communities that need them while giving the students an opportunity to connect with the local African American community and give back.

Interestingly, in contrast to racial conflicts prevalent throughout higher education, African American male student athletes often report that race is not an issue in their team community. A suggestion would be to look at the athletic programs producing students who report positive experiences with regards to race and to then develop programs for the general student population (St. John, 2000). For African American male student athletes to persist, it is vital that academic affairs, student affairs, and athletic departments collaborate and share resources to develop programs for students.

CONCLUSION

The ability of African American male student athletes to successfully obtain a college degree is contingent on many factors. This population may encounter several factors that may aid or inhibit their progress toward degree completion. On a positive note, the structure of many Division I athletic departments provides comprehensive academic support services. Orientation programs, tutoring, mentoring, and financial support are all shown to benefit African American male student athletes, thereby assisting them in their pursuit of a college degree. On the other hand, there are issues that inhibit these students from being successful. African American male student athletes, recruited mainly for their athletic prowess, may arrive on campus academically underprepared, which can lead to poor performance in the classroom. Because they are in the spotlight on the field, they also find themselves in the spotlight in the classroom; performing below average in that setting can lead to diminished self-confidence and the inability to see themselves as successful. Negative stereotypes and perceptions visited upon these students by faculty and peers often add more stress. Given the myriad of challenges facing this population during their college experience, educators must explore ways to improve their retention and increase their graduation rate.

As early as during the recruiting stage, before the student is enrolled at the university, coaches and administrators should outline what the university expects of the student athlete as a *student*. It is vital for coaches or recruiters to explain verbally to African American athletes their responsibilities and obligations as college students, but this must be reinforced through ongoing efforts. Creating a pamphlet or including a section in a recruitment video outlining the academic and cocurricular aspects of being a student athlete are effective ways of doing so. Continued collaboration between the athletic department and faculty—such as mid-semester monitoring reports, joint academic advisor training, advisor handbooks that provide advisors with contacts and resources in both athletic and academic departments—can benefit the student athletes through the departments that serve them.

More coaches, faculty, administrators, and staff of color should be employed to provide African American male student athletes with more role models and potential sources for mentoring relationships. Athletic departments should also rely on their African American male student athlete alumni as a resource, using them as guest speakers, mentors, and career connections. African American male athletes should be charged with getting involved in the life of the campus outside of the athletic arena.

Given the time commitment that athletes must make to their sport, it should be required of athletic departments to create off-season opportunities for community service, research, or cocurricular endeavors. For example, at the University of Louisville, student athletes have an opportunity to give back to the surrounding community through the CardsCARE (Community Action Response Effort) program. U of L student athletes, along with coaches, administrators, and staff members, volunteer their time with many organizations in an effort to assist the community. In 2004, a total of 5,475 hours were donated to the greater Louisville community, reaching over twenty thousand individuals (University of Louisville, 2005). Partnerships among campus service organizations, activities offices, and academic departments are paramount to the success of this initiative.

Because emphasis may be placed on a career in professional sports, career education should be developed for this population, specifically aimed at continuing nonprofessional careers that use their sports expertise. African American male student athletes should be given opportunities to explore sports-related careers such as entertainment law, physical therapy, journalism, or sports writing. This would allow the students to make the connection between the love of sports and the necessity of completing a degree to take advantage of the many career opportunities in the field, not just *on* the field.

Those of us who are practitioners in educational institutions have a mission: to create an environment that is conducive to helping all students be successful. That includes helping African American male student athletes to work to the best of their ability in all areas of their campus life and to use the resources provided to assist them in being successful—and to challenge the institution when it seems that those resources are nowhere to be found.

References

Adler, P., & Adler, P. (1991). *Backboards and blackboards: College athletics and role engulfment.* New York: Columbia University Press.

American Institutes for Research (AIR). (1989, March). *The experiences of Black intercollegiate athletes at NCAA Division I institutions* (Report No. 3). Palo Alto, CA: Center for the Study of Athletics.

Arno, K. S., (1990). A descriptive study of how student-athletes perceive the use of study skills as they relate to success in college and beyond. Dissertation Abstracts International, 50(12), Publication No. 9312145.

Barbalias, P. (2004). Black student-athletes: Improving their collegiate experience. Retrieved Dec. 4, 2004 from http://www.uvm.edu/~vtconn/v17/barbalias.html.

Benton, M. A. (2001). Challenges African American Students face at predominantly White institutions. [On-line]. Retrieved Dec. 4, 2004 from http://www.colostate.edu/Depts/SAHE/JOURNAL2/2001/Challenges.htm.

Berry, R. D. (2002). Athletic commodities: The African American male student athlete in higher education. Dissertation Abstracts International, 62(11), University Microfilms No. AAT 3031407.

Bowen, W. G., & Levin, S. A. (2003). Reclaiming the game: College sports and educational values. Princeton, NJ: Princeton.

Brice, B.E.G. (1992). A study of persistence of freshman males at two historically Black institutions of higher education. Dissertation Abstracts International, A54(01), p. 35.

Campbell, L. (2004). The real March Madness is in poor academic record of athletes. Knight Ridder newspapers. Retrieved Dec. 4, 2004 from www.highbeam.com/library/doc1.asp?ctrlInfo.

Carr, P. (1992). College success and the Black male. Research report no. 138. San Jose, CA: San Jose State University, Evergreen Community College District.

Clark, M., & Parette, P. (2002, March). Student athletes with learning disabilities: a model for effective supports. College Student Journal.

Dixon, J. C. (1999). A qualitative study of perceptions of external factors that influence the persistence of Black males at a predominantly White four-year state college. Doctoral dissertation, Columbia University Teachers College. Retrieved from http://www.pvc.maricopa.edu/~lsche/resources/dissertation.htm.

Edwards, H. (1984). The Black "dumb jock": An American sports tragedy. College Board Review, 131, 8–13.

Endecavage, C. (2000). The role of internal attribution and social support in the college success of African American males. Dissertation Abstracts International A60(12), p. 4339.

Figler, S. K., & Figler, H. E. (1991). Going the distance: The college athlete's guide to excellence on the field and in the classroom. Princeton, NJ: Princeton.

Fleming, J. (1984). Blacks in college: A comparison study of students' success in black and white institutions. San Francisco, CA: Jossey-Bass.

Funk, G. (1991). Major violation: The unbalanced priorities in athletics and academics. Champaign, IL: Leisure Press.

Gaston, J. L. (2003). A study of student athletes' motivation toward sports and academics. *Dissertation Abstracts International, A63*(07), Publication No. AAT 3059248.

Gerdy, J. (1994). Restoring trust in higher education: Athletics' role. *College Board Review, 170,* Winter 1993/1994.

Gerdy, J. R. (2000, April 27). Counterpoint: Slam dunk is not life's ultimate experience. *Black Issues in Higher Education.*

Greene, H., & Greene, M. (2001, October). The true cost of collegiate athletics-From our perspective. *Matrix: The Magazine for Leaders in Education.* Retrieved December 28,2005, from http://www.findarticles.com/p/articles/mi_m0HJE/is_5_2/ai-79961355.

Hale, J. A. (1999). The effects of personal background and psychosocial variables on student-athletes' academic performance and retention at Black private colleges. *Dissertation Abstracts International, A60*(02), Publication No. AAT 9920418.

Harris, O. (1989). Sport and race: A comparison of the social and academic worlds of Black and White student athletes. *Dissertation Abstracts International,* A50–07, University Microfilms No. AAT 8924161.

Hawkins, B. J. (1995). Examining the experiences of Black and White student athletes at predominately White division I NCAA institutions using an internal colonial model. *Dissertation Abstracts International,* A56–06, University Microfilms No. AAT 9536202.

Hayes, D. W. (1996). Balancing the ball. *Black Issues in Higher Education, 12*(3), 24–26.

Heath, D. (1977). Maturity and competence: *A transcultural view.* New York: Gardner.

Hill, O. F. (1997). Examining the barriers restricting employment opportunities relative to the perceptions of African-American football coaches at NCAA Division I-A colleges and universities. *Dissertation Abstracts International, A58*(08), 3036.

Hoberman, J. (1997). *Darwin's athletes: How sport has damaged Black America and preserved the myth of race.* New York: Houghton Mifflin.

Hrabowski III, F. A., Maton, K. I., & Greif, G. L. (1998). *Beating the odds: Raising academically successful African American males.* New York: Oxford University Press.

Hyatt, R. (2001). Commitment to degree attainment among African American intercollegiate athletes. *Dissertation Abstracts International, 62*(12), AAT 3035666.

Institute for Diversity and Ethics in Sport. (2004). *Analysis of the 2004 NCAA Graduation Rates Report,* University of Central Florida, Orlando.

Lapchick, R. E. (1988). The student athlete. *New Perspectives, 19*(1), 35–45.

Lapchick, R. E. (1989). Future of the Black student athlete: Ethical issue of the 1990s. *Educational Record, 70*(2), 32–35.

Lapchick, R. E. (2001). *Smashing barriers: Race and sport in the millennium.* Lanham, MD: Madison.

Leach, B., & Conners, B. (1984). Pygmalion on the gridiron: The black student-athlete in a white university. In A. Shriberg & F. Brodzinski (Eds.), *Rethinking services for college athletes* (pp. 31–49). San Francisco, CA: Jossey-Bass.

Murray, M. A. (1997, December). The counseling needs of college student-athletes. *Dissertation Abstracts International, A58*(06), Publication No. AAT 9737427.

National Center for Education Statistics. (1994). *Digest of Educational Statistics,* U.S. Department of Education Office of Educational Research and Improvement.

National Collegiate Athletic Association. (2004, October). *Graduation-Rates Reports.* Indianapolis: National Collegiate Athletic Association.

Okinaka, A. O. (1991). Social factors influencing the academic performance of student-athletes at Indiana University. *Dissertation Abstracts International, 52*(03), Publication No. 9122811.

Pascarella, E. T., & Smart, J. C. (1991). Impact of intercollegiate athletic participation for African American and Caucasian men: Some further evidence. *Journal of College Student Development, 32,* 123–130.

Person, D. R., & LeNoir, K. M. (1997). Retention issues and models for African American male athletes. In M. J. Cuyjet (Ed.), *Helping African American males succeed in college* (pp. 79–91). San Francisco, CA: Jossey-Bass.

Ridpath, B. D. (2002). NCAA Division I student athlete characteristics as indicators of academic achievement and graduation from college. *Dissertation Abstracts International, 63*(06), Publication No. AAT 3055939.

Rivas-Quinones, L. A. (2003). Career maturity exploration and identity foreclosure of student athletes. *Dissertation Abstracts International, 64*(03), Publication No. AAT 3083247.

Roper, L. D., & McKenzie, A. (1988, Winter). Academic advising: A developmental model for Black student-athletes. *NASPA Journal, 26*(2), 91–98.

Schulman, J. L., & Bowen, W. G. (2001). *The Game of Life: College sports and educational values.* Princeton, New Jersey: Princeton.

Smedley, B. D., Meyers, H. F., & Harrell, S. P. (1993). Minority student stresses and college adjustment of ethnic minority freshmen. *Journal of Higher Education, 64,* 434–452.

Snyder, P. L. (1996). Comparative levels of expressed academic motivation among Anglo and African American university student athletes. *Journal of Black Studies, 26*(6), 651–667.

Sperber, M. (2000). *Beer and circus: How big time college sports is crippling American higher education.* New York: Henry Holt.

St. John, E. (2000, May 11). Level playing fields? *Black Issues in Higher Education, 17*(6), 16–17.

Suggs, W. (2005, January 21). At its convention, NCAA preaches fiscal restraint and academic rigor. *Chronicle of Higher Education.*

Tinto, V. (1987). *Leaving college: Rethinking the causes and cures of student attrition.* Chicago: University of Chicago Press.

Tinto, V. (1993). *Leaving college: Rethinking the causes and cures of student attrition* (2nd ed.). Chicago: University of Chicago Press.

Towers, C. (2004, January 8). College football: Graduation rates: An "F" for the course diversity study: 27 of 56 bowl teams graduate less than half their players. *Atlanta Journal Constitution.*

Tracey, T. J., & Sedlacek, W. E. (1985). The relationship of non-cognitive variables to academic success: A longitudinal comparison by race. *Journal of College Student Personnel, 26,* 405–410.

University of Louisville, Athletics Department. (2005). CardsCARE. Retrieved Dec. 4, 2004 from http://uoflsports.collegesports.com/genrel/081501aab.html.

Walter, J. C. (1996). The changing status of the Black athlete in 20th century United States. Retrieved Dec. 4, 2004 from http://www.johncarlos.com/walters.htm.

Wiggins, D. K. (1991). Prized performers, but frequently overlooked students: The involvement of Black athletes in intercollegiate sports on predominately White university campuses, 1890–1972. *Research Quarterly, American Alliance for Health, Physical Education and Recreation, 62,* 164–177.

Wiggins, D. K. (1998). The future of college athletics is at stake: Black athletes and racial turmoil on three predominantly white university campuses 1968–1972. *Journal of Sport History, 15,* 304–333.

CHAPTER NINE

AFRICAN AMERICAN GAY MEN

Another Challenge for the Academy

Jamie Washington, The Washington Consulting Group

Vernon A. Wall, The Washington Consulting Group

The topics of same-sex love, homosexuality, men who have sex with men, and bisexuality are historically "don't ask, don't tell" in the African American community. Although most African Americans know of a cousin, aunt, uncle, sister, brother, teacher, pastor, choir director, or barber who "messes around" or "has a special friend," these topics are often given little serious attention in dominant culture (heterosexual) conversations. Most of the literature on sexual orientation in America estimates that 10 to 20 percent of the population would identify as gay, lesbian, or bisexual (Human Rights Campaign, 2004; Mondimore, 1996; Kennedy, 1988). If one accepts these numbers, we must consider what this means for African American men in higher education.

In this chapter we address the impact of identity development, religion, finding of role models, and self naming on the experiences of gay and bisexual men of African descent (GBMAD). We explore issues and challenges related to having two subordinated identities and the influence of religion on gay, lesbian, bisexual, transgender (GLBT) issues. We also suggest some possible campus supports and programs. Since there is very little written about the experiences of same-gender loving men of African descent in higher education, we draw from other bodies of literature to inform this writing.

Understanding of Sexual Orientation Identity Development for GLBT Persons

Gay and bisexual men of African descent (GBMAD), like most college students, have very little scholarly understanding of sexuality and sexual orientation. Hence, many GBMAD are carrying the same misinformation and missing information about sexuality as their heterosexual counterparts. Some GBMAD believe they were "born that way"; others believe they are gay because of an absent father or strong mother or sexual assault as a child. There are no conclusive data on the cause of sexual orientation, and the lack of information for persons questioning or exploring their same-sex attraction can contribute greatly to identity confusion and the absence of self-esteem.

A fair amount has been written about homosexual identity formation (Cass, 1979, 1983, 1984; Lee, 1977; Plummer, 1975; Troiden, 1989; Savin-Williams, 1990, 1995, 1998; Fassinger, 1998), but most of these theories were developed based on the experiences of White gay men and later women. Thus the dynamic of another subordinated identity impacting the developmental process is not considered in these models to any great extent, if at all.

That being said, the basis of most of these models is similar. These theories posit a general process of moving from identity confusion, to exploration and comparison, to tolerance, deepening commitment, and acceptance. Although most of these are linear stage models, they do provide a basis for understanding some of the experiences a same-gender loving person may have.

For GBMAD, these models lack the complexity of the race or religion intersection, thus making them only partially useful. Let us look, however, at the four basic stages. In the first stage, usually depicted as one of identity confusion, GBMAD are not only dealing with the confusion as it relates to their attraction to other men, but what that means for them in the context of the Black community, the church, and the eyes of God. Issues that arise at this stage for GBMAD can keep them in denial of their true feelings for years.

Without a supportive environment in which to deal with these inter-sections, these men are at a loss and often remain silent and afraid.

The second stage is that of exploration. In this stage the person is exploring his feelings and attractions through interactions with others. If this person does not have access to a GBMAD community, he is not likely to find safety in the heterosexual African American community, thus leaving him to find his way amidst the racism often present in largely White gay communities. These spaces can often feel isolating and disconnected for two main reasons. First, in the larger White gay community there is often less space to engage and explore Christian concepts or other strong religious beliefs. Second, the discussion of race is often minimized by a pseudo-understanding of all oppression because of one's status as a sexual minority.

Failure to overcome the challenges faced in the first two stages makes it really difficult for students to move to the last two stages of deepening commitment and identity synthesis. The general frus-tration and confusion in the first two stages of identity development in GBMAD can cause them to delay "coming out" until after col-lege. Identity synthesis occurs when one's sexual orientation becomes an integral part of one's being. This entire process is informed by the availability of role models and other supports and whether or not they are present and accessible to GBMAD students.

Much of the writing that has been done on racial identity development gives little attention to the impact of sexual orienta-tion on that process (Cross, 1971, 1995; Helms, 1994, 1995). Although this information is quite useful and important on its own, there is an inherent assumption of heterosexuality. The psychoso-cial developmental process of a subordinated race identity is con-founded when you add to it the psychosocial developmental process of a subordinated sexual orientation identity.

Listen to these voices, from interviews with students at the Baltimore Gay Community Center:

Student One

I grew up in this hood in Baltimore. I have lived with Black people all of my life. I went to school with all Black people and I get teased sometimes because I was feminine. When I got ready to go to college I was so glad so I could get away from my neighborhood. People would whisper and call me names sometimes, but those same boys were trying to talk to me when they were by themselves or I was sitting on the steps alone late at night. I guess most people knew I was gay, but didn't talk about it except with my gay friends. When I got to college, with all these White people, I didn't know what to do. I really wanted to party with other gay people, but I couldn't find anybody Black. The White gays were too "queeny" for me and besides there was few Blacks on campus, especially men. What would they say about me hanging around with White gay people?

Student Two

I went to private school. While I grew up my family still lived in a Black urban area. My school was predominantly White. I was the president of the Black Student Society at my private high school and I was at the top of my class. There were several people who questioned my sexuality but I just let them keep guessing. I fell in love with this wonderful Jewish boy and we kept our secret pretty well. By the time I got to college, because I interacted so well with everyone, I was not interested in hanging out with just Black people. I got seen as snotty, stuck-up, and gay. I made some friends in the gay alliance and started attending their meetings and social functions. This was fine, but I really had a hard time not being as accepted amongst Blacks, especially men.

Student Three

I went to a public school in rural North Carolina. I spent my high school years as the "asexual student leader," participating in clubs and organizations rather than having close personal relationships with my classmates. I was afraid that they would learn of my secret desires for other boys. When I arrived at college, I saw that there was a distinct separation between the African American and the Gay Community. How was I to choose? As a result, I stay in the "invisible middle," becoming involved in campus leadership positions but not connecting with either community. I would attend events in each community but never really stayed around long enough to develop relationships or close friendships.

These three men, all of whom attended predominantly White institutions (PWIs), illustrate some of the identity challenges facing GBMAD. The first two young men came from similar socioeconomic backgrounds. However, the influence of private education on Student Two made his experience at college different. Although Student Three came from a higher socioeconomic background, there were some similarities in his words with the thoughts conveyed by the other two. His experiences were informed by his connection or lack of connection to his communities.

ROLE MODELS

Finding role models and mentors for college men of African descent is challenging regardless of sexual orientation or gender identity and expression. Many students can go through their entire college experience without significant contact with an African American man in a leadership position, such as a member of the faculty, administration, or staff. Given the pressures that many African American men feel to be everything for everybody, those who identify as GBT are less likely to be willing to take the risk of being "out' and identified as both Black and gay, thus leaving students who are looking for role models at a disadvantage. Students often know who the "suspected' gay faculty or administrators are. The message that is sent by their inability to be "out" is that it's not okay to be gay and professional. Thus, most African American men have only White gay men as examples. This is not to say that mentoring cannot happen across race, gender, and sexual orientation; however, the experience is not the same.

For gay and bisexual men, an unspoken tension exists for both the students and, particularly, the staff or faculty member. Given the assumptions and stereotypes of gays as predators and recruiters, many professionals feel at risk to connect with students for fear of being accused of inappropriate behavior. The other very real risk is that if the student has never had a supportive relationship with an adult African American male, the support could be misinterpreted, putting the faculty or staff member in a difficult situation. One might ask how this is different from a heterosexual person in the same situation with a student. The simple answer is that there is a culture that allows for this dilemma to be dealt with in a fairly open way between heterosexuals. When it is between two persons of the same sex, the dynamics are not as comfortable to address and there are generally no systems in place to support both the faculty or staff person and the student. All of these issues impact how a man comes to see and name himself. Thus, some discussion about naming and labels is warranted.

Labels and Naming

College is a time in which self-identity and the politics that surround identity are often explored. How a man names himself is important. One of the issues facing a man of African descent with a homosexual or bisexual orientation is how he names himself and then how he becomes seen and named by others. Lesbian, gay, and bisexual persons of African descent continue to face the questions "Who are you first?" and "Are you Black first or gay first?"

Constantine-Simms (2001) identified two ways in which self-naming and group affiliation occurs. African American identified gays (AAIG) are those whose primary connection is within the African American community. These men look for opportunities to be fully embraced within the African American community, and they are clear that race is the more salient identity. AAIGs tend to be involved in Black student organizations, attend primarily Black functions, participate in Black religious experiences, and, in some cases, allow ambiguity about their sexual orientation. These men are not as likely to participate in gay organizations or activities without a really strong reason to do so. These men care most about how they are seen in the Black community; how they are seen in the heterosexual White or gay community is not as important to them.

Gay identified African Americans (GIAA) are more connected to their sexual orientation's identity group. This group of men often does not feel welcome in the Black community. They find themselves not as comfortable in discussion around race because of the heterosexist assumptions that often inform those conversations. At PWIs these men may be involved in the Gay Student Alliance or simply attend gay functions. They are likely to be "out" as resident assistants or student leaders, whereas their counterpart AAIGs are more likely to leave their sexual orientation unspoken. These two major categories represent the backdrop for looking at the experiences and issues of GBMAD. The other major factors one must consider are class, religion, and gender identity and expression.

It is very common for GBMAD to not feel attached or connected to the labels of gay or bisexual, because the political and cultural agendas associated with these labels often are more White and middle class than those of the Black community and not as religiously focused. For this reason some GBMAD may not identify with any label; others may name themselves as heterosexuals who "mess around" on the side. Another popular term among GBMAD is *same-gender loving*; in smaller liberal arts communities some GBMAD also choose the term *queer.* Although this term is not one traditionally accepted by African American gays and lesbians, there is a population of younger, middle- and upper-class GBMAD who find the term acceptable. What a person names himself is less important than the support he needs to move through the naming and renaming process.

Some men are more comfortable identifying as bisexual, even if they are sexually involved exclusively with men. The label of bisexual is an easier sell in some spaces in the Black community than the identification as gay. This brings us to a discussion of the currently popular term used in Black and Latino communities: *DL,* or *the down low.* This term describes gay men who are not "stereotypically gay" and therefore could pass for heterosexual. These men are more often than not involved with women to some extent, and their involvement with men is not shared with their female partners. Unfortunately, men "on the DL" don't often find the space to develop healthy sexual orientation identities. This is not a new issue. There is no research to support that there are currently more men on the DL than at other times in history; however, the Internet has made it easier for these men to find each other. Unfortunately, most of the popular attention that has been paid to the DL phenomenon has been negative. Men on the DL are being blamed for the spread of HIV and AIDS among African American women. This dynamic alone has served only to push these men further into silence. The blame is misplaced. Although each individual has to accept responsibility for what he does, we live in a culture that makes it unsafe for men who are bisexual to tell the truth.

Finally, the construction of masculine and feminine identity is also a factor that impacts how GBMAD see and name themselves. The construction of masculine identity within the Black community, although not as rigid as thirty years ago, is still centered on traditional male stereotypes. Strong men, according to such stereotypes, do not show their emotions, carry on the family name, are good financial providers, are athletic, are conquerors of women, and are not afraid to fight" (Katz, 2000). These expectations are strongly encouraged and reinforced in some households and communities. The extent to which a man finds his identity connected to these gender expectations will also inform how he identifies.

THE IMPACTS OF CLASS IDENTIFICATION AND CAMPUS COMMUNITY

The dynamics of social and economic class are important to consider as we examine the experience of being a GBMAD. Many GBMAD from poor, working-class backgrounds in urban settings are likely to be more connected to a Black gay community than those from middle-class urban or rural areas. Thus, seeing others like them and being accepted within a Black context may have an impact on how they identify. The urban middle-class or rural Black man may have only experienced a level of acceptance for all of who he is in a White gay context, not ever knowing Black acceptance; this affects how he identifies.

The intersection of race and economic class is an important dynamic to understand when discussing the experiences of GBMAD. As the African American middle class grows and more families move into predominantly White communities and schools, the context of identification shifts. Acceptance into the predominantly White community is often the focus. This behavior of blending into the predominantly White culture is sometimes modeled by parents and other family members, thus adding another level of complexity to the experience of identity development as the young man enters higher education.

For many college students, engaging the topic and dynamics of race are new. Most students come to college underprepared to have honest dialogue about issues of race. This is primarily due to lack of experience in real discussion. Thus the race politics that show up at PWIs are often challenging even for those who have come from integrated experiences. There are many dynamics that impact a person's sense of community in this campus environment. However, most people would agree that a comfortable community is a place in which you feel at home. For many African American gay, bisexual, and transgender men, finding community can be a real challenge. The identity development process described earlier will have a major impact on a person's experience, but one must consider the context and community in which the person is moving through the developmental process.

Students of color quickly learn that they are being given a "race test" by their own community that can have a profound impact on how they move through the social environment at college. Thus, GBMAD may have to think about things in new, unfamiliar ways. Like all students, finding a place where they matter and can feel at home is important. Navigating a campus climate where race and sexual orientation politics are not aligned is often very challenging for the GBMAD.

RELIGIOUS IMPACT

One aspect of the race test often involves religion. Are the GBMAD's religious views, understandings, and practices more traditionally "Black" (that is, born-again Christian fellowship, church attendance every Sunday, gospel music, services of at least two hours, and a fairly fundamentalist view of the Bible) or more "White" (that is, more Christian in a broad sense, room for other belief systems, fairly calm worship experiences, services of no more than an hour, and a less strict adherence to biblical teachings)? To understand the experiences of this population, one must carefully consider the intersection of race, religion, and sexual orientation for GBMAD.

Most GBMAD who attend PWIs face the challenge of needing to choose to connect their race, religious, or sexual orientation communities. Although these are not distinct things, they are often seen as separate. The issue of religion is always present in the Black community. Traditional religions such as Islam and Christianity have a major influence in the Black community, even if individual members do not participate or practice. Given that these two religious traditions in general do not bless same-sex relationships, the extent to which a man is connected to these faith communities can have a major impact on how he identifies. GBMAD who were raised in the traditional Black church are likely to have gotten some messages that it would not be okay to connect to the LGBT community on campus. Men without the strong religious messages may struggle with the dilemma of either connecting with an almost completely White LGBT campus community or connecting with an often homophobic or at least nonembracing and nonaffirming African American community. The importance of religious affiliation in the African American community, as long as it is Christian or Islam, is pretty well accepted and entrenched; all others are suspect. However, in the LGBT communities, there is often a silencing of one's religious belief, particularly if it is Christian, given the nonsupportive messages that have come from some of the Christian church leadership.

Although more religious denominations—particularly Christian ones—are becoming open and affirming of LGBT persons, most of those denominations are predominantly White. For GBMAD who are used to participating in a traditional Black church, this option is often not sufficient. There are some African American congregations that are open and affirming of same-sex loving persons, but they are hard to find and most people give up the search. The impact of this void cannot be overstated. For many African Americans, the church is their very foundation. For a person who has had the Black church community as home for most of his life, not having that place of support, comfort, and community is a major loss.

For GBMAD at nonpublic HBCUs, the challenge is magnified by the strong religiously based spoken and unspoken rules that inform behavior, values, practice, and the very culture on many of these campuses. Until the mid-1990s, the number of HBCUs with recognized LGBT student organizations could be counted on one hand. Although LGBT students are on these campuses—and often a very visible presence—they have not found institutional and community support to express themselves fully.

An additional impact of religion on GBMAD is the effect of the subtle (or not-so-subtle) message regarding HIV and AIDS in the Black church. For many years, from pulpits all over the country, came the message that AIDS is God's punishment to the homosexual community. Although this message has quieted somewhat, the residual impact has endured. The parents of today's college students and the students themselves have grown up hearing these messages in the church. Very little has been done to address the impact of such a damaging message. As an example, between 1999 and 2004, there was an increase in HIV and AIDS diagnoses among young people between the ages of 18 and 25 (CDC, 2004). Many of these young people suffered in silence because of guilt and shame that they carried as a direct result of the messages about God's punishment. Their level of guilt, shame, and despair often resulted in low self-esteem, deep depression, self-destructive behavior, and even suicide.

Whenever we engage in conversation about sexual orientation, particularly in the African American community, religion will surface. This conversation is never an easy one—hence, most people simply choose not to have it. This conversation must be considered with much patience and care, given the level of conservatism in Black religious communities. There are those who are perfectly content to live with inconsistent and incongruent religious beliefs. Because the Black community is largely Christian or Christian-influenced, interpretation of what the Bible says about homosexuality is where the discussion starts—and, more often than not, comes to a screeching halt.

Those who wish to engage folks on biblical issues should do their homework and be prepared for some disagreement (Boykin, 1996). However, if people are at least willing to have a conversation, there is potential for increased understanding and respect. Much writing has been done on the Bible and homosexuality. Some key writings include *Sexuality and the Black Church: A Womanist Perspective* by Kelly Brown Douglas (1999), *What the Bible Really Says About Homosexuality* by Daniel Helminiak (2000), *The Good Book* by Peter Gomes (1996); there are many others. These are useful resources for gaining a more comprehensive understanding of these issues.

It is important to note that this conversation has been going on for a long time, and it will not end in one setting. Helping students, faculty, staff, community, and, in this situation, family stay engaged is a part of the ongoing challenge for those struggling to reconcile these issues.

PROVIDING SUPPORT IN A CHALLENGING ENVIRONMENT:

We have talked about identity, community, religion, role models, and naming. All of these dynamics inform the experiences of GBMAD. We would like to offer a few suggestions for creating supportive environments for these students. All faculty, staff, and students need to be prepared to see the LGBT community as more than White and nonreligious, and the Black community as more than heterosexual. This must start with our admissions and recruitment staff and include all who may interact with GBMAD throughout their relationship with the institution. The following suggestions may minimize the division between race and sexual orientation and help to provide support in often challenging environments.

- When sharing opportunities for involvement with new students, mention the LGBT student organization to everyone.
- When students come to campus for the Black student overnight, make sure the LGBT student association is notified and encouraged to participate and serve as a host.
- When selecting and training orientation leaders, prepare them for the diversity in the Black and the gay communities.
- Hire openly gay and lesbian students, faculty, and staff of color who represent their diversity.
- Train resident assistants, program board members, student government representatives, and other organization leaders to think more broadly about the Black and the gay communities.
- Work with the athletic department to identify, at a minimum, one person to whom GBMAD athletes can go for support.
- Work with faith communities to do work that explores and engages sexual orientation issues.
- Work with the LGBT student organization to make sure that during the awareness week or month celebration the diversity of the community is represented.
- Work with the Black Student Union and others planning for Black History month events to include the diversity as it relates to sexual orientation in the program.
- Work with faculty in African American studies, women's studies, and religious, psychology, and LGBT studies to be inclusive of student diversity in the readings, examples, and potential projects.
- Work with the alumni association to identify LGBT persons of color to serve as role models, mentors, and supports for students.

This list is not comprehensive by any means, and there are many other things to be considered before trying to implement a program. This list is designed to generate some thought about ways that we can begin to create a more supportive community for GBMAD.

ADDITIONAL GBMAD TOPICS FOR EXPLORATION

This chapter focused on sexual orientation of African American men, but not all of the various aspects of that topic could be explored in this brief treatment of the subject. Among numerous other issues for GBMAD, the experience of transgender persons in the African American community needs much attention. Although some campuses across the country are developing policies and procedures for addressing issues and concerns for transgender persons, little, if any, of the work has taken into consideration the particular needs of transgender African American men. This is a topic for further research and discussion.

The diversity of ethnicities amongst GBMAD could also use further exploration. Although the experiences of immigrants from Africa and different regions of the Caribbean may be similar in the context of race to that of African Americans, there are culture dynamics that make these experiences very different and, in some cases, even more delicate. These differences should also be explored as programs and trainings are being developed.

CONCLUSION

In this chapter we have attempted to focus attention on the impact of sexual orientation on the experiences of men of African descent. We have addressed the issues of racial and sexual orientation identity development and the complexities present when one's racial and sexual orientation identities are historically oppressed. We also discussed the impact of religion on homosexuality for African American men. To achieve real understanding of and support for GBMAD, we must not understate the role of religion in their lives.

Finally, the process of identifying role models and self-naming by African American gay and bisexual men was discussed, and we suggested potential strategies for minimizing challenges and increasing supports for GBMAD. We hope to have demonstrated that for the experiences of GBMAD to reach their full potential, they must be able to find positive role models and safe spaces in the college or university community to explore issues such as naming, dating, sex, religion, and race.

References

Boykin, K. (1996). *One more river to cross: Black and gay in America.* New York: Bantam Doubleday Dell.

Cass, V. C. (1979). Homosexuality identity formation: A theoretical model. *Journal of Homosexuality, 4*(3), 219–235.

Cass, V. C. (1983). Homosexual identity: A concept in need of definition. *Journal of Homosexuality, 9*(1–2), 105–126.

Cass, V. C. (1984). Homosexuality identity formation: Testing a theoretical model. *Journal of Sex Research, 20*(2), 105–126.

Centers for Disease Control. (2004). *HIV/AIDS Surveillance Report, 2004* (Vol. 15). Atlanta: U.S. Department of Health and Human Services, CDC: 2004–1–46.

Constantine-Simms, D. (2001). *The greatest taboo: Homosexuality in Black communities.* New York: Alyson.

Cross, Jr., W. E., (1971). Toward a psychology of Black liberation: The negro-to-black convergence experience. *Black World, 20*(9), 13–27.

Cross, Jr., W. E. (1995). The psychology of Nigrescence: Revising the Cross model. In J. G. Ponterotto, J. M. Casas, L. A. Suzuki, & C. M. Alexander (Eds.), *Handbook of multicultural counseling.* Thousand Oaks, CA: Sage.

Douglas, K. B. (1999). *Sexuality and the Black church: A womanist perspective.* (pp. 93–122). New York: Orbis Books.

Fassinger, R. E. (1998). Lesbian and bisexual identity and student development theory. In R. L. Sanlo (Ed.), *Working with lesbian, gay, bisexual and transgender college students: A handbook for faculty and administrators* (pp. 13–22). Westport, CT: Greenwood Press.

Gomes, P. J. (1996). *The good book: Reading the Bible with mind and heart.* New York: Morrow.

Helminiak, D. A. (2000). *What the Bible really says about homosexuality.* San Francisco: Alamo Square Press.

Helms, J. E. (1994). The conceptualization of ethnic identity and other racial constructs. In E. J. Thicket, R. J. Watts, & D. Birman (Eds.), *Human diversity: Perspectives on people in context* (pp. 285–311). San Francisco: Jossey-Bass.

Helms, J. E. An update of Helms's White and people of color racial identity models. In J. G. Ponterotto, J. M. Casas, L. A. Suzuki, & C. M. Alexander (Eds.), *Handbook of multicultural counseling* (pp. 181–198). Thousand Oaks, CA: 1995.

Human Rights Campaign. (2004). *Annual Report.* Washington, DC: HRC 2004, 1–50.

Katz, J. (2000, June 25). Putting blame where it belongs: On men. *Los Angeles Times.* p. M5.

Kennedy, H. U. (1988). *The life work of Karl Heinrich Ulrichs: Pioneer of the modern gay movement.* Boston: Alyson.

Lee, J. A. (1977). Going public: A study in the sociology of homosexuality liberation. *Journal of Homosexuality, 3*(1), 49–78.

Mondimore, F. M. (1996). *A natural history of homosexuality.* Baltimore: Johns Hopkins University Press.

Plummer, K. (1975). *Sexual stigma: An interactionist account.* New York: Routledge.

Savin-Williams, R. C. (1990). *Gay and lesbian youth: Expressions of identity.* New York: Hemisphere.

Savin-Williams, R. C. (1995). Lesbian, gay male, and bisexual adolescents. In A. R. D'Augelli & C. J. Patterson (Eds.), *Lesbian, gay, and bisexual identities over the lifespan: Psychological perspectives* (pp. 165–189). New York: Oxford University Press.

Savin-Williams, R. C. (1998). *"... And then I became gay": Young men's stories.* New York: Routledge.

Troiden, R. R. (1989). The formation of homosexual identities. *Journal of Homosexuality, 17*(1–2), 43–74.

CHAPTER TEN

AFRICAN AMERICAN MEN AT HISTORICALLY BLACK COLLEGES AND UNIVERSITIES

Different Environments, Similar Challenges

Walter M. Kimbrough, Philander Smith College

Shaun R. Harper, The Pennsylvania State University

Since the publication of "Helping African American Men Succeed in College" (Cuyjet, 1997), scholars and practitioners alike have devoted increased attention to the experiences of African American men in higher education. Though little published research has been offered since the 1997 publication, faculty and administrators have begun developing programmatic interventions to facilitate African American men's adjustment to and success in college at several recent national meetings of higher education professional associations. The plight of the African American male collegian remains complex; fortunately, his needs and issues are making their way onto the higher education agenda.

In spite of this increased momentum, in recent years we have acquired only limited insight into the experiences of African American men attending historically Black colleges and universities (HBCUs). With much of the national attention being placed on issues facing African American students at predominantly White institutions (PWIs), particularly with regard to affirmative action, the quality of life at HBCUs for African American students—especially African American men—has gone virtually unnoticed. The contemporary experiences of and challenges faced by African American men on those campuses are discussed in this chapter.

CURRENT CHALLENGES OF HBCUS

HBCUs continue to be important venues for African American student access to postsecondary education. However, HBCUs' ability to attract, enroll, and retain significant numbers of African American students has gradually declined over the years. According to Fleming (1984), fifty years ago "over 90 percent of Black students (approximately 100,000 in 1950) were educated in traditionally Black schools" (p. 7). Hoffman, Snyder, and Sonnenberg's (1992) research showed a dramatic decline, to 18.4 percent in 1976, and to 17.2 percent in 1990. Most recently, the National Center for Education Statistics (2003) reported that in 2001, HBCUs enrolled just 12.9 percent of all African American students in higher education. Though it is often assumed that this shift is entirely related to the extension of educational opportunities for African Americans at PWIs, Harper (2001) submits that "virtually no attention has been given to other possible factors that may influence the enrollment decisions of African American students" (p. 55). Findings from his research suggest that some HBCUs, particularly public institutions, unsystematically and ineffectively market themselves to prospective students; this partially explains declining enrollments. Regardless of the reasons, the fact remains that HBCUs have forfeited control over the enrollment of African American students, especially men.

Gender disparities in the college enrollments of African American women and men are the most pronounced of all racial and ethnic groups in higher education. These trends persist at PWIs and HBCUs alike. At most colleges and universities, African American women outnumber their same-race male counterparts by a ratio of two to one or more. According to NCES data (2003), African American men made up less than one-third (31.3 percent) of the students at HBCUs in 2001. Moreover, men earned only 32.9 percent of the degrees awarded to African Americans at HBCUs in

2002. Disparities are most problematic at the master's degree level: African American women comprise 74 percent of degree earners at HBCUs. Gender gaps in degree attainment between African American women and men across all levels on historically Black campuses are shown in Table 10.1.

At least a portion of the degree attainment differences between African American women and men can be attributed to alarming attrition trends among African America men at all institutions, including HBCUs. Increased attention is being placed on the current retention rates of African American men throughout all of higher education. Though not disaggregated by institutional type, the findings of Mortenson (2002) indicate that in the year 2000 African American men had the lowest retention rates (33.8 percent) among both sexes and all racial and ethnic groups in higher education. That is, 66.2 percent of African American men—nearly two out of three—discontinued their education before completing their bachelor's degrees, compared with 56 percent of African American women and 58.1 percent of White male undergraduates.

It is often assumed that PWIs are mainly responsible for the low retention and degree completion rates among racial and ethnic

TABLE 10.1. AFRICAN AMERICAN HBCU DEGREE ATTAINMENT RATES
BY GENDER AND LEVEL.

Degree Level	Awarded to African American Men (n)	Awarded to African American Women (n)	Total Awarded to African Americans (n)	Percent Awarded to African American Men
Associate's	496	1,379	1,875	26.5
Bachelor's	8,623	16,499	25,122	34.3
Master's	1,163	3,298	4,461	26.1
First Professional	399	598	997	40.0
Doctoral	108	148	256	42.2
Total	10,789	21,922	32,711	32.9

Source: National Center for Education Statistics (2003).

minority college students. It is certainly worth noting, however, that the figures for HBCUs are fairly comparable to national college continuation and graduation trends for African Americans. Historically, HBCUs have been notably successful in enrolling and promptly graduating large numbers of African American students (Thomas, 1981; Drewry & Doermann, 2001), but this success rate has declined drastically in recent years. Twenty years ago, Braddock (1981) found that HBCUs graduated 69 percent of their African American students, compared with 31 percent at PWIs. According to recent NCES data, only fourteen of the 105 HBCUs had graduation rates above 50 percent in 2003—based on six-year graduation rates for undergraduates who began matriculation in 1997 (NCES, 2004). Interestingly, only seven HBCUs graduated 50 percent or more of their male students.

Recent policies that have been phasing out remedial programs in state systems of higher education have yielded negative results for African American student enrollments at public HBCUs. Though HBCUs have always offered courses in some form to help fill gaps in African American students' precollege educational preparation (Allen, 1986; Drewry & Doermann, 2001; Fleming, 1984), developmental studies courses were officially introduced on college campuses in the 1960s (Weissman, Silk, & Bulakowski, 1997). These programs typically provide remediation in English, mathematics, and reading. Research has confirmed that in addition to increasing access to higher education, these programs significantly improve persistence rates and the academic performance of marginally prepared students (Haeuser, 1993; Walleri, 1987). In spite of the demonstrated success of remedial programs, many state systems, including those with HBCUs, have restricted access to four-year institutions by students who need to enroll in remedial courses (O'Malley, 1999; Wright, 1998). This policy shift has had negative effects on African American men at some public HBCUs who previously relied upon developmental studies programs as a one-chance opportunity for admission to postsecondary institutions.

AFRICAN AMERICAN MEN AT HBCUs

Historically, African American men fared considerably better than African American women in many of the landmark research studies on HBCU students. For example, Gurin and Epps's (1975) data, which were collected from more than five thousand African American students at ten HBCUs in the late 1960s, indicated that HBCU male students' educational and careers goals were considerably higher than those of female students; HBCU undergraduate men were three times more likely to express the intent to enroll in graduate and professional schools (especially doctoral programs), and men were more likely to aspire to higher-prestige careers in the traditionally masculine sector of the job market (such as engineering, business, and the sciences).

Fleming's (1984) analysis of gender differences among African Americans at HBCUs was consistent with Gurin and Epps's results from the previous decade. Fleming found that African American men on HBCU campuses—much like White men at PWIs—felt potent, empowered, and "in charge." Consequently, they dominated the classroom and social environments and were far more competitive, thereby outperforming their African American female schoolmates. The primary research question in Fleming's study was "Who gets the most out of college?" Based on the findings, she concluded, "It turns out to be a man's world. Women usually bring up the rear. In predominantly Black colleges, men gain the most" (p. 138). Similar to the findings from Fleming's study, male students on the eight HBCU campuses in Allen's (1986) study had higher educational and career aspirations, reported more favorable relationships with faculty, and tended to be more engaged on their campuses than African American women.

Based on more recent data—collected through the National Survey of Student Engagement from 1,167 African American undergraduates at twelve HBCUs—Harper, Carini, Bridges, and Hayek (2004) found significant gender differences in the amount of effort African American men and women invested in academic preparation. HBCU male students devoted significantly less time to studying, reading, rehearsing, writing papers, completing homework assignments, and preparing for classes than did their African American female counterparts. The women in the sample also reported more frequently than did male students that they worked hard to meet academic standards and to fulfill faculty expectations. The male respondents in Harper et al.'s study, however, interacted more frequently with faculty members on their campuses than did the female students in the sample. However, HBCU men's and women's scores were nearly the same on the other engagement scales in the study—active and collaborative learning, general education gains, personal-social gains, practical competence, and satisfaction.

Harper and Wolley (2002) contend that African American male participation in campus activities and student organizations on both HBCU and PWI campuses is woefully low. It is important to note that although student organizations are not universally deemed as "uncool" for African American men, participation in these clubs limits their time to assert proficiency in activities that create ostensibly more masculine reputations, such as participating in sports, playing video games, obtaining material possessions, pursuing romantic relationships with women, and interacting informally with other African American male peers (p. 19). In spite of this explanation, Harper and Wolley cite a lack of strategic institutional effort to invite and encourage involvement among African American men as the primary reason for such disengagement.

Little research has been offered on African American students at HBCUs in recent years without comparing them with African American students at PWIs. Though most comparative studies have presented findings that favor HBCU environments and add much-needed credibility and legitimacy to Black colleges, this body of research has not focused on various dimensions of the HBCU student experience without comparing it to the experience at PWIs. Beyond Harper et al.'s (2004) study, insight into gender differences on HBCU campuses has not been offered since the Fleming and Allen studies in the 1980s. Consequently, little has been documented about the contemporary challenges and issues faced by African American men on those campuses.

Recent studies addressing the plight of the African American male collegian have not been disaggregated by institutional type, leaving one to wonder if the experiences are fully reflective of African American men at HBCUs. During the late 1970s and 1980s, Fleming (1984) and Allen (1986) found that African American men felt "potent" and "in charge" on HBCU campuses. Recent conversations with male students on those campuses suggest less potency in the areas of academics, leadership and out-of-class involvement, and interpersonal relationships.

AFRICAN AMERICAN MEN AT HBCUS: IN THEIR OWN WORDS

In light of recent research indicating numerous challenges confronted by African American men in higher education, it is important to gain some insight from the men themselves regarding their issues and challenges and how they can be addressed in contemporary times. Although a fair amount of evidence exists, there is a need for more qualitative research that describes the experience of African American men on contemporary college and university campuses. Furthermore, though much of the concern is in reference to African American men at PWIs, the challenges facing men at HBCUs may be more disturbing in some ways, given the belief that these institutions ostensibly provide a safe haven of sorts for African American student growth and development.

To explore the issues facing African American men at HBCUs, focus groups were conducted and major themes regarding their collective experiences were identified using inductive analysis (Patton, 2002). The first group consisted of men attending a public, historically Black institution in Georgia. These students represented a broad spectrum of backgrounds in terms of majors, hometowns, and involvement, including Student Government Association (SGA) officers, orientation leaders, and Residence Assistants (RAs). The second group consisted of men attending the *Sixth Annual National Student Leadership Institute for All Student Leaders Attending HBCUs,* held in Bowie, Maryland, in May 2002. The National Association of Student Affairs Professionals, an organization primarily comprising student affairs officers at HBCUs, sponsored this event. These men were SGA presidents, fraternity presidents, and RAs representing eight different HBCUs, both public and private.

The focus groups were designed to elicit responses from the men in several broad areas. In all cases, the men engaged in open, semistructured dialogue that yielded interesting perspectives on their experiences at HBCUs. Using the inductive analytical approach, recurring themes were clustered and identified in the following five areas: (1) predisposition to college, (2) academic achievement, (3) involvement and leadership development, (4) interpersonal relationships, and (5) perceptions of PWIs. What follows is a summary of findings from the major themes that emerged from the focus groups.

Predisposition to College

The men openly acknowledged their sparse representation on their respective campuses. With most ratios of women to men at HBCUs being at least two to one, the first logical question was, why was there this imbalance? What were the factors that prevented African American men from attending college?

The participants offered many explanations. One of the most frequently cited reasons was that African American men were expected to fill some traditional roles, particularly as providers for their current family members. This was even expected for those who did not have children. In many cases, this meant that they were expected to begin gainful employment as soon as possible, which meant that college was not necessarily the first option. Several participants indicated that they were expected to learn a trade and take up the family business, or they were advised by their family members to seek a career in the military. The expectations for immediate work were also seen as a by-product of the perceived lack of financial resources to attend college, so learning a trade or enlisting in the military were seen as viable, respectable options for many African American men once they completed high school, if not before.

Reportedly, this was contrary to the expectations of African American women in the participants' families. They felt that women were nurtured more, and part of that nurturing included setting the expectations for them to go to college and then become gainfully employed afterward. In fact, some men appeared to be disappointed that they did not receive the same level of nurturing or familial expectations for college attendance as the young women in their families.

One of the more interesting themes was the effect of popular culture on the transmission of college-going messages to African American men. The participants consistently indicated that their African American male peers lacked maturity and were negatively affected by popular culture. They also noticed that the aspirations of many boys and teens in their home communities did not revolve around higher education, but instead were largely influenced by the instant gratification and materialism expressed in many hip-hop songs and music videos.

One student indicated, "They are most comfortable with media images that seem to represent themselves." He felt that younger people could relate better to rappers and entertainers who looked and talked like the average person in their communities, and they had difficulty relating to men in suits and ties. Furthermore, those same younger people were also thought to identify with the materialism flaunted in hip-hop videos and by professional athletes, and they were under the impression that it would be easier for them to acquire those items through means other than higher education.

For these men, there reportedly are not enough professional, college-educated role models who promote higher education as a better alternative to the lifestyles that many young African American males see on television. Some noted that they grew up in families where few, if any, men pursued any form of higher education; therefore it was not a familial expectation for them. This critical issue of the lack of role models appeared throughout the focus groups as a significant impediment to the prematriculation and success of African American men in college everywhere, including HBCUs.

Academic Achievement

The participants explored reasons why African American men at HBCUs perform so poorly in comparison with their same-race female peers (as confirmed through the retention and graduation statistics referenced earlier). The major theme was an issue of maturity. The participants thought their male peers did not see the "big picture" and consequently struggled to stay in school and graduate. They felt this was a serious issue at HBCUs because they perceived their institutions to be highly social. Focus group participants identified many factors—opportunities to attend parties in the middle of the week, along with the abundance of female classmates to "chase," or even the preoccupation with planning to join a fraternity—that led to a lack of focus, underachievement, and ultimately attrition among African American male undergraduates at HBCUs.

One student disclosed his personal story of spending his first year of college partying and not realizing how important it was to attend classes and attain good grades. He indicated that by his second year he realized those habits would hurt his chances for graduate school or obtaining a good job; thus he became serious about his schoolwork. Others said that many of their peers did not make this kind of adjustment because they had no real interest in college to begin with. They spoke often of peers who, because their parents had made them attend college, were perfectly comfortable with spending their time socializing rather than studying.

The most interesting discussion revolved around perceived gender differences with regard to academic achievement at HBCUs. Some felt that their female classmates were more organized and mature and therefore earned higher grades. There was also a strong sentiment that professors expect more of women, which enhances their achievement. They believed female students were nurtured more in class and were catered to more often on HBCU campuses. Some even indicated that women get preferential treatment by an overwhelmingly male professoriate because of their physical appearance. Several participants indicated that their African American male peers were, in general, not prepared mentally or academically for college, which hindered their success. One student simply stated, "They just don't want to study."

The dialogue then shifted to determining if HBCUs provide the kind of support and resources that African American men could take advantage of to improve their academic standing. The consensus was that academic support programs and various resources do exist at HBCUs—the issue was whether their male peers took advantage of those resources. There was some division in the responses. Some men indicated that their peers do seek services, such as tutoring, and participate actively in study groups to improve their grades. But a prevailing voice indicated that African American men at HBCUs do not take full advantage of these resources. One student who served as a tutor for a first-year experience program indicated that for the entire academic school year, none of the students to whom he provided individualized academic assistance were male. These behaviors were primarily attributed to male pride and male egos. One participant jokingly likened this resistance to asking for help to the cliché of the male driver who is obviously lost, but refuses to stop and ask for directions. Another student admitted, "It's hard for me to ask for help. I'm a grown man. I'm supposed to take care of my own problems and responsibilities."

INVOLVEMENT AND LEADERSHIP DEVELOPMENT

The focus group dialogues shifted to discussions of the levels of involvement of African American men in out-of-class activities and student organizations. The general consensus was that men at HBCUs are not involved in student organizations as a whole, and even fewer hold leadership positions. Although the participants noted the already glaring disparity in the ratio of men to women on their campuses, this gap was further widened when they considered those who were active participants in out-of-class activities. They provided many examples of the imbalances between male and female involvement on campus. At one institution, in an SGA of twenty-four members, only five were men. At another, the student senate consisted of twenty-five people with only two men, both of whom were impeached in the course of the year. Two students seeking SGA presidencies on their respective campuses indicated that they targeted their campaigns to women because they knew their male peers would not participate in voting. Reportedly, their African American male peers did not care about the elections or any type of campus leadership and involvement.

The same imbalances were noted even at fraternity and sorority interest meetings. The sororities were estimated to have four hundred or more prospective members attend interest meetings on most campuses (six hundred at one institution), whereas fraternities normally had fifty or fewer. The poor academic performance of male students often made them ineligible for membership, as most of the historically Black fraternities require at least a 2.5 cumulative GPA to join. This was offered as one key reason for the low numbers of prospective members at fraternity interest meetings on HBCU campuses.

Other theories were offered to explain the low levels of out-of-class involvement. Most men preferred to participate in athletics (intercollegiate and intramural), the participants indicated, because athleticism was perceived to be more socially acceptable and "cool." Conversely, being involved, even in a fraternity, or being a leader on campus was not "cool." The students at the institution in Georgia indicated that the shortage of male applicants for positions as RAs in Residence Life was a clear indication of this fact. Although some of their peers felt that leadership was "uncool," the focus group participants believed they had earned the respect of uninvolved African American men on their campuses. Part of this respect was believed to have been earned through the leadership these men displayed and their assumption of roles as spokespersons, advocates, and problem-solvers for uninvolved students.

Another theory for the overall lack of involvement and leadership by African American men at HBCUs was the perceived difficulty that men have with working together. Participants indicated that they have been taught as men to compete rather than collaborate. They felt that men have problems working collectively, and therefore women are more involved because of their ability to collaborate. One student indicated that African American women, unlike their male counterparts, are not afraid to take orders from each other or empower someone else to be the leader.

The consensus was that men need more attention at home to prepare them for college, especially for an active role as a leader. One student provided an interesting insight into this problem. He thought that girls were developed by participation in middle school and high school clubs, the arts, pageants, and other constructive activities. Thus, he felt, girls acquired a certain collaborative skill set and confidence that boys did not develop. Other participants felt that parents were too aggressive in pushing boys to play sports, even those boys who preferred to read. This was also seen as a detriment to the overall success of African American men in college.

One of the issues surrounding student involvement was the place for and availability of mentors for men at HBCUs. On the surface, this may have appeared to be an irrelevant question, as HBCUs are perceived to be institutions that have an overabundance of same-race mentors, particularly for African American men. However, the students complained that there were too few role models and mentors, that the few there often had schedules that did not permit them to be involved with students, and that students lacked the initiative to interface with the role models. Several indicated that HBCUs purport to offer a familial environment, "but the students receive horrible treatment most of the time." Therefore, the few caring and committed mentors are sought by all students, which often creates a burden on those few faculty and staff persons. Yet the students clearly felt a need to have more committed mentors to improve African American male involvement as well as academic success.

INTERPERSONAL RELATIONSHIPS

The focus group participants engaged in lively discussions about male-female relationships. They were very aware of the numerical imbalances on their campuses, and they acknowledged the ways, many of them negative, that this disproportion presented itself. Despite the overrepresentation of female students on their campuses, the participants indicated that there was clearly a competition amongst African American men for romantic or sexual relationships with women at HBCUs.

Some felt that many women were sent to college to find mates. One student discussed an instance when a woman indicated that her mother would love him because he was a leader at the university. But the overall climate on campus was viewed as one of excessive sexuality. One participant said, "No one is meeting their spouse in college—they are meeting their sex partners." Although these students felt that men played a significant role in the advancement of sexual promiscuity, they felt that women were equally to blame. They indicated that music videos and television series like *Sex and the City* legitimized college women's attitudes toward casual sexual relationships.

Despite the efforts of men who sought more serious relationships, the participants overwhelmingly acknowledged that many of their male peers took advantage of women at HBCUs, particularly first-year female students. They felt that this happened not just at HBCUs, but in all educational settings. Again, they pointed to hip-hop culture as creating a climate in which the abuse and objectification of women was not only accepted, but also glamorized.

The men acknowledged that women are routinely manipulated, and they revealed an even darker side to the extent of this problem. They described "freak lists" on a few campuses, which were developed by men who got together, compiled, and distributed amongst themselves lists of sexually "overactive" female students. The lists were described as explicit and vulgar, providing details of sexual encounters and sexual acts (such as oral sex) in which these women engaged. Although many students did not believe the contents of the lists, the students indicated that they sometimes had first-hand knowledge of the activities. These lists were known to be hurtful and damaging to the reputations of the women, many of whom were first-year students.

The participants also pointed out that some female students took advantage of men as well. They pointed to attractive women they saw dating unattractive men who were involved in drugs and had nice possessions, such as cars. They likened such behavior to prostitution. Others complained about the hassles they felt when attempting to date women. Some felt as if they were completing applications in order to prove their worthiness, and that the women looked down on them. As for their future prospects, they felt comfortable in finding mates, but also expected to see more African American women dating and marrying White men.

PERCEPTIONS OF PREDOMINANTLY WHITE INSTITUTIONS

The final area of discussion involved the participants' perceptions of the climate for African American men at PWIs, and their speculations as to which institutional type provided the best environment for their growth and development. African American men attending HBCUs appear to be split in terms of their feelings on the subject.

Thoughts about students attending PWIs varied. Some felt that African American students attending PWIs perceived themselves to be superior to their HBCU counterparts. They believed those students' parents were primarily responsible for such beliefs, as they advanced misperceptions about the quality of HBCUs. Others felt that African American students at PWIs really envied the experiences of students at HBCUs. They were cited as especially trying to experience HBCU life and culture through big social events, such as homecoming. These participants also believed their peers at PWIs desired more opportunities to learn about their culture and Black history, which they believed to be characteristic of HBCUs.

Others explained that despite some unique challenges they had encountered on historically Black campuses, it was definitely an experience they would not trade. They discussed the familial nature of HBCUs, but specifically indicated that feeling was produced and managed by students, not faculty or staff. These perceptions were largely due to the hassles and hurdles they encountered when interacting with staff in various offices on their campuses. Despite these issues, they felt that HBCUs were important in teaching them how to interact positively with other African Americans, appreciating their unique cultures, and recognizing their own skills and self-worth. Particularly from a socialization perspective, including an appreciation for their culture and heritage, there was a great deal of agreement that HBCUs offered the better environment.

Those who felt PWIs were better indicated that those institutions provided a higher-quality academic experience. They knew that those institutions could easily offer the resources they needed that were often absent at HBCUs. They also believed PWIs would likely provide better opportunities for their futures with regard to graduate school or employment.

DISCUSSION AND CONCLUSIONS

The experiences of the participants in this study mirror many of the challenges noted in recent literature on African American undergraduate men, but also raise other poignant issues that must be addressed. To some extent, it appears that this group has been neglected on HBCU campuses. Although the general thought is that HBCUs provide nurturing and supportive environments, it is clear that for many students, particularly African American men, these institutions are overlooking some of their basic needs for connection and nurturing, especially since this group is less likely to reach out for assistance when in trouble. It is apparent that greater attention is warranted from faculty, staff, and administrators on those campuses.

A major part of the problem lies in a continued struggle to determine what is "cool" for African American men. Majors and Billson (1992) introduced the concept of *cool pose,* which is a double-edged sword that African American males use to express their masculinity and respond to environmental oppression. Some aspects can be linked to pride and self-respect, yet cool pose also involves dropping out of school, succumbing to negative peer pressure, and getting into trouble. (Chapter One contains a somewhat more detailed explanation of cool pose.) Clearly, contemporary African American men at HBCUs battle this modern-day double consciousness on a daily basis, appearing to fall victim to it, as noted by the low graduation and retention rates at many HBCUs.

Furthermore, like their same-race male peers who attend PWIs, African American men at HBCUs often struggle to define success through the attainment of a college degree and gainful employment, instead of by the competing images of success portrayed through popular culture, most notably hip-hop. Potter (1995) more directly described the "gangsta ethos" of hip-hop as "based in part on a refusal of bourgeois notions of 'work' and 'responsibility,' and [rejecting] the Black middle class and its values as essentially traitorous" (p. 138). Therefore, this powerful culture negatively affects many African American men, despite their educational level and aspirations, and subsequently skews their views regarding educational attainment, success, family, and, even more disturbingly, the treatment of African American women (Evelyn, 2000; George, 1998; Rose, 1994; White & Cones, 1999).

Although there are many benefits to the historically Black college experience, it must be stated firmly that there is a great need for improvement. The declining percentage of African American student enrollments, along with retention and graduation rates that are often below those of PWIs, indicate that the HBCU experience leaves much to be desired for many African American students, particularly men. Hurd (2000) indicated that students and graduates of HBCUs tell of "institutional disorganization, problems with financial aid, staff 'with attitudes' and the red tape" (p. 45), which hinder their progression through degree attainment and minimize the likelihood that they will encourage future generations of African American college-goers to choose those same institutions.

HBCUs can begin to respond to the plight of African American men years before they arrive on a college campus. Given the historic mission of HBCUs to provide access to African American students who may not otherwise have a chance to attend a postsecondary educational institution, more outreach is needed to attract larger numbers of male students to those campuses and higher education in general. The aforementioned statistics on enrollment trends, coupled with responses from the focus group participants, suggest that African American men disproportionately choose alternatives other than college on completion of high school. Admissions officers and HBCU recruiters should have a stronger presence in high schools and in predominantly Black communities. Given that most HBCUs are nestled in the heart of Black neighborhoods or in close geographic proximity to large concentrations of African Americans, they are in a unique position to reinforce college-going messages to young boys and teenage males. After-school, summer, and special outreach programs should be created to nurture pools of prospective African American male college-goers.

The findings in the Predisposition to College section suggest that HBCUs have a role to play in educating African American parents and families about options for postsecondary education. Many of the participants admitted that college attendance was not commonplace in their families; thus their parents frequently expected them to do other things after high school, such as joining the military or working full-time. Colleges and universities (including both HBCUs and PWIs) that are interested in increasing African American male student enrollments must do some early seed-planting by informing African American families about the doors that college attendance can open for their boys and young men, as well as the array of financial aid options.

The shortage of mentors and role models available to African American boys and teens prior to college also merits special attention. HBCUs could use their current African American male students, as well as their male alumni, to provide this much-needed support in predominantly Black communities. Interacting meaningfully with men who are currently in college or have attained college degrees will positively affect the lives of young African American men. Moreover, these young men will have an opportunity to become acquainted with professional African American male role models who provide an image that differs from those depicted in hip-hop songs and music videos.

Obviously, getting more African American men to HBCU campuses is only half the battle—keeping them there and graduating them in larger numbers is the other half. The underutilization of support programs and academic resources clearly impairs academic achievement among African American men on Black college campuses. Many of the focus group participants noted that services existed on their campuses but were not used by their male peers. Efforts should be made to inform all students of various services on campus during orientation programs and throughout subsequent semesters of matriculation. Simply hosting a student services fair during orientation week is an ineffective way of ensuring that students are aware of the existence of campus support programs.

Academic advisors at HBCUs must keep track of the classroom performance of African American men and encourage them to utilize student support services when in trouble. Advisors should strongly encourage proud and stubborn strugglers to "stop and ask for directions." Constant support from academic advisors, though seemingly annoying to some undergraduates, will show low-performing African American male students that someone is paying attention to and investing in their academic success.

In addition to the academic advising staff (which on some campuses includes faculty), those who offer instruction in HBCU classrooms also have a role to play in providing academic support to African American men. Harper et al. (2004) found that men interact with faculty inside and outside of class far more frequently than do women on HBCU campuses. Thus, it seems only proper to suggest that professors use these periods of interaction to assess and inquire about the academic performance of African American male students. Also, since instructors are responsible for the evaluation of student work, they are in an ideal position to pull academically low-performing men aside and suggest that they get the help they need. A recommendation from a professor to seek academic assistance could very well be the single most potent means of motivating students to put aside their male egos and pride.

Greater attention must be devoted to improving the out-of-class involvement rates of African American men at HBCUs. Although there appears to be some male participation in certain activities (such as athletics), the average male student chooses not to become involved in leadership experiences that are so critical to the overall educational process. Sutton and Terrell (1997), as well as Harper and Wolley (2002), offer several strategies that can be used to increase involvement. Practical approaches are also offered in Chapters Three and Four of this book.

The most disturbing finding that emerged from the focus groups is the nature of the relationship between undergraduate men and women at HBCUs. The participants unanimously agreed that women were routinely being taken advantage of on their campuses. Administrators must begin to programmatically address the treatment of African American women. Open and frank discussions with men and women must be held to explore the pitfalls of casual sex from health and psychological perspectives. Orientation is a logical first step, as the participants noted that first-year female students are most susceptible to mistreatment. Sessions to build self-esteem would seem to be a critical necessity for students who take advantage of others or allow themselves to be taken advantage of. Beyond orientation, continuous programming is needed to address this issue so that both men and women can learn how to effectively navigate the numerical gender imbalances at most HBCUs.

The qualitative experiences of African American men at HBCUs deserve ongoing attention. The literature indicates that these men are facing significant challenges as they navigate higher education. The experiences of the men in this study highlight these challenges and in fact indicate that a sense of urgency is needed among faculty and administrators at HBCUs to improve the overall experience of African American men attending these institutions.

References

Allen, W. R. (1986). *Gender and campus differences in Black student academic performance, racial attitudes, and college satisfaction.* Atlanta, GA: Southern Education Foundation.

Braddock, J. H. (1981). Desegregation and black student attrition. *Urban Education, 15,* 403–18.

Cuyjet, M. J. (Ed.). (1997). *Helping African American men succeed in college.* New Directions for Student Services, no. 80. San Francisco: Jossey-Bass.

Drewry, H. N., & Doermann, H. (2001). *Stand and prosper: Private Black colleges and their students.* Princeton, NJ: Princeton University Press.

Evelyn, J. (2000). The miseducation of hip-hop. *Black Issues in Higher Education, 17*(21), 24–29.

Fleming, J. (1984). *Blacks in college: A comparative study of students' success in Black and in White institutions.* San Francisco: Jossey-Bass.

George, N. (1998). *Hip-hop America.* New York: Viking.

Gurin, P., & Epps, E. G. (1975). *Black consciousness, identity, and achievement: A study of students in historically Black colleges.* New York: Wiley.

Haeuser, P. N. (1993). *Public accountability and developmental (remedial) education.* Arnold, MD: Anna Arundel Community College, Office of Planning and Research. ERIC Document Reproduction Service No. ED 356 003.

Harper, S. R. (2001). On analyzing HBCU recruitment material. *Journal of the National Association of Student Affairs Professionals, 4*(1), 54–64.

Harper, S. R., Carini, R. M, Bridges, B. K., & Hayek, J. (2004). Gender differences in student engagement among African American undergraduates at historically Black colleges and universities. *Journal of College Student Development, 45*(3), 271–284.

Harper, S. R., & Wolley, M. A. (2002). Becoming an "involving college" for African American men: Strategies for increasing African American male participation in campus activities. *Association of College Unions International Bulletin, 70*(3), 16–24.

Hoffman, C. M., Snyder, T. D., & Sonnenberg, B. (1992). *Historically Black colleges and universities, 1976–1990.* Washington, DC: National Center for Education Statistics, U.S. Department of Education.

Hurd, H. (2000). Staying power: Colleges work to improve retention rates. *Black Issues in Higher Education, 17*(18), 42–46.

Majors, R., & Billson, J. M. (1992). *Cool pose: The dilemmas of Black manhood in America.* New York: Lexington.

Mortenson Research Seminar on Public Policy Analysis of Opportunity for Postsecondary Education. (2002, February). Earned degrees conferred by gender, 1977 to 2000. *Postsecondary Education Opportunity, 116,* 1–9.

National Center for Education Statistics. (2003). *Digest of education statistics, 2003.* Based on Integrated Postsecondary Education Data System (IPEDS) Completions Survey, 2001–2002. Washington, DC: U.S. Department of Education, Institute of Education Sciences.

National Center for Education Statistics. (2004). *Integrated postsecondary education data system.* Washington, DC: U.S. Department of Education, Institute of Education Sciences.

O'Malley, S. G. (1999). Schmidt report restructures City University of New York. *Radical Teacher, 56,* 36–38.

Patton, M. Q. (2002). *Qualitative research & evaluation methods* (3rd ed.). Thousand Oaks, CA: Sage.

Potter, R. A. (1995). *Spectacular vernaculars: Hip-hop and the politics of postmodernism.* Albany: State University of New York Press.

Rose, T. (1994). *Black noise: Rap music and Black culture in contemporary America.* Hanover, NH: Wesleyan University Press.

Sutton, M., & Terrell, M. (1997). Identifying and developing leadership opportunities for African American men. In M. J. Cuyjet (Ed.),

Helping African American men succeed in college. New Directions for Student Services, no. 80 (pp. 55–64). San Francisco: Jossey-Bass.

Thomas, G. E. (1981). College characteristics and Black students' four-year college graduation. *Journal of Negro Education, 50,* 328–345.

Walleri, R. D. (1987, May). *A longitudinal study of "guided studies" students.* Paper presented at the Annual Forum of the Association of Institutional Research, Kansas City, MO.

Weissman, J., Silk, E., & Bulakowski, C. (1997). Assessing developmental education policies. *Research in Higher Education, 38*(2), 187–201.

White, J. L., & Cones III, J. H. (1999). *Black man emerging.* New York: Routledge.

Wright, S. W. (1998). The ill-prepared and the ill-informed. *Black Issues in Higher Education, 15,* 12–15.

CHAPTER ELEVEN

MEETING THE CHALLENGES TO AFRICAN AMERICAN MEN AT COMMUNITY COLLEGES

Myron L. Pope, University of Central Oklahoma

For just over one hundred years the community college has provided American citizens, especially minority students, with an opportunity to gain a postsecondary education. For many African American men, the community college serves as the sole opportunity for access to higher education. However, despite its original mission of preparing students to transfer to senior colleges and universities, the community college has decreased its emphasis on the transfer function in the last thirty to fifty years. Critics have stressed that this mission shift will limit African American men, and others in this system, to modest jobs with moderate economic returns and no opportunity to advance toward baccalaureate and other advanced degrees. This chapter analyzes the relationship of African American men and their matriculation in two-year colleges.

BRIEF HISTORY

The American community college system had its impetus in a variety of social factors, including the Morrill Land Grant Acts of 1862 and 1890, which provided for publicly supported universities, and the suggestion of many higher education leaders that a system be developed to relieve the university of lower-division preparation so that it could focus more on research and professional development. The latter stimulus led to the opening of Joliet College in 1901. This institution's goal was to provide freshman- and sophomore-level coursework, in addition to counseling and guidance, to prepare students for the transition to the four-year institution—the transfer function. The focus on the transfer function was the goal of these institutions, recognized as "junior colleges," as they gradually grew around the country before the turn of the twentieth century (Vaughan, 2000).

The community college system experienced a tremendous increase in number during the latter part of that century due in part to the country's leadership. In 1947, the publication of Higher Education for American Democracy by the President's Commission on Higher Education, or the Truman Commission as it is more commonly called, emphasized the need for a system of community colleges that would be affordable, serve as community centers, provide a variety of curricular offerings with a focus on civic duties, and provide service to the communities in which they were established (American Association of Community Colleges [AACC], 2002). This report on community colleges—as well as the G.I. Bill and federal and state support for educational access to all citizens through legislation, executive orders, and legal proceedings—contributed to a substantial amount of enrollment growth for the system from the 1950s to the present (Diener, 1994). Additionally, the community college system has expanded beyond its original mission of preparing students for transfer to a four-year institution to include a myriad of other functions, including community service, remediation, vocational and technical education, and continuing education (Cohen & Brawer, 1996).

The system has grown to a total of approximately 1,600 institutions, with a presence in each of the fifty states. Each state has a goal of providing access to all of its citizens; thus many have built community colleges within a thirty-mile commute of all of its citizens, offering education at a cost that is substantially less than the fees of the four-year counterparts. The average cost of attendance, consisting of tuition and fees, at a public community college in 2003–04 was $2,076, compared with an average of $9,400 at a public four-year institution (College Board, 2004). Even more significant to the issue of access is the community college's open-door policy, which essentially provides enrollment to any individual who presents the institution with a high school diploma or the equivalent. The policy, though initially revolutionary and inclusive, has presented the community college with many challenges, including the task of remediation of unprepared students. Community colleges also have emphasized their mission of providing smaller classes with instructors who focus primarily on instruction and providing a nurturing environment for students, a mission different from that of most of their four-year institutional counterparts.

STUDENT DEMOGRAPHICS

The demographics of the community college have changed significantly during the last fifty years. With the number of community colleges built during this period, in addition to the affordability and emphasis on access, the community college system has reached an enrollment of about 5.5 million students, or 38 percent of the total number of students in higher education (Phillippe & Patton, 2000). Phillippe and Patton compared this with the 1965 enrollment figure of only about 1.2 million students. This number does not account for the approximately five million students who take courses through community colleges as noncredit students in community and continuing education capacities.

Additionally, the number of minorities in the system has increased, coinciding with the overall increase in the number of minorities in this country (see Table 11.1). The National Center for Education Statistics [NCES] (2002) reported that 41.2 percent of African Americans in higher education are in the community college system, along with 50 percent of the American Indian and 55.8 percent of the Hispanic enrollment in higher education.

The background characteristics of community college students are also quite distinct from those of students attending four-year institutions. The National Center for Education Statistics (NCES), in its analysis of postsecondary students, found that 26 percent of the students attending community colleges are older than twenty-four years of age, compared with only 5 percent of the students at public four-year institutions (NCES, 1996). The overall average age for community college students is twenty-nine (AACC, 2002). Also, these students tended to receive less support from

TABLE 11.1. TOTAL MINORITY FALL ENROLLMENT BY TYPE OF INSTITUTION FOR SELECTED YEARS (NUMBERS IN THOUSANDS).

	1988	1992	1993	1994	1995	1996	1997	1998	Percent Increase 1988–98
All Institutions	2,399	3,164	3,248	3,396	3,496	3,637	3,771	3,891	62.2
Four-Year Institutions									
All minorities	1,292	1,663	1,734	1,819	1,886	1,947	2,016	2,092	61.9
African American	656	791	814	834	852	870	896	928	41.3
Hispanic	296	410	432	463	485	509	530	553	86.8
Asian American	297	407	429	462	482	501	519	539	81.1
American Indian	42	55	59	61	66	67	72	73	72.6
Two-Year Institutions									
All minorities	1,107	1,500	1,514	1,577	1,610	1,691	1,755	1,799	62.6
African American	473	602	599	615	621	636	655	657	38.9
Hispanic	384	545	557	583	608	657	689	707	84.1
Asian American	199	289	295	313	315	327	341	363	82.3
American Indian	50	64	63	66	66	70	71	72	42.7

Source: Adapted from *Enrollment in Higher Education*, National Center for Education Statistics (NCES), 2000 (as cited in Wilds, 2001).

their parents—65 percent do, compared with over 90 percent of their public four-year counterparts. Both of these factors are significant in that they indicate that many of the students in the community college system are part-time students who are working at least part-time; some are financially independent. These factors, in addition to four others—having delayed entry into college after high school, having dependents, being a single parent, and having no high school diploma—are considered risk factors that are detrimental to the success of college students (Coley, 2000). In the NCES (1996) research, community college students were significantly more likely than their four-year institutional peers to have each of these six factors. These statistics indicate that 24 percent of community college students had four or more of these factors compared with only 4 percent of their four-year counterparts (Coley, 2000).

Two other significant demographic characteristics of community college students are their family backgrounds and their level of involvement upon entering college. Dougherty (1994) points out that many community college students come from families with lower incomes and are typically first-generation college students. As community colleges are less expensive and are within commuting distance, they are the only options for postsecondary education for these students. Even though these factors are instrumental in enabling college attendance, they may also be detrimental in the long run because these students are unable to become as socially and academically integrated as their peers who are attending four-year residential institutions.

ECONOMIC BENEFITS

Achieving access to higher education has been particularly significant to African American males because it has increased their opportunities to enhance their economic standing. The American Society for Training and Development projected that by the end of the year 2000, 65 percent of all jobs in this country would require some education beyond high school (Myran, Zeiss, & Howdyshell, 1995). Additionally, compared with individuals with high school diplomas only, individuals with associate's degrees or who complete some college earn more money (Grubb, 1999). Those who completed their associate's degree were expected to earn approximately

$26,235 in 1997 compared with $22,895 for individuals who only completed high school. Those individuals who completed their associate's degree, transferred to a four-year institution, and completed their bachelor's degree (Phillippe & Patton, 2000) were expected to earn even more. This phenomenon is particularly true for African American males, but despite the significant increases in numbers of these students in the community college system because of access and the potential to enhance their social mobility, there have not been corresponding increases in the number of associate and baccalaureate degrees awarded to them.

THE DIMINISHING TRANSFER FUNCTION

One significant reason why the number of community college students achieving their baccalaureate degree has not increased is that many of them are not transferring. Since the 1960s, many researchers have identified the shift of the focus in the community college from one that offered four-year college preparation to one that has strived to meet other needs of the people (Clark, 1960; Monroe, 1977; Pincus, 1980). Rendon and Nora (1994) suggest some of the main factors that have contributed to the decline in transfer students: (1) more emphasis and enrollment in vocational and technical programs; (2) the growth of remedial education; (3) the addition of the adult, continuing, and community education functions of the community college; (4) an increase in the number of part-time students in the system; and (5) increased competition from four-year institutions for students who in the past saw the community college as their only option. As a result, the number of students enrolled in the transfer tracks fell from approximately 43 percent in 1973 to about 30 percent in 1985 and finally to about 15 to 20 percent in the late 1990s (Friedlander, 1980; Dougherty, 1994; Nora & Rendon, 1998; Tinto, 1998). Considering that roughly half of the minority students enrolled in higher education during the last three decades are in the community college system, it is important to take into account the associate's degree completion and transfer rates for these populations. The NCES (2002) indicated that even though White students made up only 64 percent of community college enrollment, they were completing 72.3 percent of the associate's degrees. Conversely, African

Americans, who made up 12 percent of the enrollment, earned only 10.7 percent of the associate's degrees awarded, and Hispanic students, who represented 14 percent of the enrollment, earned only 9.1 percent of the degrees.

Critics of the community colleges have suggested that during the last half century, since the enrollment booms, the system has neglected its minority students and turned the open door into a "revolving door"—referring to the ability of students to easily enroll in and drop out of community colleges (Moore, 1981; Ignash, 1993). One prominent criticism is directed at the community colleges' increased efforts to provide remedial education to their increasingly diverse students. The same era in which open access produced multitudes of new community colleges also caused an influx of academically underprepared students. The community college expanded its mission from the transfer function to one that increasingly incorporated services to address poverty and societal class differences, during a period when students from disadvantaged backgrounds needed remediation of their deficiencies through "appropriate educational technology" (McGrath & Spear, 1991). Regrettably, community colleges were not providing the proper curricula, student services, and pedagogy to create a productive environment for these nontraditional students. Thus, as Roueche (1968) reported, as many as 90 percent of the students admitted into community college and assigned to the remedial education programs of the time never completed the programs. It was not until the 1970s that community colleges began to develop distinct programs to address the needs of these students (Roueche & Kirk, 1973). Despite these improvements, students who began their academic careers in remedial courses have continued to have high attrition rates and often failed to graduate (Dougherty, 1994). This is of particular importance in regard to those African American males who come from disadvantaged backgrounds and take remedial courses.

Another criticism of the community college stems from the perception that community colleges are tracking and sorting African American males, as well as other minority students. One study suggested that minority students experience a "cooling out" effect when they enroll in community colleges (Clark, 1960, 1994). "Cooling out" refers to the perception that community college officials are encouraging minority students to pursue vocational and remedial tracks rather than transfer programs. If this perception is true, many African American males are preparing to enter occupations that relegate them to lower-middle- to middle-class jobs with little opportunity for advancement beyond that level from a socioeconomic perspective.

There are several factors in play in the community college system that impede African American males' efforts to successfully complete the transfer to a four-year institution and graduate. Many students of color find the transfer process particularly difficult in that they lose credit and experience either transfer shock or a decrease in academic performance upon entering the four-year institution (Townsend, 1999). Additionally, research has shown that mentoring plays a significant role in retaining students (Stromei, 2000). Mentors are instrumental in helping these students deal with problems they may encounter in the college environment, which is especially important for those students who are first-generation and have no family members to whom they can relate about the college experience. Finally, the campus climate must be welcoming and compatible to African American men to enhance their opportunities for success in transfer. Community colleges can achieve this, in part, by providing programs and services that focus on creating a diverse campus climate. Such programs and activities include creating diverse orientation programs, providing monies for minority student group and club operations, and including diversity in the curriculum (Clements, 2000).

There have been many efforts to enhance the transfer function since Brint and Karabel's (1989) critical analysis of the community college system. One such effort, conducted during summer 2001, was a conference entitled "Transfer: The Forgotten Function of Community Colleges" (Johnson County Community College, 2001). The conference, focused exclusively on the diminishing mission of transfer in community colleges, was hosted by Johnson County Community College and Oakton Community College and endorsed by the AACC and the League for Innovation in the Community College. The purpose of the conference was to explore the realities of community college transfer programs, the transfer patterns of community college students, statewide transfer initiatives and policies, and the curricular and support services that facilitate transfer.

One presentation, focusing on African American male retention in community colleges in the state of Texas, demonstrated that
the most influential strategies for assisting this group in succeeding academically should focus on identifying at-risk students at
enrollment and monitoring their academic progress; providing a
friendly, inclusive, and helpful student body and faculty; and implementing orientation courses for credit and required tutorial programs (Glenn & Glenn, 2001). Such research and conferences will
be significant in community colleges' analyzing and solving the
problem of African American men's low rate of transfer to four-
year institutions.

AFRICAN AMERICAN MALES' ENROLLMENT AND ACADEMIC SUCCESS

Many are concerned about the educational plight of the African
American male population in community colleges, particularly
their declining enrollment, retention, and graduation numbers
(Hrabowski, Maton, & Greif, 1998; Cross & Slater, 2000). Critics
addressing this population's lack of academic success have particularly focused on the community college system, pointing out the
inability of these institutions to reconcile open admissions with academic standards.

In 1996, there were 231,183 African American males enrolled
in community colleges (see Table 11.2). Even though this was an
18.7 percent increase over the 194,765 population of 1976, it was
far less than the 45.7 percent overall increase in population that
community colleges experienced during the same time span from
1976 to 1996. It's also significant that in 1976, more African American men were enrolled in community colleges as full-time students
(100,095) than as part-time students (94,670), but by 1996 these
enrollment statuses had reversed: more African American men
were enrolled in community colleges as part-time students
(139,248) than as full-time students (91,935) (AACC, 2002).
Clearly, this population is in jeopardy of not achieving academic
success in community colleges, because being enrolled part-time
is considered to be a risk factor that Coley (2000) suggests is detrimental to this success.

TABLE 11.2. COMPARISONS OF COMMUNITY COLLEGE ENROLLMENT
FOR AFRICAN AMERICAN MALES, FEMALES, AND ALL STUDENTS.

	1976	1986	1996	Percent Change From 1976 to 1996
African-American Men				
Overall	194,765	179,568	231,183	18.7
Full-time	100,095	83,075	91,935	−8.2
Part-time	94,670	96,493	139,248	47.1
African-American Women				
Overall	220,548	274,598	392,710	78.1
Full-time	111,274	115,445	154,131	38.5
Part-time	109,274	159,255	238,579	118.3
Overall Enrollment				
Overall	3,743,480	4,467,849	5,454,020	45.6
Full-time	1,582,984	1,633,724	1,984,141	25.3
Part-time	2,160,496	2,934,125	3,469,879	60.6

Source: American Association of Community Colleges, as adapted from U.S. Department of Education, National Center for Education Statistics, Integrated Postsecondary Education Data System (IPEDS).

In the years between 1976–77 and 1999–2000, the total graduation of African American males from community colleges with associate's degrees has increased, but it has not been comparable with their female counterparts. NCES (2001) reported that between the 1976–77 and 1999–2000 academic years, African American women students' associate's degree completion increased by 120 percent, from 17,829 to 39,230. Conversely, during that same time period, African American men only increased their completion rates by 36.7 percent, from 15,330 to 20,951 (see Table 11.3). Even though the completion of this degree by community college students is not a guarantee that they will graduate from a four-year institution, it is one of the factors that has been shown to be conducive to achieving this academic success, as it provides career opportunity and social mobility (Laanan, 2001).

TABLE 11.3. ASSOCIATE'S DEGREES COMPLETED BY AFRICAN AMERICANS
BY GENDER IN SELECTED YEARS.

	1976– 77	1980– 81	1984– 85	1990– 91	1995– 96	1999– 2000	Percent Change 1976–77 to 1999–2000
Females	17,829	21,040	21,607	23,939	33,818	39,320	120.5
Males	15,330	14,290	14,184	13,718	17,854	20,951	36.7

Source: Adapted from National Center for Education Statistics (2002).

Another consequence of African American males not maintaining enrollment and graduating from the community college is the detrimental effect that this has on their possibility of advancing to higher degrees. Research has shown that at the end of the twentieth century, as in the completion of associate's degrees, African American men were earning fewer master's, doctorate, and professional degrees than men in other demographic groups (Cross & Slater, 2000). This has a significant impact on the progress of this group toward racial, economic, and social equality. Based on both the increase over the last twenty years and the expected near-future increase in the number of African American males in community colleges, these students need to be given ample opportunity and support to succeed so that they will ultimately have a chance to achieve an associate's degree and progress toward advanced degrees.

Within the African American population is a special subpopulation: student athletes. In the twenty years between 1983 and 2003, starting with its initiation of Proposition 48, the National Collegiate Athletic Association (NCAA) has attempted to increase the academic standards for admission to their member institutions, while also increasing the graduation rates of those who are admitted. Under Proposition 48, student athletes are required to have a minimum SAT score of 700, or an ACT score of 17, and a minimum GPA of 2.0 in at least eleven courses in core classes in order to compete for Division I colleges (http://www.hardnewscafe.usu.edu/archive/june2002/0606_ncaa.html). The former initiative has resulted in policies—especially the recommendations of the Knight Foundation

Commission on Intercollegiate Athletics (Knight Commission, 1991, 1992, 1993, 2001)—that have resulted in more African American male students beginning their academic careers in the community college system and later transferring to a four-year institution. Research in this area has neglected this population thus far, but in the future it is important that these results be chronicled to address the specific needs and success rates of African American males who matriculate first at community colleges as athletes. Those African American males who participate in athletics in the community college system may possess the motivation to succeed and advance to a four-year institution. The success of these African American athletes would be a significant finding in terms of the success of African American males in the community college, because research has consistently shown that those students in the community college who are unsure of their ultimate academic and career goals typically do not succeed. This finding also would be significant to community colleges' efforts to recruit more African American males to participate in athletics on their campuses rather than at a four-year institution.

As anti-affirmative action legislation is enacted and/or court rulings—such as California's Proposition 209, Washington's Initiative 200, and Hopwood v. State of Texas—are decided to discontinue the use of race in consideration for admission to public higher education institutions, the community college and its open-door policy may become the primary opportunity for African American males to enter higher education (Kaufman, 2000). The community college, which is more accessible and affordable overall compared to HBCUs, may be the principal portal of entry into higher education for African American men. Thus it is important that community college leaders be proactive in developing diverse learning communities that emphasize retention and educational achievement. Many such efforts are presently in place, but it is important to evaluate them to assess whether they are producing the intended results.

A RESEARCH STUDY

In the fall of 2001, the author developed an instrument to assess minority student perceptions of campus diversity. The instrument requested that the students assess several environmental factors related to diversity on their campuses through six sections and forty-one questions. The study was distributed to fifteen community colleges throughout the country. From this study, data were analyzed from three of the sections of the survey for several groups, including African American male respondents. For this chapter, only the responses of these African American male students are analyzed. The three sections of the survey analyzed focus on student perceptions of campus diversity, mentoring, and college leadership.

METHODOLOGY

In spring 2002, 375 surveys were sent to student affairs representatives at fifteen community colleges around the country. These institutions varied in size from a total head count of approximately eight hundred students to ten thousand students. The representative at each institution distributed these instruments to twenty-five racial minority students, including African American, Asian American, Hispanic, and Native American, on the campus or campuses. The students were asked to complete the survey and return it in a sealed envelope to the representative, who returned the collected instruments to the researcher. Through the first distribution, the researcher received 250 instruments, for a return rate of 66.67 percent. Of those instruments returned and used in this study, seventy-four were from African American male respondents. The respondents represented all fifteen of the community colleges that were originally solicited to participate in this study.

RESULTS

The first section that was analyzed focused on minority student perception of campus diversity. The students rated their responses on a Likert scale from 1 to 5, with 1 being "I do not agree with this statement," 3 being "I do not agree or disagree with this statement," and 5, "I agree with this statement." All of the responses were rated just at a moderate level, indicating that the respondents were not in total agreement or disagreement with the statements (see Table 11.4). Of the seven statements, the one that rated the lowest was "All students are receptive and supportive of diversity,"

TABLE 11.4. AFRICAN AMERICAN MALE STUDENT
PERCEPTIONS OF CAMPUS DIVERSITY.

	M	SD
The administration is friendly to diverse students.	3.84	1.11
Faculty is friendly to diverse students on campus.	4.00	0.91
All students are receptive and supportive of diversity.	3.41	1.06
The college's curricula reflect support for diversity.	3.62	1.00
The college's resources are considerate of students from all backgrounds.	4.08	0.95
Staff are welcoming to students from different cultures, backgrounds, and races.	3.86	0.97
This institution treats me, as a person of color, in a friendly manner.	3.92	1.00

Note: n = 74.

which had a mean of 3.41. The statement that rated the highest (M = 4.08) indicated whether students felt the college's resources were considerate of students from diverse backgrounds.

These students seemed to be fairly comfortable on their campuses, thanks to the support that they received from faculty and their colleges' conscious effort to provide resources that respect diversity. However, the students seemed to have some concerns regarding fellow students' support of them on campus and about the curricula not reflecting diversity. Both these issues reflect the literature on campus climate regarding reasons why minority students do not persist in the community college.

The second section of the survey to which the students responded consisted of two-part questions. The first part was similar to the first section in that students indicated their level of agreement with the statement. The second part asked whether they perceived that particular aspect of mentoring to be important: respondents answered yes or no. As with the first section, the level of agreement in the responses was relatively marginal overall for each of the statements (see Table 11.5). The highest-rated statement related to the students' perception of mentoring being a key to success at the institution (M = 4.11). The lowest-rated statement related to whether the student mentored other students (M = 3.35). In each case except one, the positive (yes) responses concerning the importance of each of the statements produced overall ratings of 70 percent or higher. The one exception—again, concerning the respondent's mentoring other students—received a lower overall positive response percentage (62.2 percent).

African American men in this study recognized the importance of mentoring to their success at their respective community colleges. However, the problem seems to be that many of these students are not encountering many administrators and faculty of color to mentor them. Also, it seems that many of these students do not have peer mentors, nor do they mentor other students. This

TABLE 11.5. AFRICAN AMERICAN MALE STUDENT
PERCEPTIONS OF CAMPUS MENTORING.

	Aspect of Mentoring Is Important		*Number of Responses (Percent)*	
	M	*SD*	*Yes*	*No*
There are persons of color in administrative roles at this institution.	3.70	1.17	54 (73.0)	20 (27.0)
There are persons of color in faculty roles at this institution.	3.65	1.20	52 (70.3)	22 (29.7)
There are peer-mentors who can advise me.	3.46	1.14	54 (73.0)	20 (27.0)
The institution supports student-to-faculty interaction.	3.62	0.98	62 (83.8)	12 (16.2)
Faculty serve as mentors for all students.	3.57	1.04	52 (70.3)	22 (29.7)
Staff members mentor students.	3.62	0.95	58 (78.4)	16 (21.6)
I mentor other students.	3.35	2.17	46 (62.2)	28 (37.8)
Mentoring is important for success at this institution.	4.11	0.77	56 (75.7)	18 (24.3)

Note: n = 74.

indicates a need for programs to encourage students who are succeeding to assist new and struggling students. Additionally, in the face of the apparent perception that peer mentoring is not important, it is important for administrators to emphasize the need for successful students to participate in such programs. This task will undoubtedly be a major development challenge because many of these students are nontraditional students, and they have little time to participate in such activities either as mentors or as individuals being mentored.

The final section analyzed focused on perceptions of the community college leadership's support of diversity. The students rated the statements based on the same Likert scale mentioned previously. Each of the statements was rated by the respondents, on average, at 3.19 or slightly higher; compared to the original 1 to 5 Likert scale this is marginal (see Table 11.6). The highest-rated statement related to the college leadership making a positive difference in the lives of diverse student populations on the respondents' campuses (M = 3.73). The lowest response was related to the college president's visibly valuing diversity (M = 3.19).

TABLE 11.6. AFRICAN AMERICAN MALE STUDENT
PERCEPTIONS OF COLLEGE LEADERSHIP DIVERSITY.

	M	SD
The college's leadership values diversity and promotes it on campus.	3.38	1.16
The college president visibly values diversity.	3.19	1.09
College leadership is visible to diverse student populations.	3.22	1.08
The college's administration actively promotes diversity.	3.49	1.09
Institutional leadership interacts frequently with diverse students and their activities on this campus.	3.38	0.95
Creating a multicultural environment is a priority for the college.	3.51	0.98
College leadership makes a positive difference in the lives of diverse student populations.	3.73	1.16

Note: n = 74.

As many of the responses of the latter section were marginal at best, it is apparent that African American students in the community college do not have a very high regard for the administration's leadership in institutional diversity efforts. The administration must be visible to diverse students not only through participation in their activities and programs, but also in providing positive leadership in promoting diversity to the campus and community.

Recommendations

The challenge of improving African American male academic success in higher education has been supported, to a degree, through this research study. Many of the respondents emphasized the need for a campus climate that is conducive to their success. This includes hiring of more administrators and faculty of color, efforts to mentor effectively, and participation and promotion of diversity by community college administrators. However, these are only some of the recommendations that will enhance the academic success of this group of students in the community college. These factors are twofold in that they focus on specific retention-related issues (Martens, Lara, Cordova, & Harris, 1995; Hackett, 2002), and also transfer-related issues (Rendon & Nora, 1994).

Retention Strategies

Since the community colleges are the matriculation venue for large numbers of African American male students, helping them to stay in school and to obtain associate's degrees must be a priority for those who wish to see more African American men receive postsecondary education. The road to degree completion may not be a smooth one. These students may encounter a campus climate that is not conducive to their success, or they may not have the tools or support necessary to succeed. Thus, it is important to attempt to create a climate that is beneficial to African American men at community colleges. This following set of recommendations are interventions designed to keep African American male students in community colleges engaged and motivated during their quest to successfully complete their program of study there.

Academic and social integration. Community colleges must make a conscious effort to ensure that African American male students integrate completely into the fabric of the institution. This process should include faculty, staff, and present students, who provide these students with a sense of community. It is important also that these individuals serve as mentors and role models to help African American male students navigate through community colleges.

Eliminate racism and promote diversity. Diversity consciousness refers to an individual or organization becoming fully aware of and accepting diversity (Buchner, 2000). Institutional leaders must strive to achieve this diversity consciousness by providing proactive leadership in the development of curriculum, their hiring practices, and their support of diversity-based programs and services. Additionally, it is important that these individuals encourage the members of their institutional community, including staff, faculty, and students, to become more diversity conscious also.

Assist students in overcoming triple consciousness. In his novel *The Souls of Black Folks*, W.E.B. DuBois used the term *dual consciousness* to refer to the dual roles that African Americans face in American society as people of African descent, who were once physically enslaved, and as Americans. I would like to submit a third consciousness, that of these individuals as students in higher education. As previously mentioned, many of the students are first-generation college attendees and are from adverse backgrounds. Thus, it is important that community colleges provide sufficient support services to assist them in striking a balance among these three roles. These should focus on study skills enhancement, goal setting, effective counseling (academic, personal, and family), and career development.

Enhance counseling. As many of these students are nontraditional, with multiple responsibilities beyond attending college, it is important to provide services that will assist these students with assistance in balancing these competing demands. This assistance should include job counseling and placement. Job counseling services will particularly benefit African American males who are unsure of their future career goals and are blindly taking courses.

Provide effective orientation programming. As many of these students are not sure of their expectations of college, it is necessary to ensure that they understand what to expect from college and likewise what college expects from them. Many institutions have summer bridge programs specifically designed to provide those students who may be underprepared with an opportunity to attend college immediately after high school. There they can develop the necessary skills to succeed while simultaneously gaining an orientation to college. Unfortunately, as many of these students in the community college are nontraditional students, it may be difficult for them to attend such programs. Administrators must gain a sense of times and information that would be pertinent to these students to ensure that they are enticed to participate in such programs. Thus it is important that institutional leadership create mandatory orientation programs or courses that address similar issues.

Evaluate program effectiveness. The importance of monitoring program success to determine institutional effectiveness cannot be overstated. Administrators must analyze programs and services and determine the impact that these efforts have on student retention, grades, transfer and graduation rates, and service usage. These assessments are important in eliminating programs, policies, and practices that inhibit African American male student success and promoting those that positively influence their academic success.

Hire more African American administrators, faculty, staff, and students. It is important that African American males see individuals "like themselves" in various positions during their matriculation at community colleges. The presence of African Americans in these positions provides encouragement to African American men, as they feel that they can be successful also. Thus institutions must strive to be intentional and diligent in their efforts to hire African Americans at various levels of the community college. Additionally, these individuals can serve as mentors to African American males—relationships that African American male students perceive to be more positive than cross-racial or cross-gender mentoring (Pope, 2002).

Create ethnic, cultural, and social support groups. In her assessment of such programs for African American women, Hackett (2002) notes that such programs provide support to participants as they relate to important ethnic, family, and social values and experiences. Such organizations can be instrumental for African American men also. The Brother-to-Brother program at St. Petersburg College is just such a program: it encourages its participants to focus on the academic and social factors that contribute to their being at risk of not succeeding in college (Leach, 2001). This particular program encourages academic success by promoting high levels of campus involvement and through positive encounters with faculty and staff. It also serves as an impetus for connecting the African American male participants with their local community, through attendance at concerts, films, and luncheons that present positive images of African Americans.

Create programs that connect with African American males' communities. The connection of community colleges with community organizations that are prominent in the lives of African American males can also help promote the success of these students. The Alliance for Excellence is an example of such a relationship (Darr, 1995). This organization, created in 1986, is founded on the notion that the Black church continues to be a significant and effective factor in African American communities, as it has been historically in terms of leadership and influence (for more on this factor, see Chapter Six). Due to the lack of higher-education attainment of African Americans in south central Virginia, five community colleges (originally four) have worked with local communities to provide programming such as motivational seminars, conferences on African American males, awards programs, and youth rallies, with the ultimate goal of enhancing opportunities for African American success in higher education.

Transfer Success Strategies

As the community college is the primary portal to higher education for many African American males, it is important that these institutions not only promote the success of these students on their campuses, but also encourage them to consider their transition to four-year institutions of higher education and support them in that effort. Several strategies may be conducive to promoting this success. These are efforts that would be conducive to the success of all community college populations, but it is important that community college leaders promote these efforts through programs in which African American males participate.

Improve external articulation agreements. Even though many states have articulation agreements that broadly define the process among the institutions within it, it is critical that individual systems and institutions provide the framework to implement these initiatives. Community colleges must make a valiant effort to enhance communication with four-year institutions. They must be able to cooperate with these institutions to create a common course-numbering system, general education core, and identifiable course equivalencies, so that students can transfer easily with or without an associate's degree.

Improve internal articulation agreements. The 2+2 program has been particularly effective at quelling much of the criticism regarding the "glass ceiling" that many students encounter on earning a vocational or technical degree. Through curriculum reform, community colleges have developed programs like this on their campus so that while the students complete the technical-based coursework, they also complete transferable general education coursework. This ensures these students an opportunity to matriculate at a four-year institution without running into the roadblock of not having their coursework transfer and having to completely start over to attain a bachelor's degree.

Create transfer centers and hire transfer counselors. The transfer process can be intimidating for community college students. The transfer center and counselors can provide the information and assistance that these students need to navigate successfully this complicated process. These resources are significant in providing print and on-line copies to explain the college matriculation process and also providing visits to four-year colleges, assistance in application completion, and so on.

Connect African American males with mentors at four-year institutions. As previously mentioned, it is imperative that African American males have mentors as they matriculate through the community college system. It is also important that these students continue to receive this support as they transition to four-year institutions. Thus, deliberate efforts to connect African American males with potential mentors at four-year institutions before they transfer are paramount. Special luncheons or formal "matching" programs where the connection is made between these two groups should be promoted as African American males declare their intention to transfer to a particular institution. These matches will serve as the bridge for African American males as they make visits to these four-year institutions, and as they formally begin their matriculation at these institutions.

Conclusion

For the last fifty years community colleges have provided African American males with a significant opportunity to gain access to postsecondary education. Given this opportunity, these individuals have had a chance to potentially increase their socioeconomic status by completing associate's degrees and possibly more advanced degrees if they enroll in transfer-based programs. However, for African American male students in the community college system, this has not always been a natural transition. As the focus of the community college has diversified so much, this and other factors have adversely affected this population's record of retention and graduation. Additionally, many are critical of the community college and its dealings with African American male students because they perceive the system as merely providing job preparation for these students that relegates them to a lifetime of lower-level positions with minimal opportunities for advancement and low pay. The community college can play a critical role in salvaging African American male students' opportunities to achieve bachelor's degrees by revitalizing the transfer function.

Community colleges can benefit African American men in their collegiate experience in many additional ways. Because the community college student population is more diverse than those of most institutions of higher education, the campus climate is typically more conducive for African American male success. However, institutional personnel must work to ensure that this campus climate is monitored and diverse student interaction is promoted, as well as community college interaction with these students, faculty, and other institutional personnel. By manipulating the campus climate in this way and promoting success mechanisms such as mentoring and advising, the potential of African American men in community colleges will become more equal to that of their counterparts who attend four-year institutions.

Community colleges should also consider their hiring practices when thinking about improving the campus climate for African American men. As many of these students may rarely encounter individuals "like them" in administrative and faculty roles, it is important that institutional leaders encourage minorities and more specifically African American males to apply for vacant positions. These new individuals will greatly benefit the campus in general in that students can see minorities in leadership roles and also gain the opportunity for formal mentoring relationships.

Overall minority student success in the community college is increasing, as demonstrated by the increased number of degrees received in recent years. However, despite these increases, the graduation rates for African American men lags behind other race and gender groups, especially African American women. Even though this issue exists at all levels of education, community colleges should evaluate the success of those African American males who graduate, as well as those who do not, to determine what attributes of the community college contributed or were detrimental to the success of this group. The community college has been criticized in the past for failing to adjust fully to the diversity of its student populations, so these colleges may be overlooking some specific needs that may be conducive to the success of African American males.

Even though the enrollment of African American men in community colleges does not constitute the majority of their enrollment in higher education, as is true for other minorities, the community college still provides a primary entry point into postsecondary education for a significant number of these students. Despite this, the number of African American men enrolled in community colleges and completing associate's degrees—a factor significant in transfer student success in completing bachelor's degrees—is behind those of other groups. Thus it is imperative that administrators in the community college system provide adequate resources and services to ensure the retention and graduation of these students. Part of that solution lies in making the community college environment a more welcoming one for African American male students.

References

American Association of Community Colleges. (2002). About the community college. Higher Education for American Democracy. President's Commission on Higher Education. Retrieved on May 10, 2002, from http://www.aacc.nche.edu/.

Anderson, J. D. (1988). *The education of Blacks in the South, 1860–1935*. Chapel Hill: The University of North Carolina Press.

Brint, S., & Karabel, J. (1989). *The diverted dream: Community colleges and the promise of educational opportunity in America, 1900–1985.* New York: Oxford University Press.

Buchner, R. D. (2000). *Diversity consciousness: Opening our minds to people, cultures and opportunities.* Upper Saddle River, NJ: Prentice Hall.

Clark, B. R. (1960). The cooling out function in higher education. *American Journal of Sociology, 65*(6), 569–576.

Clark, B. R. (1994). The "cooling out" function revisited. In J. L. Ratcliff, S. Schwarz, & L. H. Ebbers (Eds.), *Community colleges. ASHE Reader Series,* 2nd ed. (pp. 67–78). Needham Heights, MA: Simon & Schuster Custom Publishing

Clements, E. (2000). Creating a campus climate in which diversity is truly valued. In S. R. Aragon (Ed.), *Beyond access: Methods and models for increasing retention and learning among minority students.* New Directions for Community Colleges, no. 112 (pp. 63–72). San Francisco: Jossey Bass.

Cohen, A. M., & Brawer, F. B. (1996). *The American community college* (3rd ed.). San Francisco: Jossey-Bass.

Coley, R. J. (2000). *The American community college turns 100: A look at its students, programs, and prospects.* Policy information report. Princeton, NJ: Educational Testing Service.

College Board. (2004). *Trends in college pricing in 2004.* Retrieved on January 20, 2005, from www.collegeboard.com/prod_downloads/press/cost04/041264TrendsPricing2004_Final.pdf.

Cross, T., & Slater, R. B. (2000). The alarming decline in the academic performance of African-American males. *Journal of Blacks in Higher Education, 27,* 82–87.

Darr, S. (1995). Alliance for Excellence: A partnership of colleges and African American churches designed to enhance access and success in higher education. *VCCA Journal, 9*(2), 24–29.

Diener, T. (1994). *Growth of an American invention: From junior to community college.* In J. L. Ratcliff, S. Schwarz, & L. H. Ebbers (Eds.), Community colleges (2nd ed.) (pp. 3–12). Needham Heights, MA: Simon & Schuster.

Dougherty, K. J. (1994). *The contradictory college: The conflicting origins, impacts, and futures of the community college.* Albany, New York: State University of New York Press.

Friedlander, J. (1980). An ERIC review: Why is transfer education declining? *Community College Review, 8*(2), 59–66.

Glenn, F. S., & Glenn, A. (2001, July). The retention of black male students in Texas public community colleges. Paper presented at "Transfer: The forgotten function of community colleges" conference, Johnson County Community College and Oakton Community College, Overland Park, Kansas.

Grubb, W. N. (1999). The economic benefits of sub-baccalaureate education: Results from the national studies. CRCC Brief, no. 2. New York: Community College Research Center, Columbia University.

Hackett, T. J. (2002). Survival strategies for African-American women in the community college. *Learning Abstracts: World Wide Web Edition*, 5(11). Retrieved on January 25, 2005, from www.league.org/publication/abstracts/learning/lelabs0211.htm.

Hrabowski III, F. H., Maton, K. I., & Greif, G. L. (1998). *Beating the odds: Raising academically successful African-American males.* New York: Oxford University Press.

Ignash, J. M. (Aug. 1993). Challenging the revolving door syndrome. ERIC Digest (Identifier: ED361057). Los Angeles, CA: ERIC Clearinghouse for Community Colleges.

Johnson County Community College. (2001, July). Transfer: The forgotten function of community colleges. Conference, Johnson County Community College, Overland Park, KS. Retrieved May 15, 2002, from http://www.oakton.edu/resource/transfer.

Justiz, M. (1994). Demographic trends and the challenges to American higher education. In M. J. Justiz, R. Wilson, & L. G. Bjork (Eds.), *Minorities in higher education* (pp. 1–21). Phoenix, AZ: Oryx Press.

Kaufman, J. (2000). California may change admissions. *Michigan Daily.* Retrieved on May 15, 2002, from http://www.pub.umich.edu/daily/2000/sep/09–26–2000/news/03.html.

Knight Foundation Commission on Intercollegiate Athletics. (1991). *Keeping faith with the student-athlete: A new model for intercollegiate athletics.* Charlotte, NC: Author.

Knight Foundation Commission on Intercollegiate Athletics. (1992). *A solid start: A report on reform of intercollegiate athletics.* Charlotte, NC: Author.

Knight Foundation Commission on Intercollegiate Athletics. (1993). *A new beginning for a new century: Intercollegiate athletics in the United States.* Charlotte, NC: Author.

Knight Foundation Commission on Intercollegiate Athletics. (2001). *A call to action: Reconnecting college sports and higher education.* Charlotte, NC: Author.

Laanan, F. S. (2001). Community college students' career and educational goals. In S. R. Aragon (Ed.), *Beyond access: Methods and models for increasing retention and learning among minority students.* New Directions for Community Colleges, no. 112 (pp. 19–34). San Francisco: Jossey Bass.

Leach, E. J. (2001). Brother-to-brother: Enhancing the intellectual and personal growth of African-American males. *Learning Abstracts: World Wide Web Edition*, 4(5). Retrieved on January 25, 2005, from www.league.org/publication/abstracts/learning/lelabs0111.htm.

Martens, K., Lara, E., Cordova, J., & Harris, H. (1995). Community college students: Ever changing, ever new. In S. R. Helgot, & M. M. Culp (Eds.), *Promoting student success in the community college.* New Directions for Community Colleges, no. 69 (pp. 5–15). San Francisco: Jossey-Bass.

McGrath, D., & Spear, M. B. (1991). *The academic crisis of the community college.* Albany: State University of New York Press.

Monroe, C. (1977). *Profile of the community college.* San Francisco: Jossey-Bass.

Moore, W. M. (1981). Community college response to the high-risk student. ERIC Clearinghouse Monograph.

Myran, G., Zeiss, T., & Howdyshell, L. (1995). *Community college leadership in the new century: Learning to improve learning.* Washington, DC: Community College Press.

National Center for Education Statistics. (1996). *1995–96 National Postsecondary Student Aid Study (NPSAS), Undergraduate Data Analysis System.* Washington, DC: U.S. Department of Education.

National Center for Education Statistics. (2002). Fall enrollment survey, 2000–01 and Completion survey, 1999–2000. *Digest of Education Statistics, 2001,* based on Integrated Postsecondary Education Data System. Washington, DC: U.S. Department of Education.

Nora, A., & Rendon, L. I. (1998). Quantitative outcomes of student progress. Report prepared for the Ford Foundation. New York: Ford Foundation.

Phillippe, K. A., & Patton, M. (2000). *National profile of community colleges: Trends and statistics* (3rd ed.). Washington, DC: Community College Press, American Association of Community Colleges.

Pincus, F. (1980). The false promises of community colleges: Class conflict and vocational education. *Harvard Educational Review, 50*(3), 332–361.

Pope, M. L. (2002). Community college mentoring: Minority student perception. *Community College Review, 30,* 31–46.

Rendon, L. I., & Nora, A. (1994). Clearing the pathway: Improving opportunities for minority students to transfer. In M. J. Justiz, R. Wilson, & L. G. Bjork (Eds.), *Minorities in higher education* (pp. 120–138). Phoenix, AZ: Oryx Press.

Roueche, J. E. (1968). Salvage, redirection, or custody? Remedial education in the community college. Washington, DC: American Association of Community and Junior Colleges.

Roueche, J. E., & Kirk, W. R. (1973). *Catching up: Remedial education.* San Francisco: Jossey-Bass.

Stromei, L. K. (2000). Increasing retention and success through mentoring. In S. R. Aragon (Ed.), *Beyond access: Methods and models for increasing retention and learning among minority students.* New Directions for Community Colleges, no. 112 (pp. 55–62). San Francisco: Jossey-Bass.

Tinto, V. (1998). Colleges as communities: Taking research on student persistence seriously. *Review of Higher Education, 21,* 167–177.

Townsend, B. (1999). Preface. In B. Townsend (Ed.), *Two-year colleges for women and minorities: Enabling access to the baccalaureate* (pp. ix–xii). New York: Falmer Press.

Vaughan, G. B. (2000). *The community college story* (2nd ed.). Washington, DC: American Association of Community and Junior Colleges.

Wilds, D. J. (2001). *Minorities in higher education, 2000–2001: Eighteenth annual status report.* Washington, DC: American Council on Education.

Wilson, R. (1994). The participation of African-Americans in higher education. In M. J. Justiz, R. Wilson, & L. G. Bjork (Eds.), *Minorities in higher education* (pp. 195–209). Phoenix, AZ: Oryx Press.

CHAPTER TWELVE

HELPING AFRICAN AMERICAN MEN MATRICULATE

Ideas and Suggestions

Michael J. Cuyjet, University of Louisville

This book is based on a premise that African American men on college and university campuses have some particular issues, concerns, and needs that make them notably different from African American women, from other collegiate men, and from most other populations of undergraduate students. Consequently, the issues to be addressed, the programmatic offerings established to meet these various special needs, and the probable solutions to the problems identified as particular to African American men may be somewhat different from those for the broader student population—or indeed completely unlike them. Even those issues that African American men share with other campus populations (such as adjusting to the campus environment, maintaining satisfactory academic achievement, or developing positive relationships with others in the campus community) may require that the interventions used to help African American men address these situations successfully be particular to the characteristics and needs of Black men. This is why we have chosen to examine the status of African American men in a variety of circumstances and to offer some suggestions for how to assist these men to succeed in their college matriculation.

This chapter attempts to summarize some of the more salient ideas presented in the preceding chapters of the book and to offer a brief compilation of some of the suggestions and ideas offered by the various authors to assist African American men in their matriculation. Of course, readers are directed back to the particular chapters for more comprehensive explanations of these ideas and suggestions.

SOME BASIC ISSUES AND CONCERNS

The characteristics and circumstances of African American men are particularly significant to note in light of the observation in Chapter One that campus administrators, as well as many researchers who study college students and their issues, tend to focus their attention on African American students without taking notice of the differences between men and women. Thus when examining the outcomes of African American students in a variety of situations on the campus, the successes and failures of the entire population may mask the variant behaviors of one portion of the group. For example, a mean of the grade point averages of African American students would undoubtedly reveal how the group is faring in comparison to the entire student body or another representative group, such as all White students. However, if African American women as one subgroup of this population achieve substantially higher grade point averages than do their African American male counterparts, the poorer performance of the men is concealed. Hence, one of the first and foremost recommendations of this book is for college and university administrators, faculty, and service providers to disaggregate their data and information about students whenever possible to get a true perspective of the relative achievements and failures of relevant subpopulations such as African American men.

A second general recommendation expressed in Chapter One is for college administrators, staff, and faculty to make a concerted effort to understand the African American male culture and its variance from the cultural characteristics of other identifiable population subgroups, particularly the dominant American male culture. A number of researchers (Lee & Bailey, 1999; Majors & Billson, 1992) have documented that the persistent denial of opportunities for a high percentage of African American men to achieve the typical dominant culture benchmarks of success, such as educational achievement, consistent employment and job advancement, and economic stability, have resulted in the creation and adoption of alternate manifestations of "manhood" achievement. Various manhood rituals involving physical prowess or confrontational interactions among peers are often-misunderstood demonstrations of behaviors signaling the achievement of manhood and power, when other means of expressing one's masculinity are not available. The wearing of particular clothing, efforts to acquire certain automobiles and other possessions, use of particular speech patterns, and other physical behaviors different from those of the dominant culture may be judged as aberrant when in fact they are structured demonstrations of masculine achievement recognized among African American men. College and university personnel would be well-served to adopt an attitude that "different is not deficient" and attempt to learn the meaning of such behaviors within the African American male community.

THE ACADEMIC CLIMATE FOR AFRICAN AMERICAN MEN

Chapter Two examined the academic climate for African American men on the campus and how their perception of the climate for their academic achievement might differ from the viewpoints of other students. The authors suggest five areas in which useful interventions could be developed to provide support for African American male students. First, staff can enhance the positive effects and diminish the negative impact of peer group influence. Students can be provided with environments in which they can learn from each other and develop habits of emulating good behaviors that result in increased academic success. At the same time, it is important to monitor and eliminate any negative peer influence that perpetrates the perception that academic success is not "manly" or is associated with "acting White." A second area of intervention is through family influence. Many African American men have strong ties to nuclear and extended family members, particularly to their mothers. Efforts to help students and their family members stay in contact over the distance that separates them when the students move to the campus will provide an important source of emotional and psychological support. These efforts should also include programs that routinely keep family members informed of the campus goings-on and that facilitate bringing the family members to campus for structured programs and informal visits.

A third area of concern is student-faculty relations. We may have to teach African American men that asking for help from faculty is not unmanly. As the authors of Chapter Two address this topic they also strongly recommend the hiring of more African American male faculty to serve as positive role models for African American male students. In the absence of success in that endeavor, campus administrators may want to help any African American young men who have never had a positive relationship with a White male in an academic setting to find ways to identify and connect with such mentors. The fourth area identified by the chapter's authors is the development of self-esteem among African American men, particularly as it relates to academic success. The internalization of negative images, along with messages they have received during their precollegiate education, may leave some African American male students with a low perception of their academic ability and low self-worth as members of the academy. Assessing such issues and bolstering their self-esteem is critical to academic success.

The fifth area of focus in assessing the academic climate for African American men is the general environment of the institution itself. It is critical to understand how African American men perceive the institution—and, perhaps more important, how they perceive that the institution sees *them*. Two suggestions are presented: to pay particular attention to the early adjustment of African American men to the campus and to combat any negative stigma attached to academic support systems provided for African American male students. The latter issue can easily undermine even the most effective academic support programs and must be addressed if it develops.

AFRICAN AMERICAN COLLEGE MEN'S OUT-OF-CLASS ACTIVITIES AND LEADERSHIP PARTICIPATION

The influence of cocurricular and extracurricular activities is deemed so important to the success of African American men in college that two chapters were devoted to this topic. Both Chapter Three and Chapter Four present results from research studies involving African American college men. The first of these studies looks at the perceptions of one group of African American men about some traditional extracurricular opportunities; the second study explores the behaviors of a group of highly successful, high-achieving African American college students.

Chapter Three presents some not-so-surprising results: that African American men have a general lack of out-of-class involvement and profess not to trust the student government organization; thus they have little desire to get involved with it or its various components. These African American men generally do use intramurals and other recreational facilities as a social outlet, but even though they may use the student union for this purpose, they profess to find it not a welcoming place. Recommendations from the author to address some of these issues include efforts to introduce African American men to the availability and benefits of many opportunities for out-of-class involvement beyond sports and physical recreation. The author also suggests that the leadership training given to ethnic majority student leaders should include suggestions of ways to help them understand some of the cultural differences between White and Black students and to try to attract African American male students to become more involved in campus organizations. One additional set of suggestions relates to the effort to help African American male students build a sense of community on the campus by supporting the activities and events that they deem important and by helping them develop healthy, strong interpersonal relationships.

Chapter Four continues this discussion by describing the outcomes of a qualitative assessment of a group of highly successful African American male leaders. The group chronicles a list of significant benefits they have gained from their involvement. Included in that impressive list of accomplishments are practical leadership skills obtained from their positional roles, the ability to work with a culturally diverse population across the campus, time-management skills born of their need to balance many different tasks as campus leaders, teamwork and team-building skills, enhanced skills in public speaking and interpersonal communication, experience in delegating tasks and responsibilities, and political astuteness honed through their interactions with campus and community administrators.

In addition to providing this list of impressive skills and abilities that we might all endeavor to help student leaders acquire, the author offers a number of recommendations that could enhance these efforts. One very important suggestion is that we pay more attention to the collection of empirical data on how African American student leaders are using their time, so we can compile the sort of information the author did as a guide to our actions. Among the other suggestions are making intentional efforts to recruit African American student leaders and to encourage those young men who come to the attention of the administration to seek and obtain positional leadership roles, holding other student leaders accountable to reaching out to African American student leaders and working closely with them as fellows, providing institutional support—financial and advisory—to help African American leaders succeed in their efforts, and developing a sensitivity to and awareness of any issues of racism so they can be addressed quickly to avert any impact that might distract African American student leaders from performing at their peak capability.

DEVELOPMENTAL MENTORING OF AFRICAN AMERICAN COLLEGE MEN

General benefits of mentoring are well documented in the research literature and in a wide range of books written on this topic. Rather than redundantly review the merits of mentoring, Chapter Five calls attention to the difference between typical "instructional" mentoring and "developmental" mentoring, which the author describes as a form of mentoring that promotes the protégé's ability to actively participate in his or her own development, rather than simply following the directions and guidance of the mentor. Readers wishing to make use of the information presented in this chapter might first examine the mentoring opportunities for African American men on their own campuses to determine if they fit the description of developmental mentoring. If not, a restructuring of such programs to allow for active participation in the decisions about the nature and content of developmental activities may be in order. Among other characteristics, a developmental mentoring program should provide opportunities for protégés to make some of the important decisions about the mentoring relationship. Developmental mentoring also allows for building helpful relationships other than the primary mentor-protégé pairing.

Additionally, the author offers several suggestions to enhance the effectiveness of mentoring programs for African American college men. Primary among these is a recommendation that developmental mentors receive comprehensive training, which includes the ability to express to their protégés a strong sentiment of caring and clear interest in their welfare. Other suggestions include adequate financial support; opportunities for intercampus communication, meetings, and symposia; and campuswide activities, particularly those that provide affirmation and celebration of the mentoring relationships and positive outcomes.

SPIRITUALITY AND RELIGIOUS ACTIVITY AMONG AFRICAN AMERICAN COLLEGE MEN

Chapter Six starts with the premise that spirituality and religion are important elements in the lives of many African American college men and thus merit some attention by those campus administrators who endeavor to understand and assist these students. The chapter author reports on the results of an empirical study that reveals, among other things, that African American college men are committed to holding on to the value of spirituality and religion as a means of coping with the struggles of their college experiences. The author describes two elements of spirituality—creative soul force and resistant soul force. The former refers to the interpretation of reality through the creative construction of Black culture; resistant soul force is described as spiritual creativity that allows one to overcome oppression. Administrators wishing to better understand the role spirituality plays in the lives of African American male students might wish to develop the ability to discern these two forms of "soul force" and how they are manifested in the lives of their students. Readers are also advised to reflect on their own spirituality before engaging in such an examination and to remain as open as possible to students notions of spirituality, which may differ from their own.

AFRICAN AMERICAN COLLEGE FRATERNITY MEMBERS

Chapter Seven presents a comprehensive and balanced examination of the impacts—both positive and negative—of fraternity membership on African American college men. Acknowledging that the institutional environment plays a significant role in determining which of these characteristics is more prevalent on any given campus, the authors advise readers to review this list of possible effects and determine which ones are evident on their campus, which positive ones they might want to cultivate, and which negative ones administrators could work to eliminate. In particular, the positive outcomes of fraternity membership—such as leadership development, practical competencies in such skills as event planning and program marketing, and any demonstrated accomplishments in cognitive development or its manifestation through successful academic measures (that is, grade point averages) should be noted and publicly celebrated. Unfortunately, besides encouraging these few ideas, neither the chapter author nor this writer has a list of suggestions for counteracting the continual problems with hazing, general academic mediocrity, and declining public perception that seem to affect many African American fraternity chapters.

AFRICAN AMERICAN MALE COLLEGE ATHLETES

Although it's recognized that athletics is often a self-contained and somewhat isolated entity on many campuses (particularly at NCAA Division I schools), readers who perceive that they might be able to have some effect on the environment for African American men are encouraged to make overtures to include African American male athletes in their programming and activities to benefit all African American men on campus. This effort can have the additional benefit of enhancing the academic and social integration of African American male athletes into the rest of campus life, which has been shown to have a positive effect on this group of students. The author of Chapter Eight mentions the importance of academic supports such as tutoring, mentors, and peer advisors. If such programs are not already in place in the athletic department (or even if they are), administrators can target such services to athletes. Campus administrators are also encouraged to provide exposure and support for participation by African American men in certain programs specifically designed for the athletes' involvement on the campus (e.g., STAGS—Skills To Achieve Growth and Success) or the surrounding community (e.g., CHAMPS—Challenging Athletes' Minds for Personal Success).

AFRICAN AMERICAN GAY MEN

Chapter Nine offers a number of suggestions to help campus administrators develop a better appreciation of gay or bisexual men—one of the least understood groups among African American male college students. The author suggests that understanding the various factors that impact identity formation is a key to appreciating the difficulty that gay African American men experience on the typical campus. Because of the multiple aspects of a Black gay man's identity—whether he identifies first as an African American or as a gay person, what label he uses to describe himself, and how others label him—this is a complex set of issues. One particular issue that affects African American gay men in a manner differently from other gay men is their relationship with religion; given the impact of the Black church on most African American students, we are advised to pay special attention to the impact of religion on African American gay college males. Developing the trust of key members of the African American gay men's community is the first step to gaining the personal knowledge of this population's circumstances, struggles, and resources on a particular campus. Once a trust relationship is established, other interventions that are viewed by gay African American men as important and supportive— such as hiring openly gay African American male faculty and staff, and openly supporting GLBT organizations and insisting that their services be equitably available to African Americans—can follow.

AFRICAN AMERICAN MEN AT HISTORICALLY BLACK COLLEGES AND UNIVERSITIES

To explore the issues and circumstances of African American men at historically Black colleges and universities (HBCUs)—one of two special environments examined in chapters of this book—the authors of Chapter Ten conducted a qualitative analysis using two focus groups drawn from students at several HBCUs. They identified five general theme areas that administrators are advised to examine on any particular campus for their impact on the African American male students there: (1) male students' lack of predisposition to attend college as opposed to entering the workforce or the military after high school; (2) their lack of academic preparation and their lack of maturity for engaging in the relationships that usually will develop during college years, and their general failure to take advantage of supports provided on the campus; (3) their lack of involvement in activities and organizations (except for a preference to engage in athletic competition) and in leadership roles in which men can learn to work collaboratively; (4) a general deficiency in healthy male-female interpersonal relations, a problem for which both men and women must accept some responsibility; and (5) HBCU African American men's perceptions of predominantly White institutions (PWIs) as superior to their own schools—a perception unfortunately shared by their parents in many cases. Fortunately, however, these men did express that they see HBCUs as a much better environment than PWIs to foster their understanding of Black culture.

In addition to suggesting the development of a better understanding of these issues, the authors offer a few recommendations for addressing these matters. Their advice includes carefully tracking college men's academic performance to have a clearer idea of where the problems may lie, using peers and personal invitations to attract African American men to support programs until they begin to see the benefits of participating, and encouraging and facilitating student-faculty interactions focused on engaging African American men with their instructors outside of the classroom.

AFRICAN AMERICAN MEN AT COMMUNITY COLLEGES

The second special environment examined in this book is that of the community college. Recognizing that, as a group, when compared to their counterparts at four-year institutions, African American men in community colleges are more likely to be the first in their families to attend college and to come from families with lower income, the author of Chapter Eleven recommends some interventions that should be particularly helpful to African American male students in community colleges. As a population that attends community college in lower numbers and fails to persist in higher numbers than other demographic groups, African American men can benefit from efforts to carefully monitor their academic progress, particularly as it relates to the transfer function that makes them eligible to continue their education at four-year schools. Corresponding to this attention to the students' progress in the transfer function, the author recommends training of counselors in transfer offices and centers so they are particularly sensitive to issues of racism on the campus and African American male cultural characteristics that can affect the relationship between such employees and the students they are serving.

The author also suggests the enthusiastic use of cultural and social support groups that focus on the interests of African American men and will attract them to participate in such organizations. Encouraging these commuter students to be on the college campus for purposes other than simply going to classes promotes a sense of belonging and community that can positively affect African American male students' retention.

CONCLUSION AND SUGGESTIONS FOR THE FUTURE

By examining various components of higher education as they relate to African American men, we hope to have provided a context in which an assessment of the conditions of African American men on any particular campus can be accomplished more easily. We recognize that there are aspects of the campus life we have not addressed in this work that can have an effect on students in general and African American men in particular. The limitations of this volume did not accommodate the inclusion of several other characteristics that one might need to consider when looking into the circumstances of African American men on any particular campus. For example, this book focused primarily on undergraduate students and did not talk about the particular aspects of graduate education that might have an impact on African American men's achievement. Although we discussed some of the specific issues of gay African American men, African American male athletes, and African American fraternity members, there are other subpopulations within the African American male student body, such as a subgroup mentioned only briefly in Chapter Four: the small but important group of African American men who are academically gifted and high academic achievers. Because they tend to defy the stereotype of African American college men as underprepared for college and consequently academic underachievers, these talented young men are often off the radar of the administrators who monitor the progress of students of color.

Although there is some attention paid here to African American men in two particular environments—HBCUs and community colleges—there are nuances and circumstances manifested by other environmental factors that have not been addressed. For example, rural institutions, particularly in mostly White communities, offer a very different environment from an urban school, especially an urban school in proximity to a substantial Black community. There is almost certainly a situational impact on African American men at small colleges compared with those at large universities, particularly if the percentage of African Americans among students at the small school is quite low. In fact, the size of the African American student population and the ratio of men to women within that populace will have an effect on African American male students by impacting the roles they are expected to play in a particular environment. For example, at some of the larger universities in the country there are literally thousands of African American students (a population of African American students larger than that at all but a very few HBCUs), and the ratio of men to women may come closer to being even. That is a very different environment from many of the schools across the country, where African American men represent about one-third of a small group of perhaps a few hundred African Americans amid a large group of Whites.

The parting suggestion here is to focus on the particular environment of each college or university and carefully assess its impact on the various aspects of the lives of the African American men attending school there. Careful assessment, careful observation, open communication, an honest expression of a sense of caring, and true concern for the welfare of African American men on the campus are a healthy beginning to any effort to support this critical population of students.

A final recommendation for those interested in helping African American men to finish college successfully is to find examples of places where colleagues are getting it done. There are numerous efforts, from large programs to small group activities, by which student affairs professionals, academic administrators, faculty, and student peers are assisting African American men to thrive in the college environment and earn their degrees. The final part of this book is a place to start; but these nine examples are only a brief, tantalizing taste of the many fine efforts being made across the country each day to enhance the graduation rates of African American men, one man at a time.

References

Lee, C. C., & Bailey, D. F. (1999). Counseling African American male youth and men. In C. C. Lee (Ed.), *Multicultural issues in counseling: New approaches to diversity* (2nd ed.). (pp. 123–154). Alexandria, VA: American Counseling Association.

Majors, R., & Billson, J. M. (1992). *Cool pose: The dilemmas of black manhood in America.* New York: Lexington.

PART TWO

PROFILES OF SOME SUCCESSFUL PROGRAMS

Recognizing that many student affairs practitioners and academic administrators across the country are actively engaged in efforts to enhance the collegiate experiences of African American men, it seemed useful to invite some of them to describe their programs for the rest of us. The individuals who have contributed these profiles of their support programs were asked to describe the program's structure and function and to explain any measurable results that have been observed.

These profiles are offered so readers can use them to generate ideas for activities, programs, and services that can be developed on other campuses. Readers are invited to borrow freely from the examples presented. Realizing that each of these profiles is probably only truly applicable to the campus at which it was originally devised, readers are particularly encouraged to select certain parts of programs that might be applicable to their own campuses. For, example, the Meyerhoff Scholarship Program profiled here was originally funded with a very large foundation grant. Since most schools are not that fortunate, it is unlikely that administrators can easily emulate this entire program on other campuses. However, on a particular campus it might be possible to replicate one or several of the individual components of the Meyerhoff program, using available (or attainable) resources, and thus provide some of the benefits to other African American men that the Meyerhoff administrators have been able to offer on that one campus.

Of all the possible choices of literally hundreds of programs in existence on campuses across the country, only nine are represented here, for several reasons. First, this sampling is not intended to be a comprehensive representation of programs for African American men in college. These profiles are not the primary focus of the book; rather, they are mainly intended to demonstrate some of the ideas and suggestions beneficial to African American college men that are offered in Part One of this book. The idea is to give readers a small sampling from which to glean ideas and to develop their own programs that fit the particulars of the individual campus, not a lengthy list from which to select programs to use in their current form. A second reason for limiting the number of program profiles was an editorial decision to allocate the space in this book to the discussions of research and the dissemination of ideas in the preceding chapters rather than by anecdotal example using a larger sampling of programs.

A third limiting factor was the relative difficulty of collecting enough useful, comprehensive information about these programs and presenting those data in a uniform and easily understandable format. More than two dozen invitations were extended to obtain the nine programs presented. It is an ironic and fitting tribute to many of our colleagues that they would often rather run the programs than write about them. One other factor that limited the identification of sample programs was that each one included here is known to the editor. Having stated that, apologies are extended to any reader who is involved in a wonderful program that you feel would be a great addition to this collection of programs, but is not here simply because the editor did not know about it. It is hoped that this work will motivate those of you around the country who have established viable, productive programs to support African American men on your campus to share information about what you are doing by e-mail, internet websites, listservs, conference presentations, journal articles, books, and other publications.

As mentioned above, this sampling of programs is intended to showcase a wide range of idea and suggestions, so each profile includes at least one particular characteristic that sets it apart from the others.

The first offering is the Student African American Brotherhood (SAAB), a program begun at a single campus in 1990 that has since developed chapters at more than eighty colleges and universities across the country. The SAAB model is perhaps the most versatile of the programs presented here because it has been adapted to large and small institutions, urban and rural schools, and four-year institutions and community colleges, and exists at PWIs as well as HBCUs. The national office in Toledo, Ohio, provides support to all recognized chapters.

The Meyerhoff Program is one of the most widely cited examples of a major initiative to increase the production of members of underrepresented populations with college degrees in the "hard" sciences, engineering, and mathematics. It is one of the longest-running and most established programs of this kind in the country. Originally begun in 1988 as a program just for African American men, it was later expanded to include women and members of other ethnic groups. As mentioned above, we include the Meyerhoff Program here not because we think other campuses are likely to have access to an endowment such as the one that began the program at the University of Maryland–Baltimore County, but because its various elements—such as the summer bridge program or the personal advising and counseling component—may serve as useful examples for others.

Bowling Green State University's Black Men on Campus (BMOC) program is presented here as a program with several related components that can be used together or as separate elements. In fact, when the funding for the "rap session" portion of the original BMOC program was discontinued, the other parts of the program persisted. That particular one-time session is a good example of the use of resources from within and outside the campus community to staff a purposeful program. The first component of the BMOC program is a noteworthy example of the adaptation of a typical freshman orientation credit course for use specifically to enhance adaptation of African American men to the campus.

The Black Men's Collective (BMC) is another program located on a state-supported campus, but it is more inclusive of both student and nonstudent participants than the programs just described. Rather than a program of events presented *by* administrators *for* students, the BMC includes students, faculty, staff, and alumni from throughout the university in a collective that examines various topics of interest to the members of the entire group. Although the BMC has several organized subunits and identified leaders of those committees, it is less structured in its program delivery than some other men's support groups described here, choosing to sponsor various programs on the campus as the members so determine.

The Black Male Rap Session (B-MRS, pronounced "beamers") at the University of Louisville is less formally structured than most programs among these examples. As the name suggests, it is a biweekly opportunity for a group of African American undergraduates to come together to "rap" with each other about topics of mutual interest. Membership is fluid; whoever happens to show up on a particular day participates in that session and is not obligated to any particular set of additional responsibilities. B-MRS does not exclude women if they wish to attend a session.

The African American Men of Arizona State University (AAMASU) is an example of a structured intervention developed to address the concerns about the low rates of recruitment and retention of undergraduate African American men on this large public research university campus. It is sponsored by Arizona State University's Multicultural Student Center (MSC), with support from other university agencies such as the Admissions Office, the Educational Opportunity Center, and the Upward Bound program. The AAMASU program has two major components: a "high school to college" recruitment program focused on the surrounding community and a college programming component that sponsors efforts to support African American male students and keep them in school to graduation.

The Black Man Think Tank at the University of North Texas was a one-day program held in 2001 that brought together African American students for a series of presentations and discussions to provide a sense of brotherhood and community among the students at UNT and other surrounding campuses. It was modeled after the original Black Man Think Tank Conference, developed by Dr. P. Eric Abercrumbie at the University of Cincinnati and held for fourteen years in Cincinnati. The UNT spin-off is profiled here, rather than the original program, for several reasons: first, to demonstrate how one campus can emulate and adapt a program from another university, and second, because there is a good amount of information already available about the Cincinnati program. Other campuses besides UNT have already adapted the Think Tank model.

Two aspects of the It's Easier Than You Think program make it a special addition to this review of example programs. First, it is the only one on this list solely at an HBCU, although both SAAB and the Collegiate 100 have chapters at HBCUs. Second, it is the only program among these examples conceived and produced by a single undergraduate student. In that sense, it could be unique. The program's creator was not performing academically as well as he wished. He then identified a series of steps to take, turned around his own academic achievement, and decided to share his plan with his fellow African American male students. The program consists of the five principles of good study habits that he was able to use to produce remarkable results in his own academic success, as well as examples of how they can be adopted by other students.

The Collegiate 100 program completes this short set of sample programs. The 100 is a national organization of successful African American men who strive to offer mentoring and support for elementary- and high school–age African American young men in their communities by providing role models, personal mentoring experiences, and other civic community service. Like SAAB, Collegiate 100 is located on a number of campuses across the country. Each chapter is sponsored on a college or university campus by a local chapter of the 100 Black Men of America, Inc., in a proximate city or community. The Collegiate 100 chapters were developed to provide additional manpower from among the campus undergraduate population for these efforts in the community, but they also provide a medium for the members of 100 Black Men to provide similar mentoring and role modeling to the undergraduates themselves.

Although not an extensive set of examples, it is hoped that each reader of these profiles can find some element of these collective efforts to support collegiate African American men that the reader can use to develop similar efforts on his or her campus.

CHAPTER THIRTEEN

STUDENT AFRICAN AMERICAN BROTHERHOOD

Tyrone Bledsoe, University of Toledo

Kevin D. Rome, Sr., Morehouse College

The Student African American Brotherhood (SAAB) organization was founded on November 10, 1990, by Dr. Tyrone Bledsoe to address the academic challenges to African American males at Georgia Southwestern State University. The organization's mission evolved out of the belief that there was a need to enhance the experiences of African American males in college. SAAB relies on the belief that the challenges facing African American males can be resolved by providing student development interventions and support to its participants.

How should African American males themselves respond to the critical situation of the majority of young Black men entering college failing to complete the baccalaureate degree? One response would be to ignore the situation and place the blame on our institutions and systems. Another would be to take positive steps by demonstrating that there are alternatives to the self-destructive path too many Black men take. Indeed, SAAB has accepted the challenge of carrying the shield to overcome obstacles to a brighter side of life. The organization offers the younger generation a means by which to think, act, and prepare for a better future than that which befalls too many of their brothers.

The SAAB organization is one of the most dynamic and fastest-growing associations in the country. It serves to assist its members to excel academically, socially, culturally, personally, and professionally. The goal is for all Black males at participating institutions to take full advantage of their academic years and to better understand and practice their full responsibilities, rights, and privileges as citizens of this country. Also, SAAB provides an opportunity for its members to work in the community with other younger Black males in need of guidance and direction. To further serve the community, SAAB has also adopted Habitat for Humanity and Big Brothers and Sisters as its official service projects. To accomplish its goals, educational and cultural activities are offered to all student participants. Services such as tutorial assistance, career planning and counseling, cultural and social activities, personal development opportunities, community service and service learning, and spiritual enrichment opportunities are offered. All of the organization's programs are designed to promote positive thinking and high self-esteem in African American male students. The primary objective of the organization is that all Black male members will be role models for each other as well as for other Black males in their community. Values-based leadership serves as one of the cornerstones of the organization. Additionally, it is hoped that SAAB members will be well prepared to enter the workforce of professionals and compete with the best for a meaningful place in our society. By offering these services, by providing positive role models, and by employing its three-pronged approach to mentoring, SAAB increases the chances for successful college matriculation for African American males. The SAAB three-pronged approach to mentoring involves (1) peer-to-peer transactions among college students, (2) advisor-to-student transactions, and (3) older student (collegiate) to younger student (high school and middle school) transactions. Many students in SAAB reported their satisfaction with the three-part mentoring component of the organization in that they experienced success in adjusting to college, the ability to connect and bond with other male students in a nonthreatening manner, the positive effect of faculty and staff mentors on their academic prowess as reflected in their grade point averages, and the personal fulfillment of serving as individual mentors to others.

SAAB STRUCTURE

Although each chapter is somewhat different from the others in that it is individualized to meet the particular needs of the men in each campus environment, there are some commonalities in the structure among the various chapters of SAAB. The basic structure of each chapter in the organization consists of six committees addressing the following areas: (1) personal development, (2) service, (3) academic, (4) financial affairs, (5) spiritual-enrichment/social, and (6) membership/public relations. Each committee is headed by a chair and cochair.

The personal development committee is responsible for creating and offering programs to foster student development and learning among the membership. An important component of this committee is the "teachable moment," an educational seminar conducted by one or more SAAB members during the regular meetings of the organization.

The service committee is responsible for organizing service learning initiatives for SAAB members. SAAB has formed national partnerships with Habitat for Humanity and the Big Brothers and Big Sisters programs.

The academic committee is responsible for coordinating with student support services (such as career services, academic support centers, student and leadership development) on members' campuses. The committee serves to enhance recruitment and retention efforts at members' universities, with particular emphasis on first-year African American males.

The financial affairs committee is responsible for developing financial seminars for the membership, with sessions on money management, tax preparation, consumer credit information, stocks and bonds, mutual funds, investment clubs, entrepreneurial opportunities, business plans, and general accounting practices.

The spiritual-enrichment/social committee is responsible for providing opportunities for the membership to bond and socialize. It plans activities such as church visits, bowling, movies, golf, the theatre, athletic sport events, and many other civic and community events.

The membership/public relations committee is responsible for maintaining the membership roster and database, developing the web site, promoting the use of technology (such as using e-mail, searching the Web, joining listservs, creating PowerPoint presentations, accessing the Blackboard Learning System, and so on), new member orientation, and promotion of all organizational activities and programs.

PUTTING THE SAAB MODEL INTO OPERATION

The student leaders and advisors within the organization work to define and embrace SAAB's four core values: proactive leadership, accountability, intellectual development, and self-discipline. One benefit of SAAB membership is that participants have the opportunity to discuss issues germane to African American males with their peers. Another is that faculty members and advisors provide an understanding of the importance of academic achievement. SAAB members also have opportunities to develop public speaking and group presentation skills by making presentations to their peer group. For example, as a means of actualizing the personal development aspect of the organization's mission and achieving appropriate goals and outcomes in that area, a SAAB organization may choose to recognize a member's in- and out-of-class involvement with the faculty. Or the group may intentionally choose to structure discussions focusing on what the members are currently experiencing in college.

A very important part of SAAB is the constant, supportive involvement of its advisors. They are expected to form a relationship with each chapter member and to coordinate the systematic effort to enhance the development of all individual participants and the organization as a whole in ways that support both the members and the respective university or college.

SAAB EFFECTIVENESS

The SAAB organization has attracted national attention as an innovative prototype for personal and academic enrichment, and has been successfully replicated at public and private schools, at four-year institutions and community colleges, and at both PWIs and HBCUs. To this end, the organization can regularly provide its members information and referrals on financial aid, part-time employment opportunities, public service opportunities, academic assistance, counseling services, and medical and health-related services. SAAB encourages its members to participate and get involved with other aspects of campus life, such as campus activities boards, student governmental boards, resident assistants, and other key student leadership opportunities. While SAAB is purposeful, just, and disciplined as well as open, the key characteristic that makes its objectives work is the way the members relate to one another. The organization creates an environment in which every individual member is affirmed and every activity of the organization is humane. Caring as a value is the key to creating the ethos within the organization. The members cherish their independence and accept as commonplace an organizational climate that is open and relaxed.

Perhaps the most significant reason SAAB is effective as an organization is the development of incentives for its members to make active commitments to one another and to their own personal development. Each chapter's personal development committee is committed to connecting the day-to-day life of the organization with the goals of the committee. Opportunities for members to mature—in ways such as achieving academic success, taking a leadership position, providing service to the community, setting organizational standards of behavior, and assisting members with resolving interpersonal conflicts—strengthen the organization's effectiveness.

SAAB ASSESSMENT INITIATIVES

For SAAB to develop the talents of individual participants, it is important to assess the climate of the organization, as this significantly influences the direction and extent of the personal, social, and intellectual development of its members. A number of surveys are administered to SAAB participants throughout the year. Also, each chapter uses focus groups in an effort to detect positive and possible negative implications associated with the institution's climate for the academic and personal development of its members. This strategy provides a clearer understanding of the manner in which the group's values and organizational structures and processes influence members and thus gives members an active role in shaping the organization's environment.

SAAB MEMBERSHIP

SAAB has active chapters or initiative groups on more than one hundred college campuses. At the time of this writing SAAB also had established pilot sites at four community colleges and five high schools. SAAB collegiate chapters are composed primarily of African American undergraduate male students, who strive for academic excellence and make a commitment to plan and implement programs that benefit themselves, their respective colleges, and the community at large. The organization membership is diverse in that some chapters have graduate student members while others have non-Black members (Whites, Latinos, Asians). The typical SAAB chapter has between fifteen and forty members, representing many different social and economic backgrounds, a wide spectrum of academic majors, varying levels of academic achievement, and different amounts of campus involvement—although all chapter members are encouraged to participate in other student organizations (including social fraternities, if they so desire).

SAAB CHAPTER UNIQUENESS

Although every SAAB chapter employs the basic structure and committee organization described in the previous section, each chapter also has unique characteristics. The specific needs of the chapter members are an important influence on the unique focus of each chapter. For example, one chapter might determine that academic support of the members is paramount to other issues. Another chapter, in which the members feel that the campus is delinquent in providing adequate social opportunities for African American men, might choose to emphasize the social bonding aspects of the chapter's brotherhood.

Another influence on the nature of each chapter is the size, affiliation, and location of the institution at which the chapter is located. The organization comprises chapters at colleges and universities of different types. The following are seven examples of SAAB chapters that demonstrate both the diversity and unique nature of each chapter and how the type of institution influences the focus of its SAAB chapter:

- Georgia Southwestern State University (small public university in a small rural town)
    Enrollment—three thousand or fewer
    Impetus—SAAB support is needed for the African American male students, many of which are first-generation college students who live within an hour of the university. SAAB

supports the institution's goal of keeping students connected to the university as well as with faculty members
and other students.

- University of Texas-Austin (large public research I university)
  Enrollment—30,000 or more
  Impetus—SAAB support is needed for the African American
  males who may feel lost or isolated at this large university
  in a big city; the student population is extremely large and
  the African American student population is fairly small.

- Ohio University (large public university in a small town)
  Enrollment—25,000 or fewer
  Impetus—SAAB support is needed for African American
  males, as African Americans are a small percentage of all
  students at the university and there are very few African
  Americans in the local community.

- University of Toledo (large public research-based university)
  Enrollment—21,000 or fewer
  Impetus—SAAB support is needed for the African American
  males at this large metropolitan university with an urban
  mission and a fairly substantial first-generation college student population. SAAB has served to connect and engage
  African American males at the institution. Many of the students maintain jobs off campus and extremely demanding
  schedules that may include family commitments away from
  campus, making it imperative to provide a forum to connect
  African American males to the university environment.

- North Carolina Wesleyan College (small private liberal arts
  institution)
  Enrollment—2,000 or fewer
  Impetus—SAAB support is needed for the African American
  males at this private college in a small town. The average
  age for the student body tends to be twenty-five or older,
  and many students maintain an extremely demanding
  schedule alongside their studies. The older students need
  a means to facilitate connections with other African American men with similar interests. Because SAAB recognizes
  their spiritual needs, the men at this religiously affiliated
  college are free to express their beliefs among their peers.

- North Carolina Central University (small public historically Black institution)

  Enrollment—6,000 or fewer

  Impetus—SAAB support is needed for the African American males at this small public HBCU in a large city. SAAB provides African American males with a forum for developing strong male relationships and positive social and academic integration within the context of a Black-oriented environment. North Carolina Central University was the first historically Black institution to establish a SAAB chapter.

- Foothill College (mid-size multicultural community college)

  Enrollment – 17,000 or fewer

  Impetus – SAAB support is needed for the African American and Latino males at this community college in a large city. SAAB serves as a link between the African American and Latino males, who have many similar needs and issues, and establishes a community in which they interact easily. Foothill College was the first community college to establish a chapter of SAAB.

CONTINUOUS DEVELOPMENT ON A NATIONAL LEVEL

This brief set of examples is intended to demonstrate the flexibility of the SAAB model and the potential for its benefits to serve as a strong retention tool for a broad segment of the African American male undergraduate population. At the time of this writing there are more than eighty-four active SAAB collegiate chapters across the country and initiative chapters seeking permanent status at approximately forty-one other institutions of higher education. Efforts have begun to establish chapters at community colleges and high schools. (For an up-to-date list of SAAB chapters and other information about the organization, go to http://www.2cusaab.org.) There may very well be SAAB chapters on hundreds of campuses within a few more years. All of these efforts are coordinated through the national office, established in 2004 in Toledo, Ohio.

CHAPTER FOURTEEN

MEYERHOFF SCHOLARSHIP PROGRAM

University of Maryland, Baltimore County

Earnestine Baker

Editor's note: Although it is not anticipated that many institutions are fortunate enough to secure a grant of the size given to UMBC by the Meyerhoffs, the program is presented here as a model because of the success of its various components in improving the matriculation of the participating students. Other schools may wish to emulate some of these components to fit their needs and assist their African American male students in the science, engineering, and mathematics areas, as well as students in other majors.

In August 1988, nineteen African American men embarked on a life-changing academic journey that would take them from the University of Maryland, Baltimore County (UMBC), to the highest echelons of academia and research. Their extraordinary academic and professional success—and that of the several hundred students who have followed them—is attributable to the goals and specific structure of the Meyerhoff Scholarship Program, a philanthropic initiative established at UMBC to address the dearth of minority students earning advanced degrees in science, engineering, and mathematics (SEM).

Begun as a collaboration between UMBC and Baltimore philanthropists Robert and Jane Meyerhoff, the Meyerhoff Scholarship

Program now annually enrolls over two hundred students and has graduated more than three hundred students, nearly all of whom are currently engaged in or about to complete graduate studies at some of the most prestigious schools in the United States. Building on an initial $500,000 gift from the Meyerhoffs, by 2005 the Meyerhoff Scholarship Program's endowment had grown to nearly $7 million, making it the largest scholarship program for minority education in the sciences in the United States. In 1989, the program was opened to women, and it now enrolls nonminorities who pass the program's rigorous selection process.

The Meyerhoff Scholarship program also demonstrates that generous financial endowments alone are not the sole predictors of academic success, particularly for African American students, whose retention rate in the sciences has historically been poor. Although many programs directed to minority students address remediation and deficits, the Meyerhoff Scholarship Program operates on a "strengths model," which assumes that every student selected to participate is capable of succeeding in the sciences and engineering, given the appropriate resources and opportunities. As a consequence, the Meyerhoff Scholarship program is now one of the leading sources of minority students pursuing graduate degrees in the sciences, mathematics, and engineering and is widely regarded as a model for success to be emulated nationwide.

The Meyerhoff Scholarship Program's success is based on fifteen key components, detailed as follows.

RECRUITMENT OF HIGH-ACHIEVING MATH AND SCIENCE STUDENTS

Meyerhoff Scholars are recruited from among the top science and mathematics students across the United States. Demand for the coveted scholarships far exceeds availability. Culling the best and brightest is the first step in ensuring that Meyerhoff Scholars will fulfill their promise. In 2005, forty-six freshmen with an average SAT score of 1309 and a grade point average of 3.95 were selected from over 2,200 applicants and nominees nationwide. Meyerhoff Scholars achieve grade point averages of 3.54 (of a possible 4.0) in science, engineering, and mathematics curricula. Prospective students cannot have received lower than a B in any high school science or math course, and many have already completed a year of calculus or advanced problem-solving courses in high school.

After recruitment, top prospects receive an invitation to a two-day Selection Weekend at UMBC, during which students and their families receive an intensive immersion in the rigorous expectations posited on Meyerhoff Scholars. This in-depth screening process helps identify students who not only are academically prepared for a science, engineering, or math major, but also are supportive of the Program's goals and genuinely committed to a postgraduate research-based degree and career.

SCHOLARSHIP SUPPORT

Upon acceptance as Meyerhoff Scholars, students are offered a comprehensive, four-year scholarship package that includes tuition, books, room, board, and the Summer Bridge Program. Those chosen as Meyerhoff finalists receive partial tuition and the Summer Bridge Program. A study of Meyerhoff Scholar graduates conducted by UMBC president Freeman A. Hrabowski and UMBC professor Kenneth I. Maton observed that financial support was the most highly rated item among students choosing Meyerhoff Scholarships. Close to one-fourth of the students cited financial support as an important factor in their success as Meyerhoff Scholars. Providing ongoing financial support also helps encourage students to go directly into graduate programs right from the outset of the Meyerhoff Program without facing the financial and emotional burden of onerous student loans.

THE SUMMER BRIDGE PROGRAM

All incoming Meyerhoff Scholars are prepared to begin their studies through their participation in Summer Bridge, a mandatory, six-week prefreshman program that includes for-credit, academic courses in calculus and Africana Studies, along with noncredit courses in chemistry, physics, and study skills and other programs to equip students with college-oriented life skills. Because African American students in SEM majors are more likely to become academically and socially isolated on majority White campuses than nonminority SEM students (Hrabowski and Maton, 2000), the

Summer Bridge program helps to form the basis of a peer-supported network that follows Meyerhoff Scholars throughout their academic career at UMBC and beyond. Peer-supported networks, both academic and social, help establish patterns for work and study that prepare Meyerhoff Scholars for their careers at the highest levels of academe.

PROGRAM VALUES

Several core values are constantly emphasized throughout the duration of the Program. These values include understanding the importance of striving for outstanding academic achievement; seeking tutoring, advisement, and counseling from a variety of sources; supporting one's peers; and preparing for graduate or professional school. Students are actively encouraged to get to know faculty and other students who perform well in their classes.

Staving off isolation and fostering peer support in a structured environment are among the hallmarks of the Meyerhoff Program. Beginning with the Summer Bridge Program, in which students start their academic day at 6:45 A.M., with sessions often lasting until 9 P.M., Meyerhoff Scholars are provided with close supervision throughout their freshman and sophomore years. To foster a sense of community and to strengthen peer support, all Meyerhoff Scholars live in the same residence hall during their freshman year and are required to live on campus in subsequent years. Meyerhoff staff regularly hold group meetings—called *family meetings*—with students.

STUDY GROUPS

Study groups are viewed as an element critical to students' success in a SEM major. Meyerhoff Scholars consistently rank study groups as one of the most positive aspects of the Program. The importance of peer study groups is introduced during the Summer Bridge Program, in which older Meyerhoff cohorts demonstrate to freshmen the importance of study groups and group study skills. Strong relationships emerge among mandatory study groups that are supported by faculty and staff.

PROGRAM COMMUNITY

The program deliberately fosters a family-like, campus-based community for students. Staff hold regular group meetings with students, and students are encouraged to fraternize with other Meyerhoff Scholars, but not to an exclusive extent. When Meyerhoff Scholars first arrive at UMBC, they are directed to stay active and involved in the university community. To that end, Meyerhoff Scholars have served as president of the student council, participated in university varsity sports, and served as officers in organizations on campus.

PERSONAL ADVISING AND COUNSELING

A major aspect of the Meyerhoff Scholarship Program is the overarching emphasis on personal advising and counseling. A full-time academic advisor and other program staff monitor and counsel students regarding academic planning and performance goals. During freshman and sophomore years, students have regular meetings with program staff. A separate advisor counsels third- and fourth-year students along with fifth-year engineering students. In addition, the Program employs a separate advisor for graduate and professional schools. This advisor helps students obtain internships and provides counseling on corporate relations and other nonacademic and professional activities. Continual guidance is meant to teach Meyerhoff Scholars a mature method for academic foresight.

TUTORING

All Meyerhoff Scholars are encouraged to tutor others and to take advantage of departmental and university tutoring resources.

SUMMER RESEARCH INTERNSHIPS

Program staff use an extensive network of contacts with companies, federal agencies, and other research universities to arrange summer science and engineering internships and create mentoring relationships.

Students have participated in internships with NASA, NSA, NIH, AT&T Bell Laboratories, the Johns Hopkins School of Medicine, MIT's Chemical Engineering Department, the Centre International de l'Enfance in Paris, France, and Lancaster University, Lancaster, England. Students have also worked at the Howard Hughes Medical Institute Laboratory at the University of Colorado-Boulder under the direction of Nobel Laureate and biochemist Thomas Cech, now head of the Howard Hughes Medical Institute.

MENTORS

The emphasis on finding and creating mentors is one of the most important components of the Program. It begins with peer mentoring during Summer Bridge, in which older Meyerhoff Scholars serve as resident counselors for incoming freshman Scholars. As freshmen bond with their new peers, older Meyerhoff Scholars are available to offer useful insights about the Program. Each Meyerhoff Scholar also is paired with a mentor recruited from among Baltimore and Washington area professionals in science, engineering, and health. In addition, Scholars have faculty mentors in research labs both on and off campus, across the nation, and in other countries.

FACULTY INVOLVEMENT

Department chairs, senior faculty, and university administrators are actively involved in many aspects of the Program, including recruitment, teaching, research mentoring, and special events and activities. From a scientific point of view, Meyerhoff Scholars have benefited from substantive mentoring with faculty members at UMBC as well as with other scientists and laboratories around the world. Under the tutelage of scientific mentors, Meyerhoff Scholars have coauthored articles appearing in journals such as *Science, Journal of Molecular Biology,* and *Nature Structural Biology.* Through regular interaction with faculty, students develop a greater understanding of the importance of scientific and medical research. Another result of this interaction is that faculty can directly comment on students' abilities for letters of recommendation and for nominations for postdoctoral studies and research protocols.

ADMINISTRATIVE INVOLVEMENT AND SUPPORT

Like many other minority-oriented scholarship initiatives that are virtually divorced from the university at large, the Meyerhoff Program has benefited by UMBC's endorsement of the Program since its inception. As a result, rather than viewing the Program as an adjunct to the University's science, engineering, and mathematics departments, the University has worked to integrate the Meyerhoff Program into its existing academic structure. This top-down support has benefited Meyerhoff Scholars, who are regarded not as minority scholars but as exceptional students who fully participate in all of the university's SEM programs at the highest levels.

FAMILY INVOLVEMENT

Parents of Meyerhoff Scholars are strongly encouraged to join this extended academic family. Parents are regularly kept informed of student progress, invited to counseling sessions, and included in special family events. The Meyerhoff Family Association comprises present and past Meyerhoff Program family members. Meyerhoff families have felt the impact of the Program in personal ways: several Meyerhoff Scholars have encouraged siblings and other family members to pursue undergraduate or advanced degrees.

COMMUNITY SERVICE

The Meyerhoff Program's success is built on the premise that when like-minded students work closely together, their energy and enthusiasm will create synergies that will benefit all of humankind. Meyerhoff Scholars are prompted to give back not only to UMBC (Scholars serve as peer mentors and tutors as well as volunteer science and math tutors in the Baltimore city school system), but also to their communities beyond the university. For some Scholars this has meant organizing volunteer efforts for doctors and researchers in medically underserved areas. Meyerhoff Scholars understand that without giving of themselves and their hard-won expertise, nothing is truly accomplished for the communities from which they have come. In reaching out, Scholars help to disseminate the Program's core values.

EVALUATION

With grant support from the National Science Foundation and the Sloan Foundation, the program has included extensive quantitative and qualitative program evaluation from its start.

PROGRAM RESULTS AND OTHER OUTCOMES

Before the inception of the Meyerhoff Program, even talented African American students majoring in SEM fields at UMBC often exhibited poor academic performances. Educators attributed this to many factors, including failure to provide adequate financial, peer-based, and administrative support, coupled with students' feelings of isolation from the university community and lack of faculty interaction and support.

Through its unique structure and integrated implementation strategies, the Meyerhoff Scholarship Program has altered the paradigm for minority students' success in science, engineering, and mathematics. The Meyerhoff Program is successful not only in recruiting top minority SEM students, but also in ensuring that these scholars remain in SEM fields while earning outstanding grades. An outcome analysis (Woolston, Hrabowski, & Maton, 1997) shows that Meyerhoff Scholars were more likely to persist in science and engineering majors than comparable groups of African American students of the same academic ability.

Statistics tell the story. Meyerhoff Scholars routinely achieve grade point averages of 3.54 (of a possible 4.0) compared with 3.24 for other college-enrolled African American students enrolled in SEM curricula. Further, the retention rate for Meyerhoff Scholars is 96 percent versus 45.7 percent for cohorts in similar SEM programs at colleges and universities in the United States. Between 1993 and 2005, 129 pursued doctoral degrees, forty-three were enrolled in joint master's and doctoral programs, and ninety-seven Meyerhoff Scholars pursued master's degrees.

SUMMARY

Beyond the numbers, the real success of the Meyerhoff Program lies in its commitment and strict adherence to the Program's core values and its key components. UMBC was among the first six recipients of the U.S. Presidential Award for Excellence in Science, Mathematics, and Engineering Mentoring in 1996, and UMBC biochemist Dr. Michael Summers also received this award in 2000 for his work with undergraduates in his Howard Hughes Laboratory.

In praising the Meyerhoff Scholars Program, Bruce Alberts, the president of the National Academy of Sciences, has said, "The success of this program has been outstanding, and it should awaken many other universities to the potential of a different type of education. By immediately exposing young undergraduates to research and engaging them in real scientific inquiry, this program has done more than it originally set out to do. The Meyerhoff Program has not only shown us how to attract minorities to careers in science and engineering; it has also demonstrated the best way to prepare our next generation of leaders for life in a society that will be increasingly dominated by science and technology" (Bruce Alberts, personal communication).

References

Woolston, C., Hrabowski, F. A., III, & Maton, K. I. (1997). The recruitment and retention of talented African Americans in science. *Diversity in Higher Education, 1,* 103–114.

CHAPTER FIFTEEN

THE BLACK MAN ON CAMPUS (BMOC) PROJECT

Bowling Green State University, Ohio

Kevin W. Bailey

Bowling Green State University (BGSU) is a doctoral/research intensive university in northwest Ohio about twenty miles south of Toledo, located in the community of Bowling Green, Ohio, population 29,600 (including students). About 7,000 of BGSU's 20,200 students live on campus. Of the 20,200 students enrolled at BGSU, 17,300 are undergraduate students, 10 percent come from outside the state of Ohio (including more than 540 from other countries), and more than 1,680 are African American, Native American, Hispanic, or Asian American. BGSU offers more than two hundred undergraduate majors and programs in seven undergraduate colleges: Arts and Sciences, Business Administration, Education and Human Development, Health and Human Services, Musical Arts, Technology, and the regional BGSU Firelands in Huron, Ohio. BGSU's Graduate College offers sixty-six master's programs, two specialist degree programs, and sixteen doctoral programs. According to data from the Office of Institutional Research and Planning at BGSU, the percentage of African American males who enroll at BGSU steadily declined between fall 1995 (48 percent) and fall 1999 (44 percent), despite increases in the total number of African American students enrolled during the same time period.

The Black Man On Campus (BMOC) Project was initiated during fall 2000 and was intended to provide a foundation for the academic and social success of African American males at BGSU through mentoring relationships, a classroom environment that embraced their African American cultural legacy, and activities designed to promote a positive self-image.

The proposed impact of the BMOC Project on student success was defined by the four elements of the Project, also known as TIPS:

Transition – facilitate a smoother transition from high school to college by linking students with a faculty or staff mentor who can personalize and explain BGSU

Involvement – promote involvement in campus life as a way to enhance socialization, stimulate leadership development, and promote a positive self-image

Persistence – expect a greater first-to-second-semester and first-to-second-year persistence rate for students who participate in this Project compared with students who do not participate

Success – ensure a smooth transition and greater on-campus involvement for students, to increase the likelihood they will persist to graduation and be successful at BGSU and beyond

The project directors were four African American men in the division of student affairs who believed in the merits of the Project and devoted time to its success. The first fall semester pilot program was supported by a one-time internal university grant of $4,000, which covered the cost of textbooks, guest speakers, and food for social activities. The BMOC Project had three components: (1) a culturally relevant classroom experience fostered through a freshman 101-style course, (2) a one-on-one mentoring relationship with an African American male faculty or staff member, and (3) participation in a weekend rap session related to success in college for African American men.

The first component of the BMOC Project was the creation of a culturally relevant classroom experience. Approximately 40 percent of the incoming first-year class at BGSU is enrolled in UNIV 100, an optional two-credit course that introduces students to college life and covers topics such as academic skills, career and life planning, and diversity awareness. Some of the sections are themed and are geared toward special populations such as athletes or students within a particular college or major, which provided precedent in the creation of a theme-section for African American males.

Students were recruited to participate in the BMOC Project during the orientation and registration program. Staff in the Center for Multicultural and Academic Initiatives and the Project coordinators approached African American men during the six-week orientation program and handed them a one-page project description sheet. Initially, enrolling students for this theme-section conflicted with other African American male-oriented theme-sections of UNIV 100, such as student athletes and the University Program for Academic Success (UPASS, in which African American men were required to enroll as a condition of their admission to the university). However, with the help of the office of admissions, the Project coordinators were able to identify the pool of first-year African American male students, eliminate the athletes and UPASS students, and make phone calls to those who remained to assemble the twenty participants.

This section, which enrolled twenty students, was cotaught by one of the Project directors and an upperclassman African American male student, who was involved in the Black Student Union, among other campus organizations. The prescribed UNIV 100 curriculum was augmented with the use of an additional textbook, *Helping African American Men Succeed in College* (Cuyjet, 1997), which was provided to the enrolled students at no cost. As the semester progressed, chapters from Cuyjet's book were assigned that corresponded with the curriculum of UNIV 100. Class discussions and assignments addressed the pertinent issues related to being an African American male at BGSU. The president of the university, who is an African American male, addressed the class and gave his personal testimony regarding his educational life and presidential woes from the perspective of an African American male. Cuyjet asserted that positive classroom experiences, in which African American males can express their personal experiences and explore issues relevant to their cultural identity, foster integration into the campus community. This is critical to persistence and graduation (Tinto, 1975).

The second component of the Project was the creation of one-on-one mentoring relationships with African American male faculty or staff. An e-mail message was sent to all of the African American male faculty and staff outlining the Project and soliciting mentors. The expectations were that mentors would meet with their student once every three to four weeks throughout the semester and attend monthly social gatherings with all twenty students and the Project directors. Eleven men (three faculty and eight staff) volunteered to mentor the twenty students in the class. Specific guidelines for selecting mentors or creating the mentoring relationship were not articulated; rather, the end goal was to assist these young men with their transition to the university and help them become involved in and connected to BGSU.

The final component of the Project was participation in a weekend rap session related to success in college and specifically geared toward the twenty men in the class. The rap session was held in conjunction with a conference, Millennium Men & Women: Meeting the Challenges Ahead, sponsored by the Center for Multicultural and Academic Initiatives. The session included two chapter authors from Cuyjet's (1997) book, Michael Cuyjet and Michael Sutton, who were invited to speak and respond to questions about the book as well as to illuminate further critical aspects of educating African American males. The day-long conference was coeducational and included topical workshops on African American male and female relationships, Black economic empowerment, and spirituality.

Multiple methods were proposed to assess the impact of the BMOC Project, which met with varying levels of success. The primary assessment instrument was the UNIV 100 qualitative and quantitative course evaluation. The quantitative results suggested that the men learned something from the class, although it cannot be correlated with the theme-section. Over 80 percent of the students agreed or strongly agreed with the following statements:

- This course helped me to adjust to life at BGSU.
- This course has helped me become familiar with resources and services on campus.
- UNIV 100 has exposed me to social issues that affect my ability to be a responsible citizen in this and other communities.
- I would recommend this course to other first-year students.

Further, approximately 96 percent of students agreed or strongly agreed that the instructors were sensitive to issues of diversity; this was the highest score given on this question among all the sections of UNIV 100 offered.

Qualitative comments such as the following were more helpful in determining the value of the theme-section for students:

"UNIV 100 made me a smarter minority student here on the campus of BGSU. This class has taught me how to use my resources to my advantage. It has also made me more informed and educated about how to deal with the different adversities facing African American males on college campuses and even society."

"What I enjoyed about this class was that you were able to feel open to speak what's on your mind and speak your opinion on anything."

"I learned more about myself as a person and what I need to do to succeed."

The results of the mentoring relationships were mixed. Some mentor-mentee pairs met more frequently than others. The quality of those interactions also varied. Generally, the senior-level administrators who were mentors did not meet with their mentees as often as other mentors. Unfortunately, there are not many African American administrators of faculty at the university, thus mentor candidates are already limited. Despite varying degrees of interactions, the mentors believed that the components of the program were valuable and needed for the campus. What was not immediately apparent was the long-term impact of the class as it relates to student persistence.

Student persistence and grades were also measured. The university's first-to-second-year retention rate of the fall 2000 cohort was 78 percent. The overall retention rate for African American males for the same period was 80.6 percent. However, the first-to-second-year retention rate for the men who enrolled in UNIV 100 was 60 percent. Eleven of the twenty men were physically on campus in fall 2001. One student spent a semester at the Disney training program in Orlando and another student stopped-out for a semester to work full-time to earn enough money to return in spring 2002. It is disheartening to know that despite the efforts of the program, the students in the pilot project did not persist at a level similar to or higher than African American males who did not participate in the pilot. For any student who does not return, there are many possible factors, such as family and finances, that cannot be controlled despite the student's willingness and desire to obtain a four-year degree.

However, African American males who participated in the pilot project had higher grade point averages in their first semester compared with the average GPA of all African American males enrolled. Also, they were above the all-male average of 2.42 and slightly under the White male average of 2.47. Unfortunately, the students could not sustain their academic success after their first semester, as their average grades for the next five semesters were more aligned with those of all African American males, as the all male and the White males averages were significantly higher. Table 15.1 compares grades of the men in the pilot project with the grades of other male populations on campus for three academic years.

Although the BMOC Project may have contributed to the academic success of the men during their first semester, there are many other factors that could have contributed to the pendulum swing in grades after the first semester.

The academic and persistence issues addressed warrant further investigation and perhaps another project. Unfortunately, the funds to conduct the pilot were one-time. If funds were received to revamp the BMOC Project, the Project could be enlarged to offer more UNIV 100 sections to African American males or modified to provide support to other underrepresented student groups. A limitation of expanding the Project is the number of African American

TABLE 15.1. GPA COMPARISON OF UNIV 100 AND OTHER STUDENT GROUPS.

Average Cumulative GPAs	Fall 2000	Spring 2001	Fall 2001	Spring 2002	Fall 2002	Spring 2003
UNIV 100 students	2.46	2.10	2.00	2.25	2.39	2.10
All African American males	2.07	2.07	2.07	2.09	2.38	2.33
White males	2.47	2.50	2.49	2.52	2.69	2.71
All males	2.42	2.45	2.42	2.45	2.67	2.67

male faculty and staff available to serve as mentors, which limits the number of students who can be effectively served by The BMOC Project. However, "graduates" of the BMOC Project could participate in subsequent semesters as peer mentors or UNIV 100 cofacilitators.

Currently, the UNIV 100 section for African American males is still being offered and taught by one of the remaining Project coordinators. African American faculty and staff are guest speakers, but there is no formal mentoring component. Further study of the persistence and academic achievement of those students who are enrolled each year in this special section of UNIV 100 for African American male students is ongoing.

References

Cuyjet, M. J. (Ed.). (1997). *Helping African American men succeed in college.* New Directions for Student Services, no. 80. San Francisco: Jossey-Bass.

Tinto, V. (1975). Dropout from higher education: A theoretical synthesis of recent research. Review of Educational Research, *45,* 89–125.

CHAPTER SIXTEEN

BLACK MEN'S COLLECTIVE

Rutgers, the State University of New Jersey

Christopher C. Catching

Rutgers, the State University of New Jersey, is one of the nation's major state universities. The university has an enrollment of over fifty thousand students located on campuses in Camden, Newark, and New Brunswick-Piscataway, New Jersey. Founded in 1766, Rutgers holds a unique distinction as a colonial college, land-grant institution, and state university. The university is a research I institution and is part of the Association of American Universities.

The New Brunswick-Piscataway campus includes four undergraduate liberal arts colleges, including one women's college. It has a total undergraduate enrollment of approximately 27,000 students. As of fall 2004, the New Brunswick campus enrollment demographically consisted of 8 percent African American, 22 percent Asian, 8 percent Latino, and 55 percent White. That term, African American males made up approximately 3 percent of the total university undergraduate population of around 27,000 students. This was consistent with the 2002 national data on African American male college enrollment of 4 percent (U.S. Dept. of Education, 2004).

BACKGROUND

The Black Men's Collective (BMC) was created in 1992 to address the high attrition rate of African American males at Rutgers

University. The BMC was formed for the expressed purpose of increasing the interaction and dialogue among African American males (students, staff, faculty, and alumni) around academic and life issues ranging from retention to economic empowerment.

The initiative was originally a universitywide program, but become exclusive to the New Brunswick-Piscataway campus in 2000. The initiative's motto, "Each One Reach One" (originated by Julius Nyerere, founder of Tanzania), was adopted by the program. The Black Men's Collective seeks to provide a multigenerational forum for Black males to connect and discuss issues pertinent to their success through the use of diverse cultural, political, and sociological perspectives. The BMC coordinates a series of initiative and collaborates with other university departments to provide resources and supports for African American males at the New Brunswick-Piscataway campus.

PROGRAM RATIONALE

A collective of Black men provides several benefits to its participants. For the student, a forum to connect with other Black men can yield several possible rewards. First, an intergenerational connection allows students to interact with other men of varying levels of experience. For example, a first-year college student facing transitional and academic challenges might receive great encouragement from a Black male faculty member or an alumnus who, like him, also struggled in adjusting to college, but persevered to attain his goals.

The exposure of students to diverse economic, political, cultural, and social experiences and perspectives is another worthwhile focus and benefit of a Black men's collective. Black men do not come from one homogeneous experience. Interacting with individuals from different beliefs, backgrounds, and social identities can help the student cultivate an awareness and understanding of others through a broad view of the Black male experience. For example, the dialogue between a student from a working-class background and one from a middle- or upper-middle class background can yield a deeper understanding of the challenges and experiences faced by Black men from various socioeconomic backgrounds.

A Black men's collective provides the opportunity for Black men to discuss other relevant issues that transcend those of the academy. A student would greatly benefit from hearing about the postcollege experiences of older faculty, staff, or alumni at different points in their life (such as racism, professional development, and relationships) and engaging in dialogue with these more seasoned members of the collective.

Students can also benefit from the leadership development opportunities that a Black men's collective can provide. In this context, students can coordinate projects and activities for the group or serve in formal leadership roles. Involving student leaders in this way can provide vital role modeling and attract new students to join the collective. The opportunity for Black male students to mentor other students in this type of setting can be beneficial because it can assist in retention, cultivate responsibility for other Black men, and increase the visibility of Black men as leaders on campus. A successful collective would probably embrace the principles of accountability, proactive leadership, self-discipline, and intellectual development.

There are also benefits for faculty, staff, and alumni members of the collective. As a forum to discuss professional and personal experiences amongst other colleagues, it provides a venue of support for participants that may be lacking in other parts of their professional experience. The mentoring relationships that can develop between new and more seasoned faculty, staff, and alumni can provide models of professional development and success that will undoubtedly be extended to the student participants of the collective. Providing a support mechanism for Black male faculty and staff may assist a college in retaining them. In essence, the same factors that make the collective effective for students can help retain faculty and staff members. The opportunity to interact consistently and frequently with Black male students gives the faculty, staff, and alumni members a chance to be directly involved in the retention of Black male students through the relationships they develop in the collective. This synergistic relationship has a powerful and reinforcing impact on the community of Black men on campus. For alumni, being involved in such an initiative provides an outlet to give back directly to the institution through the current students.

PROGRAM DESCRIPTION

The BMC includes students, faculty, staff, and alumni from through-out the university. The steering committee consists of all African American male members who have volunteered to assist in the leadership of the BMC. Subcommittees of the steering committee handle recruitment, retention, communications/correspondence, social programming and leadership, general programming, and mentoring. Each committee has two conveners who act as cochairs of the subcommittee. The BMC is structured in this way to allow for full, equal participation and ample leadership opportunities for all members. The activities that are planned are coordinated through surveys of participants to decide what programs would be of interest to the group.

As an example of one of its successful events, the BMC, with the Paul Robeson Cultural Center, sponsors an annual Cultural and Academic Bonding Workshop for first-year African American male students. The program serves as an orientation to the university as well as a forum for addressing some of the challenges facing first-year African American male students at the university. This summer workshop connects first-year students with continuing African American male student leaders, faculty, staff, and alumni. Topics such as financial aid and course selection, skill development, student involvement, leadership development, and campus resource contacts are discussed. Students are formally introduced to the campus community and connected with the BMC. A parents' workshop is also held concurrently to inform them about university policies as well as supports and resources available to the students and to get them involved.

The BMC sponsors several other programs each year, including general membership meetings, discussions on academic and career success, a Black Men's Retreat, and a Kwanzaa celebration, to name just a few. Cross-generational mentoring and role modeling occurs in the BMC informally and through the connections made between participants. A formal peer mentoring program has recently been developed to foster an intentional link between continuing African American male students and first-year students. This supports the retention of African American male students by providing both a leadership opportunity for the continuing student and a resource for the first-year student.

Alumni play an important role in the BMC. Undergraduate participants learn about the experiences, challenges, and accomplishments of successful African American male graduates. Alumni that have formerly been a part of BMC are often eager and willing participants in discussions and activities.

RESOURCES

The BMC is an intra-university initiative that does not originate from a specific college or department. Funding for its programming comes from contributions and cosponsorships from university departments that share goals similar to the BMC's, such as the Rutgers College Educational Opportunity Fund Department, Paul Robeson Cultural Center, and Student Development and College Affairs, to name a few. Programs and events are typically held at a central location on the New Brunswick-Piscataway campus to facilitate attendance and participation throughout the university.

In addition to the BMC, Rutgers University, New Brunswick-Piscataway, provides other resources that assist in educating and retaining African American males. The Paul Robeson Cultural Center provides a source of support and guidance for African American males through its programs and initiatives. The educational initiatives serve to reinforce the efforts of the BMC by providing historical and positive depictions of the contributions of people of African descent to American culture. The Rutgers College Educational Opportunity Fund (EOF) program also acts as a resource for the BMC. The program provides access to higher education for individuals from disadvantaged educational and economic backgrounds. Support services, such as counseling, tutoring, financial aid, leadership development opportunities, and a summer residential bridge program, are provided to help students meet both their academic and personal challenges. Programs like the EOF provide a level of foundational support for participants, who often include African American males. The existence of that support provides reinforcement for a program such as BMC by serving as a place to recruit students into the BMC and by collaborating with BMC on initiatives. In addition to the aforementioned departments, partnering with other departments such as student activities, residence life, and academic services has helped with the success of the BMC. Recruiting administrators and faculty from a variety of departments helps to provide a well-rounded offering of guidance and support for the BMC.

Sources of support and education for African American males are not limited to the student affairs domain of the university. The Africana Studies Department offers a credited course entitled Blacks and Economic Structures: The Issues of African American Men in Contemporary United States of America. This course is a comprehensive exploration of African American males in contemporary American culture through an analysis of American economics, history, and politics on the psychological and psychosocial development of the African American male in today's society. Although the course is available to the general student population, it offers a unique opportunity to examine perspectives of the African American male's experience as well as insights on meeting the challenges that they face. The BMC and Africana Studies faculty work collaboratively to provide curricular and cocurricular outlets for African American males to connect and reflect upon their historical and contemporary experiences. This represents one of the mutually beneficial relationships BMC has developed on the academic side of the institution.

RESEARCH

Although there is currently no formal research being done on the success or satisfaction of the BMC, it warrants mentioning that several of the current faculty and staff participants were former student participants. In addition, students that have been active in the BMC have continued to be over the duration of their college experience. This conveys a level of success and satisfaction with the BMC. To empirically assess the effectiveness of the BMC, the institution needs to conduct a study of first-year African American male students involved in BMC in comparison with those who are not involved. It would be worthwhile to assess the GPAs of these students as well as attrition rates of BMC participants and nonparticipants to reveal findings that may assist with retaining African American males.

Overall, the BMC is perceived by the Rutgers administration as having provided a successful initial attempt to help develop and retain African American males.

Reference

U.S. Department of Education, National Center for Education Statistics, Higher Education General Information Survey (HEGIS). (2004). Fall Enrollment in Colleges and Universities surveys 1976 and 1980, and 1990 through 2002. Integrated Postsecondary Education Data System (IPEDS). Fall Enrollment Survey (IPEDS-EF:90-99), and Spring 2001 through Spring 2003.

CHAPTER SEVENTEEN

BLACK MALE RAP SESSION

University of Louisville

Edward Laster

In the book *Talkin and Testifyin: The Language of Black America,* Geneva Smitherman (1977) notes that "many black semantic concepts enter the American culture mainstream and serve to enrich the general language of Americans" (p. 69). Although young African Americans may be of the opinion that they invented rap, the oral tradition is of African origin. One of the definitions that the American Heritage College Dictionary (1993) provides for rap music is "spoken or chanted rhyming lyrics with a syncopated, repetitive rhythmic accompaniment." Another definition of rap that is considered slang suggests "discussing freely and at length." These two official definitions are only a part of what African Americans consider to be rap. This "black semantic concept" also incorporates jiving, boasting, exaggeration, and punning, just to name a few of the elements incorporated in rap. Unquestionably, African Americans have a rich oral tradition, and rap is a significant part of that tradition. Rap, therefore, can be used as a discussion format to exchange dialog and ideas. Thus, the informal, biweekly support group for African American male students at the University of Louisville, known as the Black Male Rap Session (B-MRS, pronounced "Beamers"), was created.

THE SETTING

The University of Louisville (UofL) is a state-supported four-year institution offering both graduate and undergraduate programs.

It has focused much of its attention in the past few years on becoming a preeminent metropolitan research I university. UofL is located in the largest metropolitan area (with about one million residents) in the state of Kentucky. In fall 2002, Kentucky had approximately 115,202 students attending four-year state-supported institutions, with African Americans comprising approximately 7.6 percent of the student population. In fall 2002 the University of Louisville had a student population of approximately 21,089 students. African Americans (2,446) formed the largest minority population in UofL's student body, while Latinos (267) and American Indians (59) made up a much smaller percentage of the students. At many colleges and universities across the nation, female students outnumbered male students; in Kentucky 57.4 percent of all college-age students were female. At UofL female students outnumbered male students by about 15 percent (11,320 to 9,769), but for African American students the difference was much greater: African American females outnumbered African American males by approximately two to one (1,462 to 780).

Despite this rather skewed proportion, African American men at the University of Louisville actually fared slightly better than national trends in bachelor's degree attainment compared to African American women. In 2001–02 nationwide, 39,194 African American men received bachelor's degrees while 28,577 baccalaureates were attained by African American women. Thus, Black men received only 33.6 percent of the bachelor's degrees awarded to African Americans ("Degrees Conferred," 2005). However in a three-year period from 2000–01 to 2002–03 at the University of Louisville, 213 Black men received bachelor's degrees, representing 35.3 percent of the 603 baccalaureate degrees given to African Americans over that time period (University of Louisville, 2005). (The three-year numbers offer a more stable representation since annual numbers of African American male baccalaureates fluctuated considerably—64, 82, 67—during that period.)

The Educational Philosophy of B-MRS

B-MRS is an attempt to engage the positive influences of the college environment as they relate to student development, with group techniques to enhance the potential for black males to feel more comfortable (and have a sense of belonging) in the traditionally White college and university setting. Many publications have addressed the impact of higher education and identity development (such as Astin, 1993, 1996; Chickering & Reisser, 1993; Evans, Forney, & Guido-DiBrito, 1998; Pascarella & Terenzini, 1991). Few of these publications have specifically addressed how predominantly White institutions (PWIs)—or, for that matter, some historically Black colleges and universities (HBCUs)—influence minority identity development. Only recently has a body of literature begun to evolve related to minority identity development (such as Allen, 1992; Davis, 1994; Helms, 1989; McEwen, Roper, Bryant, & Langa, 1990: Plummer, 1996; Thompson & Fretz, 1991) and alienation at PWIs (such as Suen, 1983; Stewart, Jackson, & Jackson, 1990; and Loo & Rolison, 1986). A majority of the literature continues to suggest that student involvement and feelings of belonging are key factors in student development, matriculation, and graduation. Most of the literature also notes that African American students often have feelings of alienation and lack of support, along with a paucity of opportunities to develop leadership skills at PWIs. On one hand, colleges and universities have considerable influence on student development; on the other hand, this development is not all that it could be for minority and nontraditional students, particularly Black males. Thus, B-MRS is a conscious effort to make PWIs more responsive to the needs of Black male students by providing them with an opportunity to discuss issues and concerns that are relevant to them.

B-MRS RATIONALE

The above framework provides the preliminary rationale for addressing the issues and concerns of Black males at the postsecondary institutional level. Clearly, the attempt to determine what colleges and universities do to aid Black males raises a significant number of questions:

- Can public and private postsecondary institutions provide Black males with a liberating education?
- Can a college education be humanizing for Black males?

- Can postsecondary education institutions aid Black males in recognizing and addressing the problems and issues that they must inevitably face?
- Can some of the issues and concerns faced by Black males be responded to in a constructive manner?
- Should PWIs take any responsibility in helping Black males in their institutions address the issues and concerns facing them?

This writer's response to all of these questions would be in the affirmative. For those of us who believe that we can have a positive effect on our Black male students, the reasoning is simple: we should choose to make a difference in the institution in which we work. Understanding the influences that Black males face prior to entering colleges and universities should become a rationale for making a difference in the lives of Black males, particularly if they survive the educational minefields and make it into college. Although it would be significantly rewarding to believe that colleges and universities would make Black males a priority for matriculation and graduation, the reality is that few have chosen to do so. Therefore it is unlikely that many colleges and universities will make assisting Black males a future institutional priority—and thus those of us who understand and see the issues and concerns of Black males must make it a priority to ensure their success within the sphere of our influence.

A clear goal of higher education is to instruct the next generation of American leaders, and Black males are a part of that future leadership pool. They will need the educational tools, skills, and leadership training provided by higher education to address their particular concerns. Groups like B-MRS and similar efforts to bring Black men together in a "safe" setting can provide constructive and supportive environments in postsecondary educational institutions, offering a humanizing educational experience that will aid Black males in actualizing their specific concerns and provide a liberating nuance to their college years.

B-MRS GOALS

The primary goal of B-MRS is to provide a supportive environment, specifically at PWIs, for the discussion of issues and concerns relevant to Black males. Allen (1992) reports that HBCUs provided more supportive environs and that "Black males felt greater acceptance and showed less anxiety about interpersonal relationships than on White campuses" (p. 31). Additionally, Allen reported that "Black males showed greater academic gains, more eagerness to compete, and considerably more social assertion than Black males on predominately White campuses" (p. 31). Clearly, this research implies that a positive and supportive environment has the potential to positively affect the success rate of Black male college students. If we can produce some of the positive and supportive characteristics attributed to HBCUs for Black males, then we may be able to improve our chances of helping Black males to matriculate and graduate from PWIs.

B-MRS OBJECTIVES

B-MRS has six primary objectives. The first objective is to provide a positive and supportive environment for the discussion (rap session) of a variety of topics, issues, and concerns relevant to Black males. The topics can be selected by the group leader or by student participants with the approval of the group leader. For example, at the end of a rap session participants discuss potential topics for the next or future meetings. Students are also encouraged to present or lead sessions that others might find of interest. Second, group techniques are used to facilitate the rap sessions. The group leader is responsible for keeping the discussion moving so as to involve all participants, so that person should have counseling, social work, or other similar facilitation skills. Third, Black faculty members are encouraged to participate in B-MRS; for example, they can present examples of their research or lead a group discussion. Additionally, faculty participation allows group members the chance for close contact with actual minority faculty members, who are likely to be a small percentage of many institutions' faculty. Fourth, B-MRS creates a way to facilitate the transition of Black male students to the college environment. For many Black males, adjusting to the new academic expectations in the postsecondary environment proves to be very difficult. Rap sessions can be used to address and share with others successful ways to make appropriate adjustments in the college environment, and the group can be used for exploring various coping strategies. Moreover, the rap session can be used to keep students informed of relevant academic dates (such as drop, add, registration) in the university community. Fifth, students can be provided with a snack or meal, simply because many minority males are often poor and hungry. The free food is also a way for the group to gain institutional support and for the institution to validate activities that support the development of the program. To meet the sixth and final objective, the group leader should develop an evaluation mechanism to determine the success or failure of the rap sessions and use that evaluation mechanism as a tool to improve the program.

TARGET POPULATION AND DURATION OF B-MRS UNIT

The target population for B-MRS is simply all college-age Black males at the institution who are willing to participate. Black females are also welcome to attend, but it is important to note that this research has focused primarily on Black males. Since the inception of B-MRS, a parallel female group (A Sistah's Voice) was started for Black females at the institution. Periodically the two groups get together to discuss issues of relevance; for example, male-female relationships or campus climate issues. However, group dynamics may require limiting the group to approximately thirty to forty students to make facilitating the discussion process reasonable. Training in group facilitation and counseling techniques are a critical skill for the group leader. Moreover, the group facilitator or leader (a Black male) needs a real grasp of all of the previously noted issues relevant to Black males. Without question, the group leader should be committed to the matriculation and graduation of Black males at their particular institution.

A typical semester at the university lasts approximately fifteen weeks, and during the semester B-MRS meets twice a month (on the second and fourth Friday of each month), so there are five or six rap sessions in a typical semester. Each rap session lasts one and a half to two hours. To encourage and facilitate student participation, as well as to spur participants to develop a spirit of ownership for the rap sessions, students are given the opportunity to suggest discussion topics. B-MRS participants are also encouraged to explore ideas of their own choosing and lead rap sessions. Thus an open-ended framework is established that allows for an endless variety of past, present, and future topics for discussion.

B-MRS Discussion Topics and Student Perceptions

The use of discussion (rap) and group techniques incorporates the African American oral tradition within the institutional framework to produce a model likely to prove conducive for Black male students' participation and success. B-MRS is also supported by the educational literature, which suggests that involvement and participation are cornerstones to feelings of belonging in higher education. The following titles from several years of B-MRS sessions are offered to provide an idea of the many possibilities for discussion topics:

- A dialogue on race and racism. Beverly D. Tatum (2003) suggests that "racism" is a system of advantages based on race, and she notes that racism is a form of oppression. What is your impression of race and racism in America today?
- Does the "G" in gangsta music stand for Black Genocide?
- Say it with words. What is your favorite writer, poet, rapper, and why?
- Do Black women prefer gangsters and/or athletes, but not a real brother?
- Can I get a hit of that? Drugs and their impact on the family. What is the impact of drugs on the Black family and in our community?
- Is acting White the key to being successful for African Americans?
- Campus Unity? Why can't Blacks on this campus stick together?
- How has Hip-Hop influenced America today? (George, 1998).
- Politics and African Americans under Bush. Will African Americans progress or regress in the next four years?
- Do brothers prefer hoochie mamas in thongs and not real sisters?
- How can Black men survive racial profiling and its consequences?

- Black identity development (Helms, 1990; Tatum, 2003).
- Too many ladies and too little time: Why can't a Black man be faithful?
- Sports and African Americans. Man that brother can play, but can he be an owner?
- Say Amen: What's the difference between religion and spirituality?
- *A Lesson Before Dying* (Gaines, 1993). Many of us know young people who died too early. What lesson would you like to have taught them before they died?
- Are there any Black heroes and role models today? Gaines (p. 191) suggests that a hero is "someone who does something for other people. He does something that other men don't and can't do. He is different from other men. He is above other men." Who are some of your heroes?
- The prison industrial complex. Many of us have friends and relatives who have spent time in jail or prisons. How does jail/prison time affect the family?
- Nihilism in Black America (West, 1993). Are African Americans more of a threat to themselves than external conditions?
- Does the Hip-Hop generation have a political agenda?
- When did you become aware of your racial identity? (Helms, 1990).
- Black American and African students' perceptions of one another: What are they?
- What is your perception of student climate at the university?
- Student activism: What are Black college students standing for?
- What do you see as some of the key concerns facing Black males today?
- What impact did 9/11 have on your life?
- African Americans and the media: How do you feel we are portrayed in the American media?
- KKK on campus and free speech: Where do you stand on the issue?
- Am I my brother's keeper?
- Why are all the black students sitting together in the cafeteria?
- Black male-female relationships

Public and private institutions are continuing to evolve and refine their requirements for assessing the success of any retention effort. It is critically important to determine African American male students' perceptions of efforts taken on their behalf to improve their status at PWIs, because accountability of institutional programming efforts is required in many colleges and universities. Some form of evaluation is necessary to provide a way of addressing accountability and gather data for understanding student perception of the programming activity. At each B-MRS session a one-page evaluation form (see Exhibit 17.1) is given to the students in attendance, asking them to rate the rap session, organization of the program, information provided, discussion topic, use of group interaction techniques, potential for their future attendance, willingness to recommend the rap session to other students, and the overall quality of the rap sessions.

SUMMARY AND FUTURE POSSIBILITIES

The B-MRS program was initially piloted for the male portion of African American scholarship students at the University, and a similar female group (A Sistah's Voice) is run as a parallel group for Black female students. B-MRS is a constructive attempt to bring the positive influences of the college environment into play as they relate to Black males and to give them a comfortable and supportive place that can foster a sense of belonging. Student evaluations and future research can provide the foundation for additional scholarship on students participating in programs similar to the rap sessions. Research has clearly indicated the positive impact that colleges have on students. However, findings about the influences of PWIs on minority students are continuing to evolve in the research, and the research is particularly scarce relative to Black male development among college students. B-MRS is one effort that can begin to create a foundation for additional research. Efforts like B-MRS can begin the important work of providing positive spaces for African American male students at PWIs, and these positive spaces can be used for Black males to articulate important issues, concerns, and ideas in a constructive manner that supports their development. Giving African American males access to spaces and places that support their development is in accord with relevant retention research that suggests involvement and a sense of

EXHIBIT 17.1. BLACK MALE RAP SESSION (B-MRS) EVALUATION FORM.

Black Male Rap Session (B-MRS)
Why Are All the Black Students Sitting Together in the Cafeteria?
January 26, 2001

Please take a few minutes to respond the questions listed below regarding this program. Your assessment will assist in improving future programs. Please circle one response for each question.

1. How would you rate the preparation for this program?

     Excellent   Good   Fair   Poor

2. How would you rate the organization of this program?

     Excellent   Good   Fair   Poor

3. How would you rate the information provided in this session?

     Excellent   Good   Fair   Poor

4. What is your opinion of the topic that was discussed?

     Excellent   Good   Fair   Poor

5. What is the likelihood that you will attend future B-MRS sessions?

     Excellent   Good   Fair   Poor

6. What are the chances that you would recommend B-MRS to a friend?

     Excellent   Good   Fair   Poor

7. How would you rate the group interaction of this B-MRS session?

     Excellent   Good   Fair   Poor

8. How would you rate the overall quality of this B-MRS session?

     Excellent   Good   Fair   Poor

9. What did you like about this session of B-MRS?

10. What did you dislike about this session of B-MRS?

11. What suggestions do you have for future rap sessions?

THANKS FOR YOUR TIME!

belonging are key factors in student development, matriculation, and graduation. The success of B-MRS is a clear indication that similar efforts can be accomplished in traditional institutions.

References

Allen, W. R. (1992). The color of success: African American college student outcomes at predominantly White and historically Black public colleges and universities. *Harvard Educational Review, 62*(1), 26–44.

American Heritage College Dictionary. (1993). (3rd ed.). New York: Houghton Mifflin.

Astin, A. W. (1993). *What matters in college? Four critical years revisited.* San Francisco: Jossey-Bass.

Astin, A. W. (1996). Involvement in learning revisited: Lessons we have learned. *Journal of College Student Personnel, 37*(2), 123–134.

Chickering, A. W., & Reisser, L. (1993). *Education and identity.* San Francisco: Jossey-Bass.

Davis, J. E. (1994). College in Black and White: campus environment and academic achievement of African American males. *Journal of Negro Education, 63*(4), 620–633.

Degrees conferred by racial and ethnic group, 2001–02. (2005). *The Chronicle of Higher Education Almanac,* Retrieved November 21, 2005 from http://chronicle.com/free/almanac/2005/nation/nation_index.htm#students

Evans, N. J., Forney, D. S., & Guido-DiBrito, F. (1998). *Student development in college: Theory, research, and practice.* San Francisco: Jossey-Bass.

Gaines, E. J. (1993). *A lesson before dying.* New York: Vintage.

George, N. (1998). *Hip hop in America.* New York: Viking.

Helms, J. E. (1989). Considering some methodological issues in racial identity counseling research. *The Counseling Psychologist, 17*(2), 227–252.

Helms, J. E. (1990). An overview of Black racial identity development. In J. E. Helms (Ed.), *Black and White racial identity: Theory, research, and practice* (pp. 49–66). Westport, CT: Praeger.

Loo, C. M., & Rolison, G. (1986). Alienation of minority students on a White campus: Perception is truth. *Journal of Higher Education, 57*(1), 58–77.

McEwen, M. K., Roper, L. D., Bryant, D. R., & Langa, M. J. (1990). Incorporating the development of African-American students into psychosocial theories of student development. *Journal of College Student Development, 31,* 429–436.

Pascarella, E. T., & Terenzini, P. T. (1991). *How college affects students: Findings from twenty years of research.* San Francisco: Jossey-Bass.

Plummer, D. L. (1996). Black racial identity attitudes and stages of the life span: An exploratory investigation. *Journal of Black Psychology, 22*(2), 169–181.

Smitherman, G. (1977). *Talkin and testifyin: The language of Black America.* Detroit, MI: Wayne State University Press.

Stewart, R. J., Jackson, M. R., & Jackson, J. D. (1990). Alienation and attrition of Black students on a predominantly White campus. *Journal of College Student Personnel, 31,* 509–515.

Suen, H. K. (1983). Alienation and attrition of Black college students on a predominantly White campus. *Journal of College Student Personnel, 31,* 117–121.

Tatum, B. D. (2003). *Why are all the Black kids sitting together in the cafeteria? And other conversations about race* (rev. ed.). New York: Basic Books.

Thompson, C. E., & Fretz, B. R. (1991). Predicting the adjustment of Black students at predominantly White institutions. *Journal of Higher Education, 62*(4), 437–450.

University of Louisville. (2005). *Institutional Research and Planning Analytical Tools.* Retrieved December 12, 2005, from http://coldfusion.louisville.edu/webs/ir/index.cfm?method=degree.UniversityDegreesByClass

West, C. (1993). *Race matters.* Boston, MA: Beacon.

CHAPTER EIGHTEEN

AFRICAN AMERICAN MEN OF ARIZONA STATE UNIVERSITY (AAMASU)

Alonzo Jones and Lasana O. Hotep

In fall 2004, Arizona State University (ASU) formally launched the African American Men of ASU (AAMASU) program in response to the low retention and graduation rates of its African American male student population. AAMASU is a part of a national trend to proactively address the high school dropout and college attendance rate of African American males. AAMASU gives particular consideration to the unique demographic distribution of Arizona, the high percentage of resident students attending ASU, the profile of the entering freshman class, limited community influences that shape youth culture and Black identity in Arizona, and the proximity of high-minority-population feeder schools to the institution. AAMASU is both a high-school-to-college program and a college student organization committed to increasing the recruitment, retention, and graduation of African American male students at ASU.

SIXTY YEARS OF DATA

In addition to the AAMASU program background, resources, and description, this profile includes national data on African American high school and college completion rates, high school completion rates for Arizona, and institutional data for ASU, because all of those data were important to the development and design of AAMSU.

NATIONAL DATA

Nationally, over the past seven decades the percentages of African Americans age twenty-five years and older who have completed high school and college has consistently increased year to year. According to the United States Census Bureau (2003), in 1940 7.7 percent of Black people over twenty-five had completed high school and 1.3 percent had completed four years or more of college. With some fluctuations, these numbers consistently rose throughout the twentieth century, so that the most recently reported year at the time of this writing, 2003, revealed an 80 percent high school graduation and 17.3 percent college completion rate for African Americans over twenty-five. This suggests educational advancement on the part of African Americans but does not translate into educational equity among racial or gender classifications.

In 2003, the total number of all people in the United States twenty-five and older who had completed high school was 84 percent, and 27.2 percent had completed college, compared with, again, 80 percent and 17.3 percent, respectively, for African Americans. Looking specifically at 2003 college data, 29.4 percent of White males and 25.9 percent of White females twenty-five and older had four years of college or more. The reverse applies when examining educational attainment levels and gender for African Americans. In 2003, 16.7 percent of African American males over twenty-five had four years or more of college, compared with 17.8 percent of African American females over twenty-five. This gender distribution, with few exceptions, has been the general pattern for African American college educational attainment rates since the early 1990s. From this brief analysis it is clear that, nationally, African American males have made progress regarding high school and college completion rates, but as a percentage of their racial group fewer complete high school and college than their White male and female and African American female counterparts.

ARIZONA DATA

In Arizona this pattern remains constant and is even more problematic in terms of overall high school completion rates. Unfortunately, overall state college completion rates for Arizona within race were not identified, but an examination of freshman retention and six-year graduation rates for African American students attending Arizona State University (ASU) appears in the next section.

Statewide graduation data for students who entered high school in 2000 reveal that after four years the Arizona high school graduation rate was 71 percent, placing it in the lower half of the fifty states. The Arizona African American high school student graduation rate was 67.8 percent; for males it was 62.6 percent and for females, 73 percent. Thus African American female high school students graduate above the cohort average and African American males below it.

ASU COLLEGE ADMISSIONS, RETENTION, AND GRADUATION RATES

ASU is a large public extensive research institution in the southwest region of the United States. Its enrollment is over 57,000 undergraduate, graduate, and professional students dispersed over four campuses throughout the metropolitan Phoenix area: the historic main campus in Tempe; ASU West in northwest Phoenix; ASU East, a polytechnic campus in Mesa; and ASU Capital Central Campus in downtown Phoenix. ASU offers over one hundred twenty degrees across ten academic colleges. Seventy-five percent of students are in-state residents, with the remaining students from all other states and 122 nations around the globe. In 2004, 22 percent of the campus population was minority, with those students enrolling from the following four ethnic groups: African Americans (1,670), 3.4 percent; Asian/Asian Pacific American (2,435), 5 percent; American Indians (1,112), 2.3 percent; and Hispanics (5,396), 11 percent. Of ASU's total enrollment of African American students in 2004, African American males numbered 708, or 42 percent.

Over the decade beginning in 1995, ASU African American students have demonstrated gradual increases in enrollment, retention, and graduation rates. Data for fall 1995 revealed that African American students made up 2.7 percent of the total ASU enrollment. The African American freshman persistence rate for the same year was 65.8 percent, compared with 71.2 percent for all students. The six-year graduation rate for African American students entering in 1995 was 37.8 percent compared with 49.6 percent for all students. The most recent data for ASU (fall 2003) reveals the largest and most diverse entering freshman class in the history of the institution to that date. In fall 2003 African American students made up 3.4 percent of the total ASU enrollment, reaching equity with the percentage of African Americans among Arizona residents (3 percent). The freshman persistence rate for African American students entering in fall 2003 was 72.5 percent compared with a 76.8 percent persistence rate for all freshmen. The six-year graduation rate for African American students beginning their college journey at ASU in 1998 was 46.9 percent, compared with a 54.6 percent six-year graduation rate for all students. The data reveal increases for all students, including African Americans, with African American student persistence and graduation still lagging when compared with all students.

The gradual increase in African American student achievement, and its relevance to the dialogue on African American student retention, can be attributed to a number of factors:

- An increase in the number of high school competency courses—from 11 to 16—required for ASU admissions in 1998
- Significant outreach efforts targeting African American and Hispanic elementary and middle school districts
- Increases in first-generation scholarship dollars
- An increase in on-campus living
- Restructuring of the Multicultural Student Center, with the addition of staff and programming resources to support freshman retention initiatives
- Articulated partnerships between high-minority feeder school districts and ASU to address the college readiness, admission, and retention of district students

In addition to these, another clearly significant factor was an aggressive university-wide campaign initiated by a new president to increase research, faculty prestige, merit-student recruitment, community partnerships, and the social connectedness of the institution with the economic, educational, and political aspirations of Arizona, particularly the larger Phoenix metropolitan area.

Within this institutional setting and climate the AAMASU program was officially launched in September 2004.

Program Background, Resources and Description

AAMASU is one of several retention initiatives coordinated through ASU's Multicultural Student Center (MSC). Established in the early 1980s, the MSC is a department of Student Life and a part of the larger ASU Student Affairs division. The MSC's mission is to support the retention and ultimate graduation of underrepresented minority students through a host of summer transition programs, academic collaborations, partnerships with student organizations, scholarship programs, cultural workshops, and targeted outreach programs.

Considered a targeted outreach program within the MSC, AAMASU has a full-time program coordinator and a ten-hour-a-week management intern position to staff the program. The AAMASU program and budgeting needs are also supported by an administrative assistant whose services are shared by several other MSC staff members. The program coordinator reports directly to the associate dean of Student Life responsible for the administrative oversight of the MSC. As is the case for all MSC positions, AAMASU is fully supported with technology, telephone services, office space, and institutional support services. In addition to in-kind contributions and salary lines, AAMASU receives an annual allotment of operation dollars to coordinate the two major program components: the high-school-to-college program and the college student organization. The following section describes each program component, its goals and objectives, and its activities.

AAMASU Component I: High-School-to-College Program

This program represents a university-sponsored, precollege, preparatory outreach initiative targeting African American male high school juniors and seniors and their parents in the greater Phoenix area.

Goal

The program's goal is to engage local high school African American males and their parents to support the process of university entrance, persistence, and graduation.

Measurable Objectives

1. To promote the program at Phoenix area high schools between the months of February and April, resulting in a yield of seventy-five applications by May 1.
2. To select twenty-five high school junior students and parents, and twenty-five high school senior students and parents, for the program by June 1.
3. To conduct six monthly workshops over the course of the fall and spring semester, addressing various aspects of college readiness and cultural awareness.
4. To reach 80-percent student participation in all six of the monthly workshops.
5. To achieve 90-percent student matriculation into the next high school grade level.
6. To achieve 80-percent matriculation of graduating seniors into postsecondary institutions.

The AAMASU high-school-to-college component is modeled after the Hispanic Mother Daughter Program (HMDP) also coordinated through the MSC. The Hispanic Mother Daughter Program was created in 1984 as an early outreach program to increase the number of Latina women who complete a baccalaureate degree. With assistance from school counselors and teachers, HMDP recruits one hundred teams of seventh grade Latina students and their mothers from local middle schools to participate in this ten-year-long program. Throughout the ten-year timeframe, HMDP provides a variety of programs and services designed to increase high school graduation and university retention rates by tracking academic development and enhancing personal growth through a support network of school counselors, community leaders, and university professionals.

There are four main components to HMDP: eighth grade, high school, university, and alumni components. Each component is designed to offer specific workshops geared toward meeting students' current and future educational needs consistent with their present academic level. To date, the HMDP has collaborated with eighty-six elementary schools and thirty-one high schools and provided outreach to twenty-seven school districts, resulting in over seven hundred mother-daughter teams receiving services through the program annually. Regarding achievement, during the program study period (1997–2002), HMDP participants persisted at the highest rate—80 percent—compared with the five-year averages of all other ASU Hispanic freshman females (77 percent), all other freshman females (79 percent), and all other freshman students (76 percent).

It is assumed that AAMASU will ultimately grow to match the HMDP program in size and scale, but in its inaugural year the AAMASU program targeted only high school sophomore and junior students and their parents. The program was designed to add a grade level every other year, eventually beginning the recruitment cycle at the seventh grade.

Recruitment efforts for AAMASU's high-school-to-college program include outreach, marketing, and publicity to school districts and community youth agencies and through local Black media outlets. Promotional support in the community is provided by the ASU admissions office, the Educational Opportunity Center, and Upward Bound programs. Additional student referrals are made through the personal and professional networks of key ASU and MSC personnel. Free to participants, the program seeks to recruit one hundred teams of sons and parents each year, beginning with the 2005–2006 academic year. The annual recruitment period is between the months of February and April. Formal programming for the first group recruited in spring 2005 began in fall 2005. Eligible participants must meet the following requirements:

- Be presently enrolled in high school as a sophomore or junior student
- Be performing at grade level in reading and math
- Have at least a 2.75 GPA in college track courses
- Plan to attend college (preferably ASU)
- Submit a student statement of interest along with application
- Submit a parent statement of support along with application
- Be able to participate along with parent(s) in monthly workshops on the campus of ASU
- Commit to participating in the program through high school and college graduation.

The proposed monthly workshop schedule for each academic year includes two tracks: one for junior students and parents, the other for senior students and parents. The workshops are designed to enhance college readiness and cultural awareness and to prepare students for admission into ASU and parents in ways to best support the college success of their sons. Following is a sample of proposed topic categories by grade level:

Juniors and Their Parents

Orientation/junior prep

Preparing for SAT/ACT

Career goals

Self-determination (students)

Preparing for senior year (parents)

Cultural awareness

Award/recognition

Seniors and Their Parents

Orientation/admissions

Seeking scholar dollars

Financial aid night

Cultural awareness

Preparing for college life

Transitioning to college

Award/recognition

AAMASU COMPONENT II: COLLEGE STUDENT ORGANIZATION

The College Student Organization is a formally recognized student group of ASU African American students designed to support the retention, leadership training, and cultural development of its participants.

Goal

To provide holistic programming at the university level to enhance the critical analysis, independent study, and programming skills of

ASU African American male participants in the AAMASU student organization.

Measurable Objectives

1. One-fourth, or approximately thirty, of incoming African American male freshman students will be involved as registered AAMASU students.
2. Freshman persistence rates for AAMASU participants will be 10 percent above the persistence rate for African American male freshmen not participating in AAMASU.
3. The organization will coordinate eight programs annually (three social and five culturally related).
4. The organization will conduct one study group per semester.
5. The organization will complete and distribute four editions of the AAMASU newsletter annually.

AAMASU, the college student organization, is a community of ASU African American men seeking to apply themselves to the task of self-development and discovery. Under the guidance of the AAMASU program coordinator, the organization is structured as a traditional student organization. The formal student leadership includes a president, vice president, secretary, treasurer, and editor of the *Voice*, the AAMASU newsletter. General members are welcome to attend bimonthly meetings, but they primarily serve on either the newsletter committee or various program planning committees. The organization's registered membership in the spring 2005 semester was twenty-two students, with ten to twelve members actively involved. The majority of those members were upperclass students. This was a result of recruiting members early in the fall 2004 semester and involving students with proven leadership skills to develop the organization during the first year. The core target audience for the organization is the entire population of ASU African American male freshman students. African American freshman recruitment efforts include registering students in AAMASU during the campus orientation information fair, a mail campaign to admitted incoming students, and transitioning male students from the African American Summer Bridge Program into AAMASU. There is additional one-on-one recruitment by current AAMASU members at university-wide and MSC-sponsored welcome activities at the beginning of the fall term and an email campaign shortly after the start of the fall semester.

The current organizational programming model consists of two major internal programs for AAMASU members and a host of external programs open to the larger ASU community. The two internal programs are the creation and distribution of the AAMASU *Voice* newsletter and the Vision for Black Men study group. All of the photos, layout design, advertising, topic categories, and articles, with the exception of the feature article, for the AAMASU *Voice* are student created. The feature articles are written by faculty, administrators, or staff members and are more vision oriented or tone setting in content. Student articles include commentary on health, edutainment, reports on past programs, current events, African affairs, historical figures, culture, and economics. This structure is based on the belief that it is important that students create and distribute their own media. This allows students to introduce and shape their environments in ways consistent with their beliefs and aspirations.

Vision for Black Men is a monthly study group session based on critical inquiry and analysis of a selected book and related readings each semester. The book selected for the fall 2004 study group was *Visions for Black Men* by Dr. Naim Akbar. The spring 2005 selection was *Mis-Education of the Negro* by Carter G. Woodson. These sessions shape the dialogue among Black men, participating in a Black male centered organization, about the state of Black affairs, with particular focus on men. On average, ten to twelve students participated in each session. Student feedback indicated a great appreciation for the introduction of new information, but mixed responses to the content. On many levels the material challenged students' conceptions about themselves, their priorities, and their allegiance—or lack thereof—to culture and community, and in many ways it charged these college students with significant responsibility in advancing the race. Some participants responded with an increased resiliency to read and learn more. Other participants actually regressed. The notion of reexamining culture—and consequently themselves—appeared to be overwhelming. They did not reject the content outright, but seem to personalize it in a way that made them feel indicted, rather than enlightened, by a broader understanding of historical influences that continue to define and mold contemporary culture. Overall, study group discussions have influenced and shaped programming content and subsequent personal and class discussions.

As a result of national interest in the study group model expressed by colleagues and students from high schools, community colleges, and other universities, the AAMASU coordinators have launched the Black Study Group Network (BSGN). BSGN is a web-based national network of students that meet locally with a local facilitator in study groups. Through the BSGN web site, the group is given a list of texts that address the historical, cultural, and political realities of people of African ancestry. The groups meet monthly, discuss questions provided by the national facilitator, and report their discussions through the web site.

The external programs open to the larger ASU community indirectly contribute to the quality and depth of cultural programming and social opportunities that should positively affect the African American campus culture and ideally enhance retention. Examples of these programs include skate nights, pool parties, intramurals, a biannual lecture series, a Fall Leadership Forum, a Kwanzaa program, an oratorical contest, program cosponsorships with other organizations, and a Father's Day program.

Assessment

Due to the newness of the AAMASU program at the time of this writing (the official start date was September 2004), to date no data exist for the high-school-to-college component or the college student organization component. However, each year participants in all MSC programs are examined as cohorts and assessed as to freshman persistence, average credit hours, GPA, and, longitudinally, graduation rates. These data can be compared by race, gender, and class standing, with other MSC program participants and with students not involved in an MSC program by the same variables. Data for the 2005–06 cohorts—including the AAMASU college student organization, high-school-to-college component, and overall African American male persistence, will be available annually beginning in fall 2007.

Conclusion

The ethnic demographics of Arizona, the need to increase the small percentage of African American ASU students, and the geographical positioning of ASU provide the ideal climate for both the high-school-to-college program and the college student organization program. In Arizona, Hispanics constitute 25 percent and Whites 63 percent of the population. The remaining 12 percent are made up of African American, Asian/Asian Pacific American, Native American, or other racial or ethnic groups. This creates a small community of African Americans uniquely connected by shared interests, common information sources, social outlets, extended family kinships, and educational, professional, and political association. The same applies to ASU. As 3 percent of the total enrollment, or approximately three hundred of each entering freshman class, African American students are a group for which the promotion and programming of African American initiatives and events is relatively manageable. As approximately 42 percent of that African American cohort, African American men are a readily identifiable group that is also relatively easy to target with events and initiatives to enhance their matriculation.

Finally, ASU is one of three major universities within the state of Arizona. ASU is in the heart of the metropolitan Phoenix area, which has the largest population base in the state and the largest African American population. The majority of high schools in the state are located within driving distance of ASU. This allows potential students much greater awareness of and access to ASU programs than is available for any other four-year institution in the state. Through community buy-in and continued institutional outreach, it is anticipated that AAMASU's high-school-to-college program and college student organization program will positively affect student success, resulting in ASU African American male students equaling and, it is hoped, exceeding ASU's average freshman persistence and six-year graduation rates for all students.

By linking a high-school-to-college recruitment program with a support group for matriculating African American male students, AAMASU seeks to develop and promote a broad continuum of longitudinal support for African American men that enfranchises these students within higher education early and keeps them engaged through graduation and perhaps beyond.

For more information about the AAMASU program, please visit the organizational web site at www.aamasu.org. The site includes contact information, high-school-to-college material, previous editions of the AAMASU *Voice,* a recommended reading list, and upcoming events.

References

Akbar, N. (1992). *Visions for Black men.* Tallahassee, FL: Mind Productions.

U.S. Census Bureau. (2003). Education attainment historical table A-2, percent of people 25 years and over who have completed high school or college, by race, hispanic origin, and sex: selected years 1940 to 2003. Retrieved March 5, 2005, from www.census.gov/ population/socdemo/education/tabA-2.pdf.

Woodson, C. G. (1990). *The Mis-education of the Negro.* Trenton, NJ: Africa World Press.

CHAPTER NINETEEN

SONS OF ALKEBULAN AND THE BLACK MAN THINK TANK

The University of North Texas

Pamela Safisha Nzingha Hill, Institute of Cultural Arts and Scholars Academy

In early fall 2001 there was a notion to develop a program geared toward Black male students at the University of North Texas (UNT). In watching Black male students interact with each other in what seemed to be a mostly confrontational manner, and seeing a decrease in those who participated in educational and cultural activities, staff felt an urgent need to give attention to this population and provide an outlet that would possibly lead to increasing critical thinking skills and intellectual dialogue. Additionally, it seemed that these young men lacked positive, real role models. A personal survey was conducted, which consisted of approaching Black male students at random and asking them to name five black males employed at the university. A majority could not name one. Likely, this was due not so much to the near absence of Black men on campus as to the lack of interest and commitment of most of the elder Black men on campus to actively making themselves visible and available to serve as role models. Although the elder Black men who are faculty and professional staff members are basically scattered around the university, and each is often the only Black man in a department or college, they tend to remain in their respective areas of the campus, seldom interacting with each other or the students outside of the classroom. In fact, only a couple of elder Black men interacted with Black students and served as advisors to student organizations. It was imperative for Black students, specifically males, enrolled at this predominantly white institution (PWI) to connect with elder Black men who can indeed serve as real, positive role models.

UNT is a four-year public doctorate-granting institution, located in Denton, approximately thirty miles north of Dallas. UNT is the fourth largest university in Texas, with an enrollment of approximately 27,500. Blacks make up 9.2 percent of the enrolled students. In 2002, the reported undergraduate population of Black males was 889, and records indicate there were 101 Black male graduate students. Statistics on the graduation rate of Black males were not available.

SONS OF ALKEBULAN

The Sons of Alkebulan was conceived with an Afrocentric approach to provide a forum or rap session specifically for open dialogue among Black males attending and working at UNT and extending to community-based alumni. *Alkebulan* is said to be the original name of the continent of Africa. The initial idea came from the realization that many Black male students at the university did not have other Black men as role models, and the forum was implemented with the intention that the elder brothers—both those employed on campus and community leaders—would be heavily involved in maintaining the Sons of Alkebulan.

The major goal of this forum was to increase retention, interaction, and graduation of Black males attending UNT. This would be achieved through the following actions:

- Developing mentor relationships with elder Black men on campus and in the community
- Instilling a sense of brotherhood among Black college men
- Promote critical thinking through intellectual dialogue
- Improving satisfaction with the college experience for Black men

The Sons of Alkebulan held its first session in September 2001 in the Student Ethnic Enrichment Center, UNT's version of a multicultural center. Twenty-two men were in attendance, five being faculty and staff members. Women were not invited. The event was publicized by passing out flyers and sending emails, and through word of mouth. The agenda for the initial program included a welcome and purpose. Afterward, a selected elder brother led an open discussion on any issue the group brought up.

The session lasted about an hour and a half, then ended with *harambee,* an African term meaning "let's pull together." Participants stand together, form a circle, and hold hands. One person makes a comment or recites a proverb, then squeezes the hand of the person to their right, and this individual makes a comment or recites a proverb. This continues until it reaches the person who made the first comment. At this point all participants raise their clenched fists to the sky and say "*harambee*" as they bring their arms down. This is done seven times, and on the seventh, the participants hold the word "*harambee*" for as long as they can. This exercise is often credited with getting participants to share something with the group, and the pulling down of the collective positive power increases energy.

The only resources needed for the Sons of Alkebulan to be successful were time and desire on the part of both the students and the elder brothers who serve as advisors and mentors.

THE BLACK MAN THINK TANK

In preparing for the first Sons of Alkebulan meeting, the planners conceived of the extended possibility of implementing a larger, regional conference geared toward Black males in higher education. At UNT, Black men did not attend educational or cultural events in large numbers, nor did they, as a group, seem to have a strong presence on the campus. The few Black males who held leadership positions, either in their fraternity or in another student organization, seemed to lack determination and tenacity. Past experiences had suggested that participants in annual African American Student Leadership Conferences were strongly affected and became more proactive; thus it was hoped that a conference geared toward Black men would likewise have a positive effect on the participants.

The most well-organized and popular meeting of this type was the original Black Man Think Tank conference, developed by Dr. P. Eric Abercrumbie at the University of Cincinnati. Dr. Abercrumbie ran a very successful conference for fourteen years, with the central purpose of building unity and brotherhood among young African American male college students. Thanks to Dr. Abercrumbie's dedication in providing this unique opportunity for the young and elder brothers to gather, it became the most significant meeting of its kind. In the past few years, the idea has been duplicated and a number of colleges and universities have hosted similar conferences. Organizers of the new Black Man Think Tank conference at UNT felt that, out of respect for the foundation first laid by Dr. Abercrumbie, it was imperative that he participate as the major keynote speaker for this event.

The Black Man Think Tank at UNT, held in October 2001, was a day-long conference that included the keynote speaker, Dr. Abercrumbie; six presenters; a networking luncheon; a panel discussion; and an African dance performance. The conference was open to anyone who registered. A small registration fee covered meals and materials. Word of mouth, flyers, and internet listservs proved to be helpful in promoting this event. Although only local attendance was expected, the Texas conference drew participants from four local colleges and universities in the Dallas-Fort Worth area as well as students from the University of Missouri at Columbia. More than one hundred men and about twenty women attended. The women who attended likely came for a number of reasons. Most came because they were interested in the conference and wanted to be supportive, which became evident by the questions posed. The presence of women did not seem to distract the men at all, and the women truly seemed to enjoy the speakers.

The selected theme was Strong Men Comin' On: Succeeding Against the Odds. This theme was significant in that the selected speakers had, in fact, succeeded against the odds. All of the speakers, with the exception of the keynote, were young men age thirty-five and under, either students in graduate or professional school or young professionals in the education field. Among them were a law student; a school teacher and current president of an NAACP chapter; a professional in higher education; a graduate student who was also the Arthur Ashe Scholar-Athlete of the year, recognized for his academic achievements as well as his athletic and leadership skills; and a school teacher who was also a rising poet.

Presentation topics included Black Man, Your Time Has Come; Building the Black Man from the Inside Out; Black Men, College

Sports, and Academic Success; and Black Men and the Push and Pull Factors of Black Student Organizations. The panel discussion topic was Black Men on Campus and in the Community, and the panel naturally was composed of students, faculty, staff, and community leaders. One of the speakers was a poet whose work reflected issues that often confront Black men.

Summary

The planning activities that eventually became the Sons of Alkebulan have spawned a number of events that benefit African American men on the UNT campus. The Sons of Alkebulan continue to meet on a monthly basis during the academic year. The local chapter of the Alpha Phi Alpha Fraternity, Inc., offered to host the Black Man Think Tank conference annually. As a part of its efforts, the fraternity has also initiated a program in the spring semester geared specifically toward African American men, called Brother to Brother, which grew out of the Sons of Alkebulan. An elder brother is invited to come and generate a variety of vital topics to be discussed in this forum, designated "for brothers only." African American men are encouraged to rap with each other about issues that directly and indirectly affect them. Another prominent program that grew out of the Sons of Alkebulan and the Black Man Think Tank was a Black history event planned and presented by the membership of the four Black fraternities on campus.

Although there is no ongoing empirical study of the outcomes of the Black Man Think Tank conference, this writer has observed a conscious effort to build brotherhood among many of the Black men on campus. More Black males seem to greet each other in a brotherly fashion as well as show more respect toward Black women on campus. It is commonly believed that the rap sessions and the conference are both paramount factors in this developmental process.

A longitudinal study is planned to determine the extent to which participation in such programming affects the academic success and psychosocial development of Black males who attend these rap sessions on a regular basis. An evaluation instrument is being prepared to conduct before- and after-program testing of

Black male students to determine the level of impact of the programs. This information should also be useful in ascertaining whether or not there is a difference in the retention and satisfaction rates of those African American males who participate in these types of programs.

CHAPTER TWENTY

IT'S EASIER THAN YOU THINK
Central State University, Wilberforce, Ohio

Tobias Q. Brown, Central State University

Amanda A. Farabee, University of Louisville

Central State University, near Xenia, Ohio, is the only publicly supported historically Black college or university (HBCU) in Ohio. It was first established in 1856 as Wilberforce University, founded by the Methodist Episcopal Church to provide African Americans access to a college education. Named in honor of William Wilberforce, a prominent eighteenth-century abolitionist, it was the first private historically Black college in the United States. In 1863, the African Methodist Episcopal Church acquired ownership of the university, and in 1887 the Ohio government began to provide Wilberforce with state funds to help finance the institution, bringing to an end the university's exclusively private status for the time being. The state-funded institution legally split from Wilberforce University in 1947, becoming the College of Education and Industrial Arts at Wilberforce. In 1951 the name was changed to Central State College, and in 1965 the institution achieved university status. Although Central State University has a predominantly African American student body (96 percent) and adheres to its core historical responsibility of educating young African American men and women, the institution is "open to all persons of good moral character" and provides equal educational opportunities to all qualified applicants (www.centralstate.edu/legacy/about/history.html).

Central State University has an enrollment of over 1,800 students, and 80 percent of the student body lives on campus in residence halls. Three undergraduate liberal arts colleges—the College of Arts and Sciences, the College of Education, and the College of Business and Industry—form the core of the institution's academic offerings, and a graduate school, the Institute of Urban Education, focuses primarily on urban education, based on the premise that an urban metropolitan school system is a socio-educational organization designed to promote and promulgate academic and social literacy.

Background

It's Easier Than You Think was created by one African American undergraduate student to achieve academic success for himself and a number of his fellow students at Central State University. The program began in 2003 as a series of specific, prescribed interventions that enhanced undergraduate students' ability to reach their collegiate academic potential. Rather than simply focusing on the problems that low-achieving students were encountering, the creator of this program observed the common characteristics of a group of more than thirty high academic achievers at Central State University. Majors or concentrations of majors of those high achievers did not seem to matter; from mathematics to music majors, the top students always had a set of internal rules that they each followed, whether they were verbalized or not. It's Easier Than You Think originated from one student's desire to identify and recognize traits and tendencies shared by those high academic achievers and emulate them. As his own plan for success evolved, it became apparent that the same activities could also provide other students who were performing at lower academic levels with supportive, intentional strategies for achieving academic success. Although the idea for sharing this series of academic success interventions was then developed merely to assist the friends of the program's creator to achieve similar results, It's Easier Than You Think was soon introduced across the Central State University campus and offered to all students interested in performing at higher academic levels.

Evans, Forney, and Guido-DiBrito (1998) indicate that "the amount of student learning and personal development associated with any educational program is directly proportional to the quality and quantity of student involvement in that program" (p. 27). Thus, theoretically, the success of It's Easier Than You Think can be attributed to the quantity and quality of student participants' engagement in the academic success activities prescribed. Students are expected to adhere to the basic tenets of the academic success model and follow academic strategies equated to successful achievement and matriculation. Using this program, the relative improvements in the academic success of participants are a direct result of the extent of the efforts that students put into their studies and the choices they make as they proceed through the educational system.

PROGRAM DESCRIPTION

It's Easier Than You Think is described as an academic achievement series because it outlines a number of specific, systematic methods for common student behaviors—including reading assigned materials, completing writing assignments, note-taking, and seeking assistance from faculty, fellow students, and other resources on campus. Although the series includes a number of suggested activities, it is a flexible program that can be redesigned by every individual student to fit his needs. This program is extremely adaptable in all settings and can be used in any environment as a tutorial intervention, a one-on-one mentoring program, or a set of activities for use in classrooms and other academic settings. Because the program was created by a student for students, it is student run and student supported, without any official university sponsorship.

The academic achievement series follows five specific principles: prioritization, goal-setting, communication, progress tracking, and time management. These five crucial principles form the foundation for creating and maintaining a successful, balanced academic college life. Because college brings changes and offers many new challenges to students, they must find ways of balancing the demands of work, social activities, and academics to be more successful in their careers as college students. These five principles for academic success—prioritization, goal-setting, communication, progress tracking, and time management—provide the means for students to successfully navigate the process of finding academic and personal balance, resulting in greater academic success in their college experience.

Prioritization

According to the first principle of the success series, the sooner students prioritize the various elements of their lives, the sooner they will find the path leading to educational success. Although college offers students opportunities to socialize and a diverse range of activities, students are encouraged to reflect on the primary reasons for attending Central State University—to receive a solid education and earn a college degree—and reminded that every other aspect of college should come second to that of intellectual growth and educational attainment. Students engaged in the academic series are taught that prioritizing means simply arranging things in order of importance and being committed to that arrangement, and they are encouraged to create guidelines to use for prioritizing their class assignments and collegiate activities. As an example, consider a hypothetical student who is involved in an organized collegial activity such as student government. In theory, the first priority at school is his studies. Issues arise when pressure is placed on a student to perform duties for SGA and to do that work before studying or in place of studying. This can have a devastating ripple effect on the student, such that he may find himself falling behind in classes and grades, and the cycle can continue to escalate. Simply making a list of prioritized activities that places academic tasks—attending all classes, doing all homework, doing library research, and completing assignments—before any cocurricular activities is an important accomplishment for the student engaged in this program.

Goal-Setting

According to Bandura (1986) and Locke and Latham (1990), the identification of academic goals is essential to the successful management of student learning. Goals, according to both Locke and Latham and Bandura, mobilize effort, increase persistence, and influence personal efficacy through the commitment and subsequent effort they generate (Schunk, 1996). The second principle of It's Easier Than You Think, goal-setting, encourages students to identify and define the aims, achievements, and values they wish to fulfill in their academic pursuits. Students are encouraged to make rational and realistic predictions about the grades they expect to receive from classes each quarter, set goals for academic achievement, and review those goals as daily reminders for the academic success they have in mind. According to this academic success program, setting goals and disciplining oneself can make the difference between receiving high grades and receiving low grades. By developing goals that are concrete and specific, students enable themselves to solidify their commitment to and ownership of those academic aspirations. An example of successful goal-setting is a student who makes a list of all of his classes for the term, determines what grades he would like to get, writes down those grade goals, and sets a course to achieve each of them. It is the action of breaking down the total job of academic success into a series of precise tasks—writing down each goal for each class and determining what tasks are needed to achieve each of them—that increases the likelihood of the success of these efforts.

COMMUNICATION

Communication with faculty, the third principle of success in academia, is critical to understanding and meeting the expectations of college professors. Although success in college is potentially within the grasp of nearly every student who gets admitted to the university, problems arise when students fail to recognize the significant advantages of communicating with faculty. According to Chickering (1969) and Spady (1971), student communication with faculty has a positive influence on academic achievement. Because professors and instructors are the primary resources of academic assistance at Central State University, building a relationship with faculty is requisite for academic success within the classroom. It's Easier Than You Think elucidates to students that communicating with professors about academic requirements and strategies for academic success is necessary for succeeding academically, and building relationships with faculty members reveals the student's interest in the class and genuine desire to do well. Students are encouraged to introduce themselves to the professor early in the semester and inquire about specific requirements for doing well in the class. It's Easier Than You Think encourages students to study the course syllabus thoroughly, to take separate notes on the academic requirements and review those requirements periodically during the semester, and to check frequently with the professor to make certain they are on track to fulfill the course requirements. In addition to the out-of-class communication with faculty that is so important, students are encouraged to maintain good communication with their instructors through active in-class participation, by both responding to instructors' inquiries and posing questions to clarify what is being presented in class. Because lack of communication with faculty can often put a student's academic success in college at risk, building strong relationships with faculty will help students succeed in class and in the university.

PROGRESS TRACKING

According to It's Easier Than You Think, creating a map of academic progress is critical to academic success in college. Students are taught to use semester mapping for assignments and tests, to create daily and weekly time management plans, and to be assertive in managing their time and academic progress. Continual monitoring and evaluation of one's education progress is indispensable; recording tests and homework grades during the academic semester and consulting with the instructor regarding any need for clarification is crucial. By tracking progress, students can detect trends—either high or low—and maintain up-to-date awareness of their standing in each of their classes. Table 20.1 gives an example of a hypothetical student's record-keeping log for his first five weekly math quizzes. In this example, by tracking his progress, the student would be able to gauge quickly the impact of the test in week four, in which he performed poorly. Because the periodic information provided by such monitoring and tracking throughout the semester is critical to academic success, the responsibility for monitoring personal academic records rests with the student. It's Easier Than You Think also encourages students to consult with faculty about their academic progress, particularly about any academic distress this tracking of academic progress reveals.

TIME MANAGEMENT

According to the fifth principle of It's Easier Than You Think, time is the most valuable commodity for college students, and time

TABLE 20.1. HYPOTHETICAL STUDENT'S PROGRESS-TRACKING LOG.

Math 165	M–F (9–10 A.M.)	Grade	Average
Week 1	Test 1: 80%	B	80%
Week 2	Test 2: 100%	A	90%
Week 3	Test 3: 95%	A	91.6%
Week 4	Test 4: 65%	D	85%
Week 5	Test 5: 91%	A	86.2%

management skills are crucial for students to achieve a sense of bal-ance. With good time management skills, the student can main-tain balance among academic, personal, and family lives and have enough flexibility to respond to surprises or new opportunities that may arise. According to research findings, time management skills, or lack thereof, can influence the college experience and level of success in college (Britton & Tesser, 1991; Horne, 2000; Nonis, Hudson, Logan, & Ford, 1998; Trueman & Hartley, 1996; Penistone, 1994). For example, Nonis, Hudson, Logan, and Ford found that college students who were perceived to have more con-trol of their time had reduced stress, and Campbell and Svenson (1992) found that students who used effective time management strategies increased their academic performance.

Although the academic success series acknowledges that sched-ules will vary from student to student, It's Easier Than You Think encourages all students to develop a schedule for allocating and managing their time. Schedules should take into account every class, lecture, laboratory, social event, athletic practice, or other work in which students engage, and should provide the students with detailed information on how they intend to spend their time. Developing a schedule that includes the opportunity to meet all their needs—academic, cocurricular, social, work-related—will allow students to get more accomplished each day.

Because the most common time management mistake that stu-dents can make is not allowing for a balanced lifestyle, It's Easier Than You Think educates students on maintaining balance in their lives by focusing on six important life areas: physical, intellectual, social, career, emotional, and spiritual. Although students are not required to have a designated set of activities in each life area, they are reminded throughout the academic series that ignoring one or more life areas may lead to ignoring important parts of themselves.

OTHER FACTORS

In addition to the five principles of success that are the main components of It's Easier Than You Think, other academic tips are offered during the success series to encourage academic success at the college level. Students are encouraged to call on anyone on campus—including faculty, college administrators, staff, or other students—who might be able to provide some assistance with any of the program's components. Program participants are advised to seek out material resources from the office of student support services or any other agencies offering skill-building or tutorial help to assist them in succeeding as college students at Central State University.

Although results from the use of the academic principles of the It's Easier Than You Think academic success series have varied among participants, the positive changes in student achievement, as measured by grade point averages, show promising academic outcomes for Central State University students. Table 20.2 presents data revealing the actual changes in grade point averages for the first six students to go through the program in 2003. They have made great academic strides, with several of them moving from one end of the academic continuum to the other. Grade point averages of many of the other students enrolled in It's Easier Than You Think have also increased significantly, and almost all participants have progressed to higher levels of academic success within the classroom. By adhering to the five principles of success in academia, students have validated that the foundation of It's Easier Than You Think is solid and effective.

It's Easier Than You Think, a self-initiated academic success series, required no special funding or contributions at its inception. Begun as an academic strategy that one student began sharing with a few of his friends, it has since been transformed into a formally designed program, applicable to increasing numbers of students across the Central State University campus, and it will soon be available as a published book.

TABLE 20.2. GPA RESULTS FOR SIX ACTUAL PARTICIPANTS.

Student	GPA Before It's Easier Than You Think	GPA After It's Easier Than You Think
Student #1	1.2	2.7
Student #2	2.2	2.8
Student #3	3.5	3.87
Student #4	3.2	3.6
Student #5	2.3	3.0
Student #6	1.0	3.91

Although at the time this was written this academic success series had been employed for several quarters by the program creator and several hundred other students at Central State University with whom he has shared the principles, no formal research had been conducted on the reliability of the academic results. However, some of the cumulative grade point average increases, as seen in Table 20.2, have been phenomenal, and the continued use of the academic success series by growing numbers of students gives testimony to its effectiveness. The program has been introduced to and utilized by many African American male students and student groups, including the football team, athletic department, and fraternities. If one undergraduate student can have that kind of impact on improving the academic success of himself and his peers, imagine what a whole team of such young men could do to raise the expectations and accomplishments of other African American male students at virtually any institution in the country.

References

Bandura, A. (1986). *Social foundations of thought and action*. Englewood Cliffs, NJ: Prentice Hall.

Britton, B. K., & Tesser, A. (1991). Effects of time-management practices on college grades. *Journal of Educational Psychology, 83*(3), 405–410.

Campbell, R. L., & Svenson, L. W. (1992). Perceived level of stress among university undergraduate students in Edmonton, Canada. *Perpetual and Motor Skills, 75*(2), 552–554.

Chickering, A. (1969). *Education and identity*. San Francisco: Jossey-Bass.

Evans, N. J., Forney, D. S., & Guido-DiBrito, F. (1998). Student development in college: Theory, research, and practice. San Francisco: Jossey-Bass.

Horne, W. R. (2000). How students spend their time. *Learning Assistance Review, 5*(2), 22–33.

Locke, E., & Latham, G. (1990). *A theory of goal setting and task performance.* Englewood Cliffs, NJ: Prentice Hall.

Nonis, S. A., Hudson, G. I., Logan, L. B., & Ford, C. W. (1998). Influence of perceived control over time on college students' stress and stress-related outcomes. *Research in Higher Education, 39*(5), 587–605.

Penistone, L. C. (1994, November). Strategies on time management for college students with learning disabilities. ERIC no. 376396. Paper presented at the annual meeting of the Center for Academic Support Programs, Lubbock, TX.

Schunk, D. H. (1996). Goal and self-evaluative influences during children's cognitive skill learning. *American Educational Research Journal, 33*(2), 359–382.

Spady, W. (1971). Dropouts from higher education: Toward an empirical model. *Interchange, 2,* 38–62.

Trueman, M., & Hartley, J. (1996). A comparison between the time-management skills and academic performance of mature and traditional-entry university students. *Higher Education, 32*(2), 199–215.

CHAPTER TWENTY-ONE

THE COLLEGIATE 100

An Affiliate Organization of the 100 Black Men of America, Inc.

Christian A. Mattingly,
University of Louisville

Carl Humphrey, 100 Black Men
of America, Inc.

The Collegiate 100 was created in the late 1990s as an organization comprising college men who share a common goal with their sponsoring 100 Black Men of America chapters: to enhance and improve the quality of life in their communities and enhance educational and economic opportunities for all African Americans. Participants in the program are committed to volunteerism and improving the community through mentoring and tutoring young African American males. A central goal of the program is for participants to gain a greater appreciation for the mission and goals of the 100 Black Men of America and, through this union, for 100 Black Men members to prepare Collegiate 100 members to become active members of the 100 Black Men of America upon graduation. At the time of this writing in 2005, incorporated chapters that sponsor a Collegiate 100 chapter, and their affiliated colleges and universities, include:

- 100 Black Men of Chattanooga; University of Tennessee at Chattanooga
- 100 Black Men of Louisville; University of Louisville

- 100 Black Men of Savannah; Savannah State University
- 100 Black Men of Charlotte; University of North Carolina Charlotte
- 100 Black Men of Metro St. Louis; Harris-Stowe State University, University of Missouri (Columbia), and Southeast Missouri State University
- 100 Black Men of Atlanta; Morehouse College
- 100 Black Men of Pensacola; University of West Florida
- 100 Black Men of Columbus, Georgia; Columbus State University
- 100 Black Men of Albany, Georgia; Albany State University
- 100 Black Men of Triangle East (Raleigh, North Carolina); North Carolina State University and North Carolina Central University
- 100 Black Men of Tampa Bay; University of South Florida
- 100 Black Men of Triad (Greensboro, North Carolina); North Carolina A&T State University
- 100 Black Men of Metro Baton Rouge: Southern University and A&M College, Baton Rouge
- 100 Black Men of Middle Tennessee (Nashville, Tennessee); Tennessee State University

For collegiate men to be accepted into the local affiliate, they must meet membership requirements. Although the precise criteria may vary from chapter to chapter, aspiring members must be students in good standing with the university, with a minimum GPA of 2.5, and must possess high moral character. Additionally, students with a prior criminal record must gain the sponsoring chapter's approval for membership.

The Collegiate 100 was created in the late 1990s as an organization comprising college men who share a common goal with their sponsoring 100 Black Men of America chapters: to enhance and improve the quality of life in their communities and enhance educational and economic opportunities for all African Americans. Participants in the program are committed to volunteerism and improving the community through mentoring and tutoring young African American males. A central goal of the program is for participants to gain a greater appreciation for the mission and goals of the 100 Black Men of America and, through this union, for 100

Black Men members to prepare Collegiate 100 members to become active members of the 100 Black Men of America upon graduation. At the time of this writing in 2005, incorporated chapters that sponsor a Collegiate 100 chapter include 100 Black Men of Chattanooga, 100 Black Men of Louisville, 100 Black Men of Savannah, 100 Black Men of Charlotte, 100 Black Men of Metro St. Louis, 100 Black Men of Atlanta, 100 Black Men of Pensacola, 100 Black Men of Columbus, Georgia, 100 Black Men of Albany, Georgia, 100 Black Men of Triangle East (Raleigh, North Carolina), 100 Black Men of Tampa Bay, 100 Black Men of Triad (Greensboro, North Carolina), 100 Black Men of Metro Baton Rouge, and 100 Black Men of Middle Tennessee (Nashville, Tennessee).

The Collegiate 100's parent organization, 100 Black Men of America, was founded in New York City in 1963, and at the time this was written in 2005 had 103 chapters across the United States, England, Africa, and the Caribbean. The 100 Black Men of America has four major program components that aid in the mission— mentoring, education, health and wellness, and economic development—factors that the organization has identified to be critical to the future of African Americans. 100 Black Men members include leading African American men who excel in the areas of business, industry, public affairs, and government.

PROGRAM RATIONALE

The Collegiate 100 began as a result of the 100 Black Men of America identifying a need to devise an intervention and prevention strategy for African American males in elementary and high school that promoted academic excellence, a solid social structure, a knowledge of the free enterprise system, and community and economic awareness among these youths. Members of the 100 Black Men of America each donate time to serve as role models for African American youth in their community. The need for such efforts is so great that additional manpower is always needed. To help meet this demand, the Collegiate 100 was created to find qualified, energetic, and empathetic individuals to provide mentoring support for their younger counterparts. The program follows the sponsoring organization's motto, "What They See Is What They'll Be," in providing quality role models to African American youth.

PROGRAM DESCRIPTION

All Collegiate 100 members must commit to at least three hours of community service per month and attend a mandatory orientation session or refresher session. Members are expected to devise a plan of service for the academic year and to submit monthly reports of volunteer service. Additionally, each year members must attend a minimum of one professional development seminar given by the sponsoring chapter. Members are expected to enhance the relationship between the sponsoring chapter and the young students with whom they work. Members must also commit that upon graduation they will maintain active participation with Collegiate 100 alumni, and they must aspire to become members of 100 Black Men of America. Adherence to university policies as well as the Collegiate 100 code of ethics is expected.

Members of a Collegiate 100 affiliate chapter participate in mentoring and tutoring young African American male students of local elementary, middle, and high schools in educational, social, and community settings. The vision of the Collegiate 100 is that through this experience, young African American males will be developed to their full potential, granted equal opportunities, and become productive members of society. As potential protégés of the Collegiate 100's mentoring activities, young African American males are assigned to one of four different grade categories: grades one through three, grades four through six, grades seven through nine, and grades ten through twelve. The purpose of stratifying the population of young African American elementary and high school students is to assess their educational, social, and cognitive needs by grade range. Key areas of focus for mentoring and tutoring visits include identifying the needs of the students, helping them to understand peer relationships, promoting educational and academic excellence, establishing values, instilling economic awareness, teaching prevention and intervention strategies, and building skills. Collegiate 100 members are trained in how to address each area and how to apply appropriate variations of strategies to different age groups. Understanding peer relationships includes gaining an appreciation of the benefit of positive relationships involving classmates, playmates, family members, and other acquaintances which also helps foster higher self-esteem. Educational and academic excellence refers to assessing the student's academic progress and determining the appropriate method of tutoring. Establishing values aims to assist students in establishing a positive and rewarding value system. Instilling economic awareness includes a goal of establishing an understanding of the free enterprise system. Appropriate prevention and intervention strategies are customized by the mentor or tutor's assessing areas that hinder or are conducive to the success, growth, and development of students. Building the student's skills entails increasing their adeptness at communication, listening, conflict resolution, and academics to excel in all fields of human endeavor.

Each Collegiate 100 affiliate chapter has a president, vice president, secretary, and treasurer. The president's responsibilities include coordinating volunteer activities with the sponsoring 100 Black Men chapter, ensuring that mentoring and tutoring objectives are carried out, ensuring that the affiliate complies with university policies for student organizations, ensuring that data is kept by the affiliate chapter to verify completion of services to youth, and serving as a liaison to the sponsoring chapter, school, and volunteer sites. The vice president is responsible for coordinating mentoring and tutoring sessions for members and coordinating professional development seminars to be presented to the affiliate chapter by a member of the sponsoring chapter. The secretary is responsible for keeping a list of active members and submitting it to the sponsoring chapter, maintaining a calendar of activities for members, and submitting monthly participation reports to the sponsoring chapter. Responsibilities of the treasurer include collecting and maintaining records of necessary fees and funds for the affiliate chapter.

As an example of the activities in which a Collegiate 100 chapter might involve itself in the community, the following is a partial list of the activities of the University of Louisville Collegiate 100 chapter over a two-year period:

2003–04

Serve as registration staff for the KAAC Prostate Cancer Walk

Serve as hosts for the 100 Black Men of Louisville Derby Gala

Participate in the Red Cross blood drive

Coordinate and staff the Derby Youth Forum for three thousand middle school students

Serve as staff for Upward Bound Junior Olympics

Participate in Louisville Urban League tutoring programs

2004–05

Serve as registration staff for the KAAC Prostate Cancer Walk

Serve as hosts for the 100 Black Men of Louisville Derby Gala

Participate in the Red Cross blood drive

Coordinate and staff the Derby Youth Forum for three thousand middle school students

Serve as staff for the Louisville Fire football clinic

Coordinate the University of Louisville Black graduation celebration

Participate in Canaan Baptist Church tutoring program

Coordinate and staff the University of Louisville Think College Now program

In addition to these activities, the chapter sponsored several social events for itself and in collaboration with the sponsoring 100 Black Men of Louisville chapter. The chapter also conducted monthly business meetings and recruitment activities leading to the induction of a new class of members for the following academic year.

RESOURCES

The most important resource for the Collegiate 100 program is the use of advisors from 100 Black Men of America. Collegiate 100 affiliates report almost all chapter activities to members of the sponsoring chapter. In addition, members of the sponsoring chapters are called on to help provide Collegiate 100 members training before beginning their mentoring and tutoring programs. Also, 100 Black Men members provide mentoring, support, and opportunities to Collegiate 100 members just as Collegiate 100 members do to the youth they serve. Networking opportunities with 100 Black men members, who are active participants in their communities, serve to provide affiliate members with strong connections for their futures after graduation. 100 Black Men members also provide support to affiliate members through periodic professional development seminars on topics such as these:

- Conflict resolution
- Peer mediation
- Leadership skills
- Communication skills writing
- Networking
- Professional dress and grooming
- Health care
- Medical careers
- MCAT/LSAT/GMAT/GRE preparation
- Business-related issues
- Government relations
- Financing higher education
- Career planning
- Financial independence

Additionally, Collegiate 100 affiliate chapters have the resource of the international headquarters office of 100 Black Men of America. Located in Atlanta, Georgia, the office provides a home base for programming as well as a central staff that is available to answer any questions. Additionally, information can be garnered on the organization's web site at www.100blackmen.org.

The code of ethics of the Collegiate 100 serves as a resource to members to help guide them in their work with the youth in their communities. The code of ethics states that members shall not (1) use profane language or display other conduct that is not consistent with that of a positive role model or objectives of the sponsoring chapter, (2) purchase or consume alcoholic beverages in the presence of students, (3) strike or threaten students with physical abuse, (4) verbally abuse or ridicule students, (5) engage in horseplay that may result in negative responses from the student, the school, parent, teacher, or representative of the sponsoring chapter, or (6) fail to honor any commitments without giving prior notice or soliciting others to act on his behalf. This code of ethics serves to hold affiliate members accountable for their actions, as well as give them guidelines to become better role models.

At least one member of the sponsoring 100 Black Men chapter is identified as advisor to the affiliated Collegiate 100 chapter. Advisors provide motivation for members and reward them for all of their hard work and dedication in their communities through rewards and incentives, such as individual recognition at Collegiate 100 gatherings, special recognition at meetings of the 100 Black Men, or scholarships sponsored by the 100 Black Men or an external funding source. This incentive program structure fosters enthusiasm in members to continue their volunteer work. At the end of the academic year, the sponsoring chapter hosts a reception or some other demonstration of appreciation in honor of the Collegiate 100 graduating seniors. Additionally, individual Collegiate 100 members who distinguish themselves are annually chosen for special recognition, such as the Collegiate Member of the Year. These actions serve to fulfill the organization's vision of helping the Collegiate 100 members become productive members of society by recognizing and rewarding their excellence in community service.

RESEARCH

Although there is no formal research assessing the effectiveness of the Collegiate 100 program, it is worth mentioning again that the success of the program depends on support from the local 100 Black Men of America chapter. In 2005, there were over ten thousand 100 Black Men members in 103 chapters, serving over one hundred thousand youth participants annually in mentoring and youth development programs. This number, although not empirically supported, seems to be evidence of the effectiveness of the 100 Black Men programs, which include the Collegiate 100. To assess the effectiveness of the Collegiate 100 program, it has been suggested that 100 Black Men of America conduct a study to determine the effectiveness of relationships between the collegiate men and the youth they serve. Additionally, the National Office, through its various chapters and in collaboration with individual college institutions, plans to study participation in Collegiate 100 affiliate chapters and compare member GPAs, attrition rates, and graduation rates with those of African American males who are not involved with the program, to gain information that may be helpful in the retention of African American males.

As of 2005, there were two intake forms available to assess the youth with whom members work, but none to assess the mentors working with the youth. The first form, the Collegiate 100 Fact Sheet, provides only general information on the individual who is being tutored: name, age, phone number, mother's name, father's name, name of school, and grade in school. The second form, the Collegiate 100 Assessment Form, is used during each visit and includes date of visit and student name, then assesses the student's skills as either above average, average, or below average in the categories of reading, math, comprehension, writing, and language.

With the increasing demand for new Collegiate 100 chapters, the future is bright for the 100 Black Men of America to continue to have a significant influence on African American youth. As of 2005, procedures are being put into place to standardize procedures for establishing new Collegiate 100 chapters, making way for additional college men to become involved in their communities. Although the number of youth served can be measured in terms of numbers, the impact that members are having on young African American males is immeasurable. Additionally, more college men will have the opportunity to become civically and morally responsible in conjunction with studying at the college level. Through its tutoring and mentoring programs, the Collegiate 100 will continue to aid the 100 Black Men of America in their quest for excellence in community service.

Name Index

SUBJECT INDEX

A

AACC. *See* American Association of Community Colleges (AACC)

AAMASU. *See* African American Men of Arizona State University (AAMASU) program

Abercrumbie, P. E., 315–316

Academic achievement: at Arizona State University, 303; of athletes, 158; and barriers to successful mentoring programs, 103–104; benefits of positive environment on, 50; at community colleges, 218–221; fraternities' obstacles regarding, 146–147; fraternity benefits regarding, 134, 139–141; at historically Black colleges, 197–198, 292; obstacles to, 33; and peer group influence, 27; and self-esteem, 33; social interaction effects on, 27; and student involvement, 140–141; of student leaders, 140; in White versus historically Black colleges, 35–36

Academic advising: for athletes, 160–161, 165–166; at historically Black colleges, 206; in Meyerhoff Scholarship Program, 269

Accountability, in peer mentoring programs, 101–102

Administrators: awareness of decisions made by, 82; communication style of, 80; of community colleges, 225–226, 228; fraternity recommendations for, 149–150; intervention responsibilities of, 15; and Meyerhoff Scholarship Program, 271; relationship with, as

perk of student involvement, 83; stereotypes of, 13; and student involvement, 75–76

Affirmations, 108–109

African American gay men: belonging of, 181–182; campus environment for, 184–186; categories of, 179; identity development of, 175–178, 180–181; labeling of, 179–181; mentoring programs for, 178–179; overview of, 174–175; recommendations for, 245; and religion, 182–184, 245; and socioeconomic issues, 181–182; student involvement of, 179

African American identified gays, 179

African American men: absence of, in college, 3–4; versus African American women, 13–15, 25, 190–191; characteristics of, 238–239; concerns of, 4, 24–25, 49–50; imbalance of, with African American women, 10–11

African American Men of Arizona State University (AAMASU) program: data affecting, 300–303; description of, 304–310; evaluation of, 310; goal of, 304, 307–308; objectives of, 305, 308; overview of, 254, 300; resources of, 304

African American people: associate degree attainment by, 216, 220*t*; disproportionate numbers of, 9; population statistics of, 5–7; subgroup characteristics of, 238; view of White colleges by, 30, 202–205; visibility of, 12–13

345